CACATUA LEADBEATERI: *Vigl.*

Simon & Schuster's Guide to

PET BIRDS

by Matthew M. Vriends

A Fireside Book
Published by Simon & Schuster Inc.
New York London Toronto Sydney Tokyo

About the Author

Matthew M. Vriends is a Dutch biologist / ornithologist of
international reputation. He holds a collection of advanced
degrees, including a Ph.D. in zoology. Dr. Vriends wrote his first
bird book at the age of seventeen, and it is currently in its
seventh printing with over 140,000 cbpies sold. He has published
more than 1,000 articles in the U.S. and Europe, has edited
numerous bird magazines, and is the author of over eighty books
in three languages—sixteen in English.

Dr. Vriends has traveled extensively in South America, Africa,
Europe and Australia to observe and study birds in their natural
environment, and is widely regarded as an expert in tropical
ornithology. A source of particular pride are the many first
breeding results he has achieved in his large aviaries, which
house over fifty tropical bird species.

A Fireside Book
Published by Simon & Schuster Inc.
Simon & Schuster Building
Rockefeller Center
1230 Avenue of the Americas
New York, New York 10020
FIRESIDE and colophon are registered
trademarks of Simon & Schuster Inc.
Manufactured in Spain by Artes Gráficas Toledo, S.A.
D.L.TO:2391–1988
10 9 8 7 6 5 4   Pbk.
Library of Congress Cataloging in Publication Data
Vriends, Matthew M., 1937-
    Simon & Schuster's guide to pet birds.

    Bibliography.
    Includes index.
    1. Cage-birds. I. Title. II. Title: Simon and Schuster's
guide to pet birds.
SF461.V736   1984   636.686   84.1331
ISBN: 0-671-50696-X (Pbk)

CONTENTS

For my parents,
my wife Lucy, and daughter Tanya
"Soyons fidèles à nos faiblesses"

KEY TO SYMBOLS

solitary

couple or
pair

colony or
group

seed-eater/
greens-eater

fruit-eater/
nectar eater

insect-eater/
commercial egg-
or soft foods-eater

singing bird or
having a nice call

talking bird

Note: This book expresses small linear and liquid measurements in their metric forms. For the guidance of readers not yet completely familiar with the metric equivalents of standard English measurements, we are including the following conversion information: one meter (m) is equal to 1000 millimeters (mm); a centimeter (cm) contains 10 millimeters and is 1/100 of a meter. One inch is equal to about 2.5 cm or 25 mm. Four inches equal approximately 100 mm; 6 inches = 150 mm; 1 foot = 305 mm; 3 feet = 914 mm. The number of millimeters divided by 10 gives the number of centimeters.

To convert degrees Celsius (or, if you prefer, Centigrade) to degrees Fahrenheit, multiply degrees Celsius by 1.8, and then add 32. (In equation form: [°C × 1.8] + 32 = °F). Some basic conversions are: 0°C = 32°F; 10°C = 50°F; 20°C = 68°F; 30°C = 86°F; 100°C = 212°F.

HISTORY

Cage birds, especially parrots and parrakeets, have been extremely popular throughout history, appealing to young and old, poor and rich. Not only are we delighted with the colors and interesting behavior of pet birds, but also with their individual personalities.

It is not known where birds were kept first in captivity; however, evidence in both the Old and New Worlds indicates that birds were kept by many different races. Paintings and hieroglyphics left behind by the ancient Egyptians contain many references to doves, parrots, ducks, and ibises as well as other birds used for hunting ducks, snipes, and herons.

Silk paintings, vases, and other ceramic objects of the ancient Chinese portray a rich collection of colorful birds. If the illustrations are interpreted correctly, most of the birds shown were domesticated. It is assumed that the history of the chicken goes back at least 5,000 years to the first settlement in India.

The Incas in South America also took an interest in birds and even tamed some species, such as the Amazon parrot, which they kept in their houses and temples. Based on this cultural testimony, we can safely assume that birds are among the animals domesticated longest. Over the centuries, while the practice of keeping and caring for birds grew, the reason for keeping them changed continually. For instance, we are aware that falconry exists today—as it has for many centuries—as purely sport. However, once falcons and hawks were used by nomadic peoples to extract a subsistence from nature, hunting other birds and small mammals. Many cultural artifacts depict the use of falcons in hunting, often as a motif in an illustration of courageous deeds of hunters. As man discovered that some birds also provided food, falcons and other hunting birds became less popular; the breeding of chickens began.

It is fairly clear that the Egyptians were the first to *collect* birds. Their literature shows that long before 4000 BC valuable bird collections existed. It is also known that Queen Hatshepsut organized an expedition around 1500 BC to add new species of birds to her apparently extensive collection.

The Greeks receive credit for discovering the charm and devotion of parrots and parrakeets. They quickly discovered how surprisingly well some species can imitate the human voice. The armies of Alexander the Great are known to have brought back ringneck parrakeets from India when they returned to Europe. Alexander was very attached to pea fowl, which were fully protected throughout his extensive domain.

In ancient Rome, emperors surrounded themselves with birds as well as other animals, and birds were popular both as pets and food. A lively trade in exotic birds and all other crawling, swimming, running, jumping, and flying animals existed, and this trade has continued to the present.

Excavations and other ancient records show that many noble Roman families of the time of Nero and earlier owned well-equipped aviaries with colorful birds. The scholar Varro, for example, who lived from 116 to 27 BC, describes a marvelous aviary in Casinum that used nets instead of metal bars to contain its birds' paradise. Siculus wrote in 50 BC that he encountered parrots during a visit to Syria—birds that probably originated in Africa. Pliny the Elder (24 BC to AD 79) offered detailed information a century later about properly training psittacines and teaching them to speak. For a time, parrots were more expensive than the best slaves and were housed in extremely luxuriously appointed cages.

In the New World at the time of the Spanish Conquistadores, the natives kept hookbills (parrots and parrakeets) that originated in Indonesia, Papua New Guinea, and South America. These birds were not caged but allowed to fly loose in and around houses and huts. In 1509, when Spanish troops under generals Hojida and Nicusco were threatening Yuibaco, a village on one of the Caribbean Islands, the tame parrots in the treetops raised a tremendous ruckus. They were alarmed at the approach of these white men, and their cawing warned the natives in time to evade the murderous troops by fleeing into the jungle. The Spanish also encountered tame parrots in 16th-century Peru, as the Incas demanded tribute in the form of a certain number of brightly colored parrot feathers from vassal tribes of the interior.

These feathers were processed in the palaces of the rulers into attractive decorations and body coverings. When Columbus landed on Guanahani, an island in the Bahamas, he encountered parrots in the huts of the populace.

These parrots did not occur naturally on the island, so they must have been imported from elsewhere. A story, probably apocryphal, is connected with the imported parrots and the discovery of America. It is too appropriate to our history not to repeat it here.

Columbus's ships had been cutting through the seemingly endless ocean. After ten weeks, the sailors were disgruntled and threatened mutiny unless the ships were turned back to Spain. Even Columbus began to doubt and was ready to give up.

"What should I do?" he asked the captain of the *Pinta*, Mr. Pinzon.

"Sir," he replied, "we have come in service of God and King. Why not follow the birds that are flying above us? They clearly are not sea birds. For the last several days, we definitely have been accompanied by birds of the forest. There must be land nearby."

Following this logic, Columbus and his party continued westward and came ashore at Guanahani on October 12, 1492. There they discovered no wild parrots, only tame ones.

Birds also figured clearly in the course of early European history. As Roman culture penetrated the west, trade increased. At the same time, connections with various eastern countries were strengthened, and tame, speaking parrots and occasionally other types of birds were moved farther and farther into Europe.

It is generally known that the ancient Romans brought several types of birds to Britain and the Continent. One was the pheasant, which has become "native" in large sections of Europe and England. Undoubtedly the Romans also brought along other brightly colored or pleasantly singing birds to the cities and villages they established in the parts of Europe that they colonized. It is presumed that they wanted to bring color and sound to enliven their new homes in the sun-starved, rainy climate they encountered.

Birds also played a recorded role in European culture. In the words of Kristan van Hamle, one of the minor Thuringian bards who expressed this wish about 1225: "*Ach, das der Anger sprechen sollte, als der Sittich in dem Glas.*" (Oh, that the meadows could speak like the parrots in the glass.) This expression indicates that at that time hookbills were kept in cages made wholly or partially of glass and represented a luxury item of the first rank. Parrots continued to be the exclusive privilege of rulers, highly placed nobility, and leading clergy through the Middle Ages and the first

Below, the earliest known fossil bird, *Archaeopteryx litographica*, found at Solnhofen, Bavaria, Germany. The bird was just over 20 inches long. Opposite page, Thebes necropolis, Sheikh abd el Gurna: tomb of Haremab. The Pharaoh and the God Horus in the form of a bird.

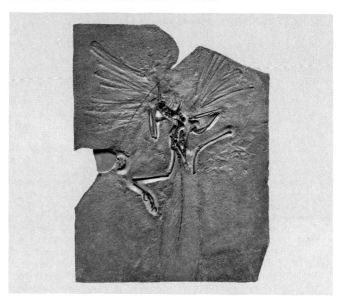

centuries following. The clergy in particular had time to study the colorful birds.

The first bird dealers came from the area of Rome. They brought all types of birds to Europe, which led to and established the interest in cage birds that continues to the present. Every day many tropical and subtropical birds are being imported through our international airports. And many one-time wild species have been domesticated and now form an integral part of the pet market—for example canaries, budgerigars, zebra finches, cockatiels, and lovebirds.

ACQUISITION

In order to decide which type of bird you want to obtain, examine the rich assortment of birds that are being kept by hobbyists. If possible visit the bird exhibitions that take place across the country during the winter, and talk to the breeders there. Look to see exactly what appeals to you: song, color, body type, or a combination of these factors. Also take a "study tour" of a good bird park or zoo, which is possible any time of year.

If you are a beginner, don't take too much hay on your pitchfork! Go for a few common types that are easy to keep and care for—zebra finches, bengalese, budgerigars, and such. Talk to other bird fanciers as much as possible. Look for a bird club in your area; there are many of these and members are always willing to help new hobbyists with advice and assistance.

Don't buy *too many* birds! Start slow and easy. If you provide the proper care, you can breed the numbers you eventually wish to keep.

An important thought to keep in mind from the first is that every living being has its time to die. Your care can be the best, and yet you may be saddened by a sudden death. Of course, you should be certain that you didn't overlook something or that there isn't an outbreak of contagious or other disease. If not, it is nature taking its course. You will just have to accept losing birds to old age from time to time.

This does not mean that tropical and subtropical pet birds are weak and nonresistant; nothing is further from the truth. In the wild these birds live three to four years on the average. In an aviary—that is, any large cage or enclosure housing birds—it's not unusual to have the same type of bird enjoy a life span of double or triple that length, if provided with proper care and housing. (The necessity of providing appropriate care for your birds—which increases longevity—should be a constant throughout the entire time of your hobby and not just at the start.)

Don't worry if at the start you produce budgies that are too small; or if you get a mix of unwanted colors in your canaries or zebra finches. That's not important for the beginner. The most important thing is that you start breeding in the first place!

The most pleasant way to start is in an aviary stocked with a rich variety of small tropical and subtropical birds. You must insure that individual birds are fit and healthy, and that the mix of birds doesn't lead to incessant fighting. Don't house large parrakeets with red-eared waxbills, for example; similarly, toucans don't belong in an aviary with canaries busy with breeding.

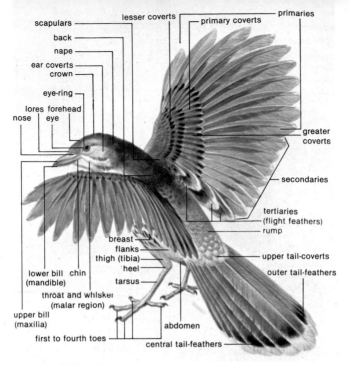

Parts of the bird's anatomy.

However, you may encounter unusual situations. You may have a couple of real aggressors among the birds you bought, and, although the species involved should get along well, the aggressors may turn the whole collection into a rowdy, fighting group. Birds with a reputation for being quiet and friendly can become fighters and killers. When you get serious fighting, constant nasty quarrels at the feed and drinking cups, continuing evening quarrels, and fights over nest boxes, watch out! Look for the aggressors that cause the ruckus, and remove them as quickly as possible.

My rule of thumb for avoiding squabbles is, as much as possible, to house together only birds of approximately the same size. Experience has shown me that although this policy doesn't eliminate the problem, it reduces the likelihood of it arising. Even so I have occasionally encountered a feisty individual that was altogether too aggressive and had to be housed apart from the rest. I suggest a daily review of the level of aggression.

Another rule I follow is never—or almost never—place new birds into an existing group in the middle of the breeding season, even if no birds are breeding at the time. Understandably, birds are considerably more watchful and therefore more pugnacious during the breeding season. A newcomer would unavoidably invade the territory of a pair of his own kind and possibly that of other species. Such a disturbance can have all sorts of unpleasant results. I also advise not to mix soft-billed birds with hard-bills; and keep hookbills from mixing with small exotics and the like. Such combinations invite trouble.

Here are some positive suggestions for a group aviary:

1. Recommended for beginners who want a reasonable chance to breed successfully:

British birds (such as the European goldfinch, serin, and linnet)
canary
cardinal species
bunting species (such as indigo bunting or rainbow bunting)
crimson finch
golden sparrow
painted quail
Pekin robin
spice finch
zebra finch
Keep all these birds in pairs and don't plan two pairs of any sort in the same aviary (to avoid constant bickering); three or more couples are okay.

2. Recommended for beginners who are not looking for immediate breeding results:
cardinal species
cut-throat finch
doves (diamond dove and the like)
Java sparrow (white, gray, and pied, for example)
painted quail
weavers (the larger species)
whydahs (the larger species)
A collection of this type could produce some breeding results, despite the description I gave it. Several species will breed satisfactorily, if they get the opportunity.

3. Recommended for somewhat experienced hobbyists:
Australian finches and parrot finches
canaries, both for song and color
Chinese painted quail
gray finch
Pekin robin
red-tailed lavender
waxbills

4. Also recommended for somewhat experienced hobbyists:
Australian finches and parrot finches
Bengalese (in several color mutations)
black-headed munia
Chinese painted quail
diamond dove (or similar birds)
gray-headed silverbill
yellow-faced grassquit
zebra finch (in several colors)

5. Recommended for anyone who likes a well-stocked group aviary:
Bengalese
cherry finch
Chinese painted quail
common waxbill
crimson-rumped waxbill
golden-breasted waxbill
gray finch
gray-headed silverbill
green avadavat
green-singing finch (Note, however, that this bird cannot be kept in an aviary also housing a pair of gray finches; these two species are almost always on the brink of battle with one another.)
Indian silverbill
nun species (the three popular species, black-headed, tricolored and

white-headed, can be placed together without problems)
orange-cheeked waxbill
red-billed firefinch
red-cheeked cordon bleu
red-eared waxbill
red-tailed lavender
spice finch
star finch
strawberry finch
violet-eared waxbill
zebra finches (in various color mutations)

6. Recommended for the experienced hobbyist:
African glossy starling
British birds
bulbul species
cardinal species
crimson finch
doves (the large species)
pagoda starling
Pekin robin
quail (the larger species)
shama thrush (and other thrush species)
song thrush
weaver species (only the larger species)
whydah species (only the larger species)

7. Recommended for hobbyists who prize song and color (while maintaining reasonable chances for breeding):
Bengalese (in several color mutations)
black-headed canary
British birds
doves (only small species)
golden sparrow
Java sparrow
saffron finch
weaver and whydah species (only the larger ones)
yellow-faced grassquit

8. Recomended for hobbyists wanting to combine song, color, and breeding:
Bengalese (in several color mutations)
black-headed canary
black-throated finch
cherry finch
Cuban grassquit (Note, however, that this bird should not be placed in the same quarters with the yellow-faced grassquit, even if there is more than enough space; sooner or later, they'll start a "war.")
diamond sparrow
indigo bunting
Java bunting
lazuli bunting
long-tailed grass finch (Note, however, that among this species there can be couples that are pugnacious, so it pays to watch them.)
nun species
quail (various species)
red-headed finch
red-winged pytilia
saffron finch
weavers and whydah species
zebra finch (various mutations)

The listed combinations basically reflect my personal preferences. They will, however, serve as a guide for creating your own collection, taking into account the size of the aviary.

Although an aviary can be stocked fully, overpopulation should be avoided at all costs. You can quickly detect signs of overpopulation from fights at the feeding and drinking stations, at perches and nest boxes and such. You can also determine mathematically the proper number of couples to keep in the aviary. Allow an average of one cubic meter of space per couple—considerably less space is needed for small exotics than rosellas, for example, but it tends to average out. Also keep in mind that a heavily stocked aviary can depress breeding success. Quiet is a prime requisite for successful breeding, and a lack of it will interfere with the desired results.

When stocking a new aviary with both small and large birds, install the small and weak species first and add the larger species several days later. The small ones can then quietly make a thorough inspection of their new quarters, so that they will later be able to hide whenever that might be necessary. The suggested combinations, you may have noticed, are designed to avoid placing large species with smaller ones. This is a good basic rule. Although the bigger ones will not harm the smaller ones in any way, they have a larger wingspan and commonly show rowdier behavior. This interferes with the quiet atmosphere that small exotics need to be happy and to start breeding.

The following list of points will prove valuable in setting up any aviary:

1. The bigger the aviary, the better your birds will get along. This rule, however, definitely does not apply if the aviary is stocked too densely. Be sure that the aviary has enough hiding places by installing ample vegetation and nest boxes—a point I will discuss later in greater detail. Preferably, install two feeding and drinking stations, so that the stronger species have a station of their own; they generally will drink and eat together if given the opportunity.

2. If you want to breed birds successfully, limit the number of birds kept in the same quarters. If you have too many birds for the available space, build one or more new aviaries or use separate breeding cages.

Although you can keep three or more couples of the same species together, don't place breeding pairs in the same quarters if they are closely related. With nonbreeding birds, house only males or only females together. As long as the population remains purely of one sex, they will get along well. As soon as a single bird of the opposite sex is added, however, you will get a full-scale war!

3. Birds coexist best if they are approximately the same size and have similar living habits. (The combinations recommended earlier reflect this rule.) However, this does not mean that the birds must originate from the same region—for example, northern Australia. Again, don't place closely related species together. They could interbreed, ruining the purity of the birds you want to breed. Of course, the situation is entirely different if your goal is to produce hybrids.

4. If you have a truly large aviary, measuring at least 5 meters in length, you can then keep quail and several species of smaller and larger doves, although I recommend that very large doves be housed in a separate aviary. The same is true for budgerigars and other hookbills, except for cockatiels. Cockatiels fit well with exotics, and they are certainly not pugnacious.

5. When purchasing birds pay attention to the following considerations. Healthy birds have smooth feathers and appear alert. (The tails of many fruit-eating birds can sometimes look a bit

ruffled, but this is usually caused by limited space in their quarters or too little water for bathing.) In contrast, sick birds tend to sit with ruffled feathers, often with their head hidden under one of their wings, like a ball of feathers shivering away in a corner.

When examining a bird, do it at a distance. If you approach it too closely, even a bird at death's door will try to get away. Of course, if you want to test a bird's reaction, do come up close. If it is healthy, it will fly up nervously and then keep a close eye on you. A sick bird may run away at the start, or it may fly away unsteadily. More often, it will only raise its head and then put it back under its wing after having thrown you a quick glance. Don't misinterpret the "tame nature" of a bird; only bright-eyed birds that look about alertly should be considered for purchase. They should also not have any dirt on their tail, legs, or underside, unless it is clearly caused by the fact that the bird has not had the opportunity to bathe regularly. Under no circumstances should you buy thin birds. Also avoid birds whose breastbone keel projects too sharply; this so called "knife effect" indicates strongly that the bird has not been fed properly. Make sure that the feathers around the anus aren't smudgy and dirty, but rather dry and clean. Feathers that are stuck together often indicate an intestinal illness that is difficult to correct.

6. Don't reject a bird solely because it is missing a few feathers. The next time it molts, the feathers will grow back. The missing feathers may have fallen out because the bird was repeatedly caught and held or moved from one cage to another. Some species of birds may have their wings clipped intentionally to keep them from flying into the cage or mesh.

7. Make an arrangement with the dealer allowing you to exchange a bird if it doesn't breed or if it fights with your other birds. It is possible that a bird won't breed for you even if it is of a type that breeds easily; often, this problem can be overcome by finding a new mate for the bird.

8. To buy wisely buy exclusively in the spring. If you are a beginner, you're best off buying birds that have already been bred locally or acclimatized to conditions in your part of the country.

Avoid repeatedly adding new birds to an existing collection in the aviary. Each bird or couple established its own territory in the aviary, even in a roomy regular or glass (vitrine) cage. A newly introduced bird or couple can wreak havoc in aviaries where earlier occupants have established territories. Occasionally, it can take a long time before peace is reestablished, especially during the breeding season. If you want to add birds, the best method is to build additional quarters for them.

9. Work with a reputable dealer and get guarantees in writing. If you are new to the hobby bring an experienced aviculturist to the store with you. In the United States, valuable birds are always sold with a certificate that clearly states that a bird may be exchanged if it doesn't form a true breeding couple with the bird sold as its mate.

10. Finally, remember that the importation of birds into most countries is legally controlled and may involve the need for import licenses, and quarantine restrictions. If in doubt, consult the appropriate authorities or your avicultural society, who will provide lists of the species concerned, before you contemplate buying.

(In Britain, certain native birds may only be bought and sold if aviary-bred and close-rung [banded] in the nest, and all imported birds require both an import license and a five-week quarantine period. Some rare species may require additional licenses.)

Whenever you want to buy new birds, you must consider the compatibility of different species and whether they will fit into your existing collection. Nothing upsets the harmony of a collection as much as an incompatible new bird. Remember that a number of larger species will not fit in with small exotics; similarly, a number of small tropical finches don't get along well with each other.

You can safely put a single dove in a collection of tropical or subtropical birds, but additional pairs would lead to quarrels within the group, interfering with their breeding and with that of other birds in the collection. A pair of quail can also enrich an aviary; but several pairs could lead to irregularities.

Parrakeets don't belong in the same aviary with small birds, and various parrakeet species don't always get along well with each other either. All this indicates that you have to be careful in considering compatibility; it pays to check out all projected changes with a dealer you trust or with a friend who has experience with cage and aviary birds. Don't experiment blindly. In nine out of ten cases, the result will be dead birds and, therefore, high expenses.

Available space will also influence your decision. Look at what you have available—a cage, a glassed-in bird-house or cage, an indoor aviary, or an aviary in the garden. Most birds, as you can imagine, can't reach their full potential and color poorly housed.

You will also have to decide whether you want to emphasize song or color. In general, the small tropical birds don't lend themselves well to a small decorative cage, with the possible exception of zebra finches and Bengalese. Generally, you will not be able to persuade them to breed, and they won't produce much in the way of song, although the zebra finches will chatter appealingly. I suggest keeping the smaller tropical birds in a somewhat roomy place where they have the opportunity to breed.

Cramped quarters are never good. Birds tend quickly to go to fat and become dopey. If you want to keep birds in a decorative cage in the living room or study, get a canary, or perhaps a white-winged seed-eater, a pair of budgerigars, or a yellow-eyed canary (green singing finch). Your are less likely to get good results with Pekin robins, orange-breasted buntings, or a pair of lovebirds. (Fortunately, people have started to provide larger quarters for these birds; they are not successful as cage birds.)

Don't just rush off to a bird dealer—even if you know one you can trust. Be aware of a proper way to house the new bird, know its feed requirements, and consider whether or not it has a quarrelsome nature. Before a purchase take plenty of time to carefully inspect the bird you're considering. Don't buy it if it looks sick or stressed, or if dirt or other matter is sticking to the legs, beak, or feathers. Be sure it acts lively and looks at you with bright eyes. The beak should be shiny and well-shaped; above all, it must close properly.

Look at the cage. If it is dirty, you can assume that the dealer is not a true professional and is likely to be more interested in your money than in his livestock. Try another dealer, even if you have to pay a little more. Trading with a reputable dealer usually, at the least, assures your purchasing a completely healthy bird. Use a special travel cage to bring new birds home. If you must travel far, place seed and some soaked bread in the cage. The soaked bread replaces a container of water, which has a tendency to spill during transportation.

No matter how good your selection and how trustworthy the dealer, your newly acquired bird or birds should be placed in quarantine the first weeks, to see if they are incubating some type of disease. Do this yourself to be sure it is done right. For two weeks place them alone in a well-lighted location that's not too cold. Next put the new birds in a cage and place the cage inside your aviary, allowing other birds to get used to the newcomers. On a sunny morning, open the cage and let them merge.

New birds need to learn where to find their feed. Scatter some extra seed on the floor of the aviary in the immediate vicinity of the feeding dish. The other birds will naturally help the newcomers find their way around the aviary; within a few hours, it will seem as if the new birds have spent many happy years there.

HOUSING

In general, this book assumes that you will keep—or are keeping—birds in pairs. If you buy birds, do everything you can to discover whether the pair you select is compatible. Look at the birds as they interact in the cage while they are still in the dealer's store. If you have selected a pair that doesn't get along once you get them home, separate them and try again.

It is not essential to keep pairs of all species. In the wild, many birds come together only during the breeding season; they may not see each other at all at other times. This is particularly true of several fruit- and insect-eating (soft-billed) birds and large parrots.

This suggests that you can successfully keep a single bird of some species—in a roomy cage, a glass show cage, or an inside or outside aviary. Large insect- and fruit-eating exotics and, above all, species that grew up tame (generally by being handraised) are often kept singly. These birds are greatly dependent on humans, and if kept alone they almost certainly will not accept a mate later. In fact, if we place another bird of the same species in such a cage, fighting, and even death, will ensue; and that's true even during the breeding season when birds normally are very interested in one another.

On the other hand, the bird world also includes species that live like Don Juans, even in the breeding season, and don't limit themselves to a single female. With the appropriate mating behavior, they happily move from one mate to another.

Not every bird belongs in a cage. Some species feel more at home in a roomy aviary, and the others need a warm indoor aviary or glassed-in show cage. Large species should not be housed in small enclosures; on the other hand, small birds may be allowed just as much room as large exotics. As a rule, you can never give birds too much room; they love space and the opportunity to move around. If you have a roomy glass show cage and want to keep only a single couple in it, don't think for a moment that you should store it and buy another type of housing. You can make it look very attractive, adding some extra plants perhaps.

The indoor aviary

Indoor aviaries are often used to house and even breed soft-billed birds, mainly because these quarters can be heated. Easy-to-breed species can also be housed indoors, although ordinarily some species, like the zebra finch, do better in an outdoor (garden) aviary.

You can buy indoor aviaries ready-made, suited to a variety of purposes. Aviaries can be placed in the living room or in an airy attic. You can grow many beautiful plants in them, and you can stock them with some colorful bird species.

Many people confuse an indoor aviary with a bird room. A bird room is a complete room in the house that is not used for any other purpose; an indoor aviary is a structure placed *in* a room. Commercially made indoor aviaries can be truly attractive and used effectively for breeding. Children playing on the floor or at the table in the same room don't seem to inhibit the birds at all.

The standard box or breeding cage

The standard, box-type cage has a trellis front plus three solid walls that give the birds a sense of privacy. It must be placed in a light, draft-free location. Don't place it in the full sun, however, as the cage will then soon become as hot as an oven. Standard cages are especially useful for breeding certain species of single pairs (canaries, budgerigars, lovebirds, finches, etc.).

Chrome-trellissed cages (which are available commercially in all shapes and sizes) should only be used if they are nice and roomy. They are especially suited for species like Bengalese, thrushes, a canary, a pair of gray finches, a couple of budgies, parrots, and so on. If you keep hook-bills, be sure to get a trellis with horizontal bars. Canaries and other tropical or subtropical birds—which rarely, if ever, climb up on the trellis—can be placed in cages with vertical bars.

If you keep birds in a standard box cage, you should give your birds the opportunity to fly free around the room for several hours each day. Remember that box-type cages are really suited only for breeding many types of birds.

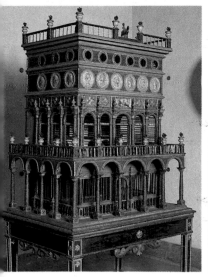

The glass show cage

The glassed show cage, sometimes called a "vitrine," is one of the most popular types of housing for birds today. It is particularly suited to soft-billed birds. Glass show cages are useful for people who have limited space but still wish to keep birds.

A variety of designs for glass show cages have been created by bird fanciers and not by commercial designers unfamiliar with raising birds. These blueprints satisfy the needs and demands of the home breeder, and are compatible with the decoration and layout of the private home. Until recently, it has been difficult to manufacture glass show cages commercially, but soon we can expect to find ready-made standard types of vitrines.

The advantage of a home-built vitrine is that you can make it compatible with the style and decoration of your home. You can make the structure more attractive by painting it (use brands recommended for painting children's furniture). People often paint pictures on the back wall, for example, an imaginary tropical landscape with mountains, a village nesting against a hill, and wild-running rivers. You should feel free to express your personal taste, of course. The back wall should, if possible, be made of wood. *However, never use composite wood (chip) board.* The fumes emitted from newly made board can be deadly for your birds, and they are unhealthy for people as well.

Ideally, the back wall should be decorative, not distracting; it is not the main attraction—the birds are! You should carefully consider the kind of illustration you want. Something sweet and

sentimental may be all right for the first week, but then get on your nerves; something loud and overdone is also inappropriate.

If you are not of an artistic bent, it may not be necessary to hire an expensive commercial artist. Perhaps you have a friend or relative who can paint well and won't have to charge you much beyond the cost of his materials. Remember, the decoration doesn't have to be complex. A few simple and imaginative flowers and plants are sufficient. In fact, painting the back wall with a soft gray tint is perfectly fine, setting a quiet nonintrusive mood. A neutral color is an effective background for the natural plants you keep in pots and planters.

Since you will, after all, build your vitrine to your own preferences, plans, and available room, its construction will be discussed only briefly. Position a glass plate in front of the back wall as protection against droppings and dirt. Make the glass removable, so that you can wash it from time to time. On the sides of the vitrine, install a number of sliding doors that make it easy to service bathing, drinking, and feeding stations. Service openings, properly situated, will also help you care for the plants in the vitrine. Such service openings disturb the birds far less than if you have to service everything by lifting off the top and working from above.

As the term indicates, a glass show cage generally has a glass front. You can, however, use woven wire with a strip of glass against the bottom to protect your room against feathers and debris from the cage. Along the sides or against the roof (which will also be partially made of mesh), install some lights; several 10-watt fluorescent lights

One of the world's most modern and splendid aviaries at Melbourne Zoo, Australia.

are ideal. The light fixtures should not be visible when viewing the birds from the outside. Since the temperature in vitrines can fall considerably during the night, especially if they are placed near windows and doors, a heating lamp should be installed. Cold is your birds' biggest enemy, so use a thermostat to keep the temperature constant. Many types of heaters are available commercially, but a heat lamp is preferable.

A vitrine should have minimum dimensions of 80 × 60 × 50 centimeters. These dimensions provide enough space for two or three pairs of birds, especially species that are not too large and can get along well with each other, such as African waxbills. The minimum cage will hold only one pair of larger species, such as the thrushes, parrakeets, and dwarf parrots.

Remember to pay special attention to plants for the vitrine. Select sturdy types of plants that have no poisonous leaves or berries.

Purchase an oblong, fine-meshed net with a short handle, which should be available in any good bird store. (Use a fine mesh, because the birds you catch could otherwise be injured.) If possible, catch birds in the evening, as you won't need a net then. Just grab the bird with your hands—carefully, without turning on unnecessary lights. This operation will make the wisdom of incorporating sliding doors on the side of the cage obvious. If you catch birds by hand carefully, the other birds will remain partly or completely unaware, which is all to the benefit of the general peace. Do your best to avoid having birds fly around in the dark, all panicky. If you don't succeed in catching the bird you want on the first try, then you're better off waiting until the next evening. If the birds panic regardless of your careful efforts, immediately turn on the lights to help them find their sleeping places once again after they quiet down.

Always construct a double floor under a vitrine—a floor that can slide out, a type of drawer. This design necessitates putting plantings only along the sides. Remember, however, that you can also place plants *around* the cage on the outside. This presents no problems and makes the bird housing look much more natural.

The aviary

This book will not provide a detailed design for building an aviary. Every breeder would still make modifications to suit his preferences and budget. Several excellent books, which provide details on building aviaries, are available, and are recommended in the bibliography. We will, however, take note of a number of general directions for aviary construction.

Nine out of ten outdoor aviaries are built in two or often three sections. (The three-section aviary is preferable.) These are the night coop (shelter); a half-open section which is covered with corrugated plastic or similar material; and an open section, usually called the run, or flight.

A key consideration is siting the aviary properly. The front (if it can be distinguished) should face south. If this is not possible, at least try to face the front as nearly south as possible; southeast is preferred to southwest. It is also advisable to construct part of the front side of glass, and this is especially important if the front doesn't face south. Don't use reflective glass; song birds and budgies will take their reflection for another bird which they may then try to attack. Use nonreflective glass.

Naturally, you should consider the whole landscape design of the property in siting the aviary. It should blend into its surroundings naturally. Select an attractive, visible location, preferably with some flowers and shrubs nearby and as a background.

Do not construct the aviary entirely with wood, unless you expect to move it from time to time. The foundation should be of brick or cement, the frame can be wood, pipe, or T-iron set into the foundation. Start with a low brick wall about 30 to 50 centimeters high on which to construct the floor of the night coop. The floor of this night shelter is best built of cement or cement blocks and covered with a thick layer of sand.

You can also build the coop floor from fire-hardened and waterproofed posts and flooring, especially if you think you may have to move the aviary at some point.

The rest of the uprights and the roof can best be built from tongue-and-groove pine board. These boards should be the narrowest size available, because they shrink and expand less. (To counteract the tendency of wood to warp, also thoroughly treat all wooden building materials with a wood preservative before you begin construction.) You will also need wire mesh, regular wire, and roofing material—which can be tile, slate, corrugated plastic, fiberglass, or wire-reinforced glass. Use the common wire mesh, which is the six-sided type; if large parrot varieties are to be kept, the preferred type is square welded wire mesh, which is available in various thicknesses (1.25, 1.47, and 1.65 mm). Other, more expensive types of woven wire, are also available. For glass use wire-reinforced or safety glass. In most cases, you will also need a gutter with drain pipe.

How big should we build? On this point, the breeder of fancy birds takes the opposite position from the breeder of chickens and ducks. A duck or chicken coop is sized depending on the number of birds to be housed. An aviary, on the other hand, is built to fit the available space and surroundings; once the size is determined, an appropriate number of birds is installed.

In deciding the shape of the aviary, keep your lines as straight as possible. Don't go for domes, towers, castles, etc. Remember, the contents of the aviary should be the main attraction. Adjust the shape of the aviary to the surroundings, including the topography and standing structures. The effect should be one of harmony between the aviary and the other small slice of nature over which you have control. Any dissonance can be softened through the use of additional bushes, trees, and flowers around the aviary.

Another very important factor to consider is not to build the aviary too low. If you want to achieve a structure that is esthetically pleasing, the minimum height of the front side must be 2 to 2$\frac{1}{2}$ meters.

Most, if not all, aviary birds should not be kept outdoors during the winter (see *Acclimatization*). The recommended procedure is to move them to keep them in roomy indoor cages. There are a few exceptions that are noted in discussions of various individual species. Birds that can be maintained outside, however, must be given protection against wind and rain, as well as a place to sleep that is protected against drafts and frost.

One section of the aviary should be open to the elements. (You will notice that a great many birds just love to take a shower in the summer rain.) The open section will have walls and a ceiling made of wire mesh. The floor is best made of sand, so that you can add the plantings that your different bird species like for building a nest (see *Plantings*). Use grass, reeds, and other low-growing vegetation to give the whole scene the effect of a natural environment—something that looks as much as possible like a piece of nature.

The covered section of the aviary requires a watertight roof, best made of light-colored fiberglass or corrugated plastic to keep the interior as light and bright as possible. You can build the back wall of wood, but consider fiberglass for this structure as well. The rest of the section is made with wire mesh. The dividing wall, which can be built so that it is removable, separates the completely open area from the covered part of the flight (which might be put into place in extended periods of bad weather) and is also made of mesh. Some fanciers even make the wall of the completely closed area (adjoining the flight) from mesh. However, this is not preferred because it does not afford enough protection against the elements. A mesh wall also means that we cannot provide the birds with some heat in the night shelter, should this ever be necessary.

The floor of the covered section can also be of sand, and you can put plants there, too. If you water them regularly, they will do fine. If you want to put concrete tiles on the floor, just cover the tiles thoroughly with a thick layer of sand. You will notice that the birds like to scratch around in it and take sand baths. With a solid floor, your aviary plants will have to be put into pots and planters. Natural furnishings such as wood are preferred; otherwise, the containers will give the place an unnatural character and violate the natural look that a good aviary should have. Be sure to supplement the living plants with one or more dead trees equipped with the necessary roosts and perches. You could also consider using cork tiles and

other materials to help achieve an attractive whole, as long as you are not planning to house psittacines (parrots and parrakeets) in such an aviary, for they will tear it up.

The night shelter is a different and more complicated matter. At the front, you will need a safety vestibule with double doors. Without this, sooner or later some birds will escape. The vestibule may even have five doors: one to the outside, one to the covered section, one to the storage area, one to the flight, and one to the completely enclosed night shelter.

The vestibule, of course, must be kept free of birds. When entering always close the door to the outside before opening the door leading to the flight cage.

The night shelter can have two floors, with the actual sleeping quarters "upstairs." Below it, you can build two rooms. One can be used as a pair-formation area, quarantine station, isolation area for rowdy birds, observation area, and so on. The other room can be used for storage—unused nest boxes, perches, bowls, dishes, etc. The floor of the lower half is best constructed of concrete or tile. The floor of the actual night shelter can also be of cement, covered with a mix of river sand and shell sand (available in any pet store), 6 to 8 centimeters deep. The side walls of the shelter should be made of reinforced glass. Other covered areas, as well as the smaller aviary previously discussed, can have walls of wire mesh, if necessary.

Here are some important general suggestions regarding construction. First, you will want to protect the aviary against mice and rats. When laying the foundations, be sure to sink the wire mesh about 20 centimeters into the earth and also work mesh into the concrete to keep it from cracking. Use vertically grooved boards for the walls and be sure that all doors and windows are hung properly and close tightly. Prevent standing water on the roof, for it causes the wood to rot. Slope the roof properly, design a generous overhang, and make sure that it is absolutely reliable and watertight.

The finishing touch is to paint or stain the aviary. Also stain the wire mesh, using a nearly dry brush. This will make your birds considerably easier to view from the outside. Paint the night shelter with a certified safe paint or use carbolic stain.

Install perches (discussed in a separate section) of several thicknesses and fasten them securely. Since droppings can contaminate food or water and cause illnesses, never position them above drinking and eating stations. If you want to supply feed and water in the night shelter, it is best to install a feeding table, about 1 1/2 meters off the ground. Note, however, that there are birds that always look for feed on the ground, and will literally die of starvation with a feeding table located right above their "noses."

The bird room
Most commonly a bird room is an unused bedroom, enclosed porch, attic, or other room. Construction work involved is simply to place woven wire screens in front of the windows and to install a wire-mesh vestibule to prevent the escape of your birds. For the rest, you can arrange the room much like an outdoor aviary.

Bird rooms are frequently used to house valuable species, such as hummingbirds, honey- and nectar-eating birds, different species of tanagers and other soft-billed bird species, as well as Australian finches (parson finch, gouldian finch, long-tailed grass finch, etc.), canaries, and lovebirds. Bird rooms are often kept by more experienced fanciers, but beginners also can use a bird room to achieve wonderful breeding results—particularly with some of the easy-to-keep insect- and fruit-eating birds. Some have said that birds in this group are difficult to raise, but experience has shown that a bird room happens to be exceptionally well-suited for these species. (Naturally, other aspects of their care should be first rate as well!)

Furnish the bird room as naturally as possible. Place tile on the floor and cover it with sand; then be sure to put down fresh sand regularly. Bring in natural plants as much as possible (see *Plantings*), although these will, of course, have to be in pots and planters. If you use your artistic sense, you will be able to create a beautiful piece of nature *inside* your house.

The breeding area
From discussions elsewhere in this book, you will have concluded that a certain amount of space is needed in which to build an aviary or vitrine. People who live in apartments are seriously handicapped in this respect. Still, although birds need space to live, to be cared for, and to breed, it doesn't have to be fancy space. I have seen birds kept in the storage rooms of apartment buildings, in the basements of office buildings, in the canteen of a factory, and in the hallway of a school. In all these places, people raised birds with enthusiasm and expertise. People who use their inventiveness can create good spaces by using proper lighting and ventilation. Canaries, budgies, zebra finches and other similar finches, Bengalese, lovebirds, and the like require relatively little space; this is also true of many fruit- and insect-eating exotics.

Bizarre living quarters for a blue-and-yellow macaw: an old beer barrel.

Restricted space is not suitable for all types of birds, however. Parrots and parrakeets, for example, need a lot of space. The important thing to remember is to provide the minimum cage space that applies to various species. If you can furnish more space, so much the better, but you can always build extra little runs and flights—the shape and arrangements of the space are not of paramount importance.

Here are the space limitations for some species that must be kept in mind for breeding and ornamental cages:
Canaries: song and color varieties, at least 45 cm long, 40 cm high, and 35 cm deep; form and posture canaries, 60 × 50 × 60 cm
Budgerigars: 65 × 50 × 65 cm
Dwarf parrots and lovebirds: 85 × 50 × 60 cm
Tropical birds the size of zebra finches: 50 × 50 × 35 cm
Mynah birds and similar species: 55 × 55 × 100 cm
Amazons, cockatoos, macaws, etc.: 65 × 75 × 100 cm

Lighting

Some bird fanciers use artificial heat and light to encourage breeding early in the spring with an eye on having birds ready for exhibit. Basically, they use artificial light to extend day length: longer periods of light stimulate birds to begin breeding. The hypothalamus is activated and the appropriate hormones are produced for reproduction. Extending day length should obviously be done gradually, or it will have no effect. Research has shown that birds retire to their sleeping coop, their roost, or other resting place when the light intensity falls to about 750 to 2,000 candlepower. (This differs for birds that are active at twilight or at night, but few of these are aviary birds and will not be discussed here.)

Some breeders begin to bring their birds into breeding condition in January and February. Starting as early as November, they begin lengthening the days for their birds. Their aim is to produce, by January 1, as many daylight hours as in a normal spring day. Their usual light sources are fluorescent lights that stimulate natural daylight, including ultraviolet and infrared. Vita Lite is widely used, and I recommend it without hesitation. In calculating how much fluorescent lighting is needed, assume 40 watts per square meter. If you use Vita Lite, consult your dealer, as it comes in various models that differ in the amount of lighting furnished. All models fit into the normal sockets,

Remember to keep a night light on (a normal 5- or 10-watt bulb) during the night hours when the fluorescent lights are off.

Heating

If you want to start breeding early in the year, you will have to arrange for artificial heat as well as artificial light. For breeding, the best results are obtained with a temperature that varies between 15 and 18 degrees Centigrade. Much lower or higher temperatures are definitely not desirable.

Many types of heaters are available: gas, oil, electric, ventilator, and so on. These all-purpose heaters are very dangerous and should not be used. Feathers can blow into them and start a fire, and poor ventilation of gases can kill off your stock—not to speak of dangers for yourself, your family, and your neighbors. I recommend only electric tubular heaters, which fit into standard light sockets and are available in various strengths—20, 100, 150, and 250 watt. They are also made in 400- and 600-watt strengths, but these are intended for very large spaces that are seldom used for bird breeding. Be sure to use a thermostat to keep the temperature constant, no matter what heating system you decide to use.

Humidity

A certain level of humidity is needed to hatch eggs, and experienced breeders know that in dry, warm summers there are often problems with hatching. Eggs dry out, the shell membranes get too tough, and the young can not free themselves from the egg. Too high a level of humidity also is undesirable, but not as problematic.

If you breed in an outdoor aviary, it isn't always easy to attain the proper humidity. In warm, dry weather, it does help, nonetheless, to spray the nest boxes regularly with a weak setting of the garden hose. Many breeders even use nest boxes with a double floor; they place a dish with water on the lower level so that water vapor rises through small holes in the upper floor, on which the nest with eggs rests. Other bird breeders have used moist moss and other spongy material to put in nesting logs and boxes. These techniques can save practically all eggs, even in extremely dry spells.

Indoors, humidity is easily controlled with a humidifier; no good breeder would be without one. Set it at 60 to 70 percent with a temperature of 15 to 20 degrees Centigrade.

If the humidity level is correct, the egg membrane stays supple, allowing the young to hatch normally. Too dry, the young birds experience problems when hatching; too wet, the unhatched young grow too fast, are unable to turn inside the egg, and die.

Roosts and sleeping shelters

There are two basic types of perches—those for utility and those for play. The utility perch should never be too thin and should always be round; it can be slightly flattened on top. The utility perch should be well anchored and is absolutely essential to the birds at mating time. Swinging perches are good for play, and so are the thinner branches that are furnished by the natural vegetation. (Of course, if plants have the right shape and location, they also have a utilitarian use for nesting.) In the summer, it is all right for birds to use trees and shrubs to sleep in, but it is advisable to furnish separate sleeping places as well.

Artificial perches should be made of hard wood stripped of bark, which stays free of lice and will be easy to clean. If they are to rest well, birds should not be able to lock their toes completely around the perch. In this way their nails will not be able to grow too long, and the muscles of the legs will stay limber, especially if all the perches are not of the same thickness. In an indoor aviary or in the covered part of the outdoor aviary, you can use rigid, round, not-too-thin rods of hard wood.

In an outdoor aviary, hang small sleeping shelters that are open on one side. Be sure to hang them in places that are protected from wind and drafts. Birds like to sleep as high as possible, so install their roosts accordingly. Provide extra roosting space to avoid squabbles at evening time. Don't place roosts one above the other, or the birds on top will foul the birds below. The same is true for colony breeding cages.

Don't install roosts in places that will inhibit the birds in their flight. In breeding cages, don't put roosts in front of the nest boxes; you don't want "uninvited guests" to be able to spy on activities that are none of their business. This will prevent fights, which are undesirable for brooding birds.

Swings, teeter-totters, and exercise wheels are nice for a decorative cage in the living room, but they have no place in breeding cages and aviaries. Playthings are all right for parrakeets and related birds, but tropical birds don't use them.

Be sure to install artificial roosts and perches so that they can be removed easily—without disturbing the birds too much.

Bath water

Whether birds are housed in a cage, aviary, or bird room, it is a fact that they need to wash themselves just as humans do. There must be facilities for bathing. The best method is to provide one or more flat, earthenware bowls filled with clear water. Use rain water if possible, especially if your tap water has a high lime level.

Place bathing bowls on a piece of flagstone or paving stone. To avoid fouling the water, be careful not to place them under locations where birds sit and sleep, and take all other precautions to keep the water clean. Be sure not to use bowls that are too deep. Remember that young birds that have just left the nest also want to bathe and are not experienced at the practice; they could easily be drowned. If you use large bowls, put a piece of flagstone in the center as a type of safety "float."

Especially in the summer months, bath water is used up rapidly. You may have to add water (or, preferably, replace all water) several times per day.

Bath water should not be used for drinking water and vice versa. Protect the drinking water with a cutoff valve or cover drinking bowls with chicken wire.

Take care to remove the bath water during cold or freezing weather. Be aware that birds still have the tendency to bathe during the winter months, even if it is cold and icy. They should not be allowed to do so because their feathers could freeze together and their legs, especially the toes, could freeze, in some cases necessitating amputation.

In this connection, it is also interesting to note that many birds like to tumble and play in high, wet grass. Psittacines, doves, and quail in particular can really enjoy a rainshower. So, if it hasn't rained in a while, it will do no harm whatever to aim a garden hose (set on a soft spray) into the aviary. You will enjoy the birds' antics.

Sandbath

If your aviary does not have any dry, clean areas with fine sand, then you should provide them with flat, earthenware saucers filled with fine, dry sand. Many birds also like to take sand baths, which work very well against bird lice and for the peeling off of new quills during the molt.

Things to watch for

First of all, avoid seams in bird cages—both vitrines and box-type. Seams are notorious hiding places for mites and other small vermin. Feed and drinking bowls should preferably be made of easy-to-wash materials: glass; smooth, hard plastic; or porcelain. All bowls and dishes should be washed daily and thoroughly dried, especially if these utensils are to be used for feed that can spoil easily. Don't leave leftovers standing around; they can quickly become reservoirs for bacteria, viruses, and other harmful microbes.

Perches and roosts should be made only of hard wood. Soft wood is too brittle and the birds gnaw and so destroy them. Perches should be washed regularly in water and disinfectant and then scrubbed down with sandpaper. You can use some commercial perches, but also provide some natural ones—ordinarily by planting the right kind of shrubs and trees.

In cages, generally use store-bought perches. Use three per cage. Two can be fastened along the side, for example, near the feed and water dishes, and the third can be above, between, or under the others so that the birds can make three hops. Be sure that perches are thick enough so that the sitting bird doesn't encircle them completely with foot and toes. Don't place perches above bowls used for feed and water and don't place perches directly under and above each other, so that birds resting above foul their fellows that are resting on a lower level. Don't place perches too close to the sides; otherwise a bird may damage its tail as it turns around on the perch. Note that insect- and fruit-eating birds have a way of jumping that differs from that of seed-eating birds. Their jump is much "flatter," quicker, and longer. These beautiful birds should therefore not be kept in narrow cages and vitrines that, of necessity, have perches placed close together.

The cage and aviary birds described in this book generally have thin but firm droppings, although the droppings of soft-billed birds are more watery. If this is true for the birds you keep, the floor of their quarters must be kept scrupulously clean, no matter what type of quarters you supply. It is best to use a thick layer of river sand with some shell sand mixed in; or, at the very least, a thick layer of newspaper or brown wrapping paper. It is essential that the floor covering be freshened regularly. Regardless of the type of birds you keep in a cage or vitrine, provide a new covering of sand or paper at least once a week. Of course, the frequency of this operation depends also on the number of birds that you have. The aviary floor should be regularly raked, hoed, or turned with a spade, except during the actual breeding season.

All birds like a lot of sunlight. If you can control it, place cages and vitrines on the south side of the house or apartment; southeast is better than southwest. Preferably place cages near a draft-free window, with a few plants placed so that birds will always find some shade when direct sunlight comes into the room.

Don't put birds in rooms where there is a lot of smoke. Cigarette and other smoke is damaging to air passages, eyes, and other organs. You can have a television set in the room, but don't position the cage in a direct line with the set, and keep it at least 3 meters away. Don't ever put a bird cage directly next to a television set because the high frequencies that are inaudible to humans are picked up by the birds and could harm their central nervous systems.

Don't house birds in a kitchen. The various vapors are bad for birds, as are the large variations in temperature and the drafts that are often found in kitchens.

Two more remarks about plants: your plantings may be plentiful, but under no circumstances should they hinder the flight of birds, whether in rooms, vitrines, outdoor aviaries, or other quarters. And remember to water plants regularly; indoors, certain types of leaves must be sponged off.

ACCLIMATIZATION

Acclimatizing means getting birds used to a strange climate and, figuratively, getting them used to a totally new environment. Both meanings certainly are applicable to tropical and subtropical birds. Pet birds are faced with difficulties not only because of the change in temperature, but also because of the changes during the time after their capture, which alone represents considerable stress. From the birds' catchers, the creatures go to buyers, then to wholesale exporters and importers, then to retailers and ultimately to the purchaser—the bird fancier. Before the fancier gets a bird in his or her possession, it often undergoes many hardships. It is worth mentioning that today, thanks to modern transportation—principally airplanes—birds arrive at their destination much faster than they once did. Fortunately, international airports now cooperate actively to offer captive animals the most professional and proper care possible under the circumstances. In some countries newly imported birds will have a few weeks to recover during their quarantine period before they can be sold. In others, of course, they may reach a retailer in a matter of days.

With all these changes a bird must cope with, it is easy to understand why a bird, reaching its final destination, deserves complete rest and total attention. Just imagine the number of cage changes the little creature experienced and how often it was exposed to high and low temperatures, strange feed, and other deprivations.

Once a bird has reached the importer, it usually starts receiving a type of food that the retailer (and the eventual purchaser) would consider acceptable. Proper feed is usually not a big problem for seed-eating birds and most parrots and parrakeets. By contrast, insect- and fruit-eating (soft-billed) birds often encounter difficulties, especially when they no longer get the exact type of insects and fruits to which they were accustomed in the wild. Exporters and importers ought to know, therefore, what feed is appropriate and which alternatives are possible.

It cannot be said that a bird has been properly acclimatized until it eats regularly. In fact, it isn't so important *what* the bird eats, as long as it is easy to digest. Honey has been a successful solution to this dilemma. Few birds (if any) will refuse this delicacy, and it is additionally advantageous in that it activates the digestive system.

It is also of prime importance for the birds to have feed and drinking water available virtually without interruption. Birds have a high body temperature (43/43.5°C) and a rapid metabolism. If for any reason the birds slow their intake of feed, the effect is almost immediate. The birds seem to deteriorate before your eyes. Their behavior changes: they become nervous, move restlessly about the cage, and constantly peck at other birds. At a somewhat later stage, they ruffle up their feathers, tuck their heads under their wings, and go to sleep in a corner of the cage.

Birds, therefore, should have their interest in feed constantly reawakened. This feed should at first be as similar as possible to that in the wild. The rations can be gradually changed to readily available feed, for example, by mixing a little of the new into the old, trusted menu. The new feed, however, should be varied and include a rich assortment of seed, fruit, and insects. Fresh drinking water should be available. En route, it can be provided in thoroughly soaked bread. The temperature of the birds environment should be

properly adjusted. Importers and others in the trade chain may have problems with this requirement, but the really good ones devote the necessary attention to it, if only to minimize their own losses.

Proper temperature should, of course, also be a concern for the retailer and the bird fancier who acquires a new bird. Newly arrived birds should be placed in quarters that are as spacious as possible and maintained at a temperature between 22° and 27°C. This is desirable, if not essential, for a gradual acclimatization since it prevents the birds' loss of body heat.

Birds that will not resume eating on their own, despite the best efforts of the caretaker, should be fed by hand. Forced feeding is, of course, easier with large birds than with small ones. Remember, however, to wear protective gloves when hand feeding large birds, like parrots and large parrakeets.

In short, keep recently imported birds in warm, spacious quarters. Cover the cage bottom with butcher's paper, matte side up, or use newspaper, for insect- and fruit-eating (soft-billed) birds. For seed-eaters, cover the cage bottom with a thick layer of rough sand.

At first offer feed in open dishes. Automatic feeders and waterers, after all, are completely strange to these birds. Set their cages in a bright, sunny place and avoid drafts at all costs. Drinking water should be at room temperature—no colder. Don't supply bathwater for the first week after arrival. Also don't furnish green feed (sprouting seedlings, spinach, chickweed, etc.) for the first five to seven days. After a week, start furnishing bathwater in shallow bowls. This also should be kept at room temperature. After the first week, furnish grit for the new arrivals; it is essential for proper digestion.

Keep a close eye on every new bird for three or four weeks. If it stays completely alert and lively, look for a pretty, warm day to put it out into the aviary. Be sure, however, that the weather is not likely to change for a while. First, introduce the newcomer *inside* its old cage, so that its future cage- or aviarymates can get used to it without being able to cause it harm. The other birds will look the new bird over quite a bit the first days. That's good; in this way they can get used to one another. After three days, you can release the newcomer.

At first, provide it feed on the ground. Its instincts will continue to drive it to look for food there. Once it has found the seedbin, of course, you can stop ground feeding.

The best place to release a bird is in the sleeping coop or night shelter. It may well want to spend its first days there, especially if you do the ground feeding there. If you release the new bird on a warm day, it isn't really so important whether it spends its first days indoors or out. It definitely is important, however, to release the bird early in the morning. That way, the bird has a whole day to look over its new quarters and discover appropriate places to retreat, hide, and sleep.

If you bought new birds in spring, as I recommended earlier (see *Acquisition*), this will be an advantage when you release them. You will usually have mild temperatures, and the sun will shine longer, so that they will have more light.

In late autumn, move tropical and subtropical birds to a protected location in which to spend the winter months. Practically all species require this. At least furnish a frost-free room, preferably a well-lit one. You can use breeding cages for inside quarters, if you want, but always be sure there is plenty of room. House the sexes separately to avoid problems. In particular, don't mix male and female zebra finches, canaries, budgerigars, and similar species. Provide the proper number of hours of light by supplementing daylight with artificial lighting. Tropical and subtropical birds need at least 13 to 14 hours of light, for example from 8 A.M. to 9 P.M.. Seed-eating birds should be supplemented from time to time with codliver oil. The best method is to mix 5 drops of cod-liver oil into 1 kilo of seed. It is also recommended to furnish old white bread soaked in milk at regular intervals (see *Nutrition*).

It is possible to overwinter properly acclimatized birds in an outside aviary, but preferably only birds that have been raised in your own country. It is better, however, to place *all* tropical and subtropical birds in lightly heated roomy cages, at about 15°C. If you want to keep them outside, this can be done only if you have an absolutely frost-free sleeping coop (night shelter) that protects the birds from draft and rain during the evenings and nights. You can release the birds to the outside flight during the day, but only during good weather. You will have to shepherd them to the sleeping coop late in the afternoon.

To be certain you are completely aware of which birds can be kept in an outside aviary during the winter, the following list includes those species that, along with closely related birds, can be considered for this practice: all Amazons, Senegal parrot, budgerigar, greater and lesser sulphur-crested cockatoo, ringneck parrakeet, Moluccan cockatoo, Moluccan lory, pennant, plum-headed parrakeet, red-rumped parrakeet, rosella, Stanley rosella, turquoisine, cockatiel, cut-throat finch, gray singing finch, green cardinal, yellow-faced and Cuban grassquit, baya weaver, red-vented bulbul, indigo bunting, Pekin robin, Bengalese, Indian silverbill, green singing finch, all nun-species, paradise whydah, red cardinal, red-headed finch, Senegal combassou, strawberry finch, and zebra finch.

Under no circumstances would I house other species in an unheated room or in a sleeping coop that is not absolutely frost free. And even with the named species, I would recommend a lightly warmed inside location (at about 10 to 15°C) if the necessary space is available.

PLANTINGS
Make your aviary as natural as possible by adding a few good bushes. In the inside aviary, you will have to do this in wooden planters filled with humus. Many plants are used by birds to play in, to find shelter from the rain, to shade themselves from strong sunlight, or to just perch. At mating time, natural perches play a very important role, and bushes also provide good nesting places. Therefore, hang some nesting baskets, pieces of heather, and similar items from the branches.

Naturally, you should select healthy bushes that are tolerant of your birds' gnawing. You can considerably reduce the tendency of birds to destroy vegetation by regularly (preferably, every day) furnishing green feed. The birds, of course, will not leave bushes entirely untouched, even if you have extensive plantings; that would be far from the truth. Cockatiels, for example, have a strong predilection for the leaves of common privet, and most birds like the berries, leaves, or bark of plants like ivy, holly, bird-cherry, and elder. Basically, the damage to growing plants can be minimized.

Planting takes planning. For example, don't plant rhododendrons in aviaries housing hookbills, like parrots and parrakeets. These inveterate gnawers could be poisoned by the leaves of this plant. For other birds, rhododendrons are no problem.

A patch of grass should be in every aviary. It is decorative and a necessity for species like quail, who "weave" a tunnel through long grass in which to nest. Parrakeets also value the grass patch. You will see that after a rain they will roll full of enthusiasm through the wet grass, all the while screeching exuberantly.

Consider planting rushes and corn plants in one of the corners of the aviary. Nun species and *Lonchura* species, among others, really appreciate these plants and they also help control the nail growth of the birds. Also plant some conifers and trees of the *Prunus* species—sturdy ones that don't grow too high. They are especially appropriate for an aviary of small exotics.

Get advice from a gardener or nursery before placing plants in the aviary; not every type of soil is suitable for the plants I am recommending.

For the sleeping coop (night shelter), supplement commercially made perches with a cut tree that is well branched. Your birds will love to climb around on it.

Maintain the plantings in the aviary or run the risk that the place will become overgrown. Trim plants regularly and consult gardening books for proper maintenance.

Plants birds like to build their nests in are:
American arbor vitae (*Thuja occidentalis*) – as hedge.
Austrian pine (*Pinus nigra*) – juvenile.
Bamboo (*Sinarudinaria*) – in small groups.
Beech (*Fagus sylvatica*) – juvenile.
Boxwood, common (*Buxus sempervirens*) – as hedge.
Broom (*Sarothamnus scoperius*) – shrub.
Buddleia (*Buddleia davidii*) – shrub, juvenile.
Climbing rose (*Rosa multiflora*) – as hedge.
Cotoneaster species (*Cotoneaster*) – dwarf and juvenile.
Douglas fir (*Pseudotsuga taxifolia*) – juvenile.
English hawthorn (*Crataegus monogyna*) – juvenile.
English holly (*Ilex aquifolium*) – as hedge.
European elderberry (*Sambucus nigra*) – juvenile.
European hornbeam (*Carpinus betulus*) – juvenile.
European larch (*Larix decidua*) – juvenile.
Falso spirea (*Sorbaria sorbifolia*) – juvenile.
Hydrangea (*Hydrangea*) – against the wall.
Ivy (*Hedera helix*) – against the wall.
Japanese spirea (*Spirea japonica*).
Jasmin (*Philadelphus*) – juvenile.
Juniper (*Juniperus communis*) – juvenile.
Lilac (*Syringa*) – as bush.
Nordmann fir (*Abies nordmanniana*) – juvenile.
Oriental (or Chinese) cedar (*Thuja orientalis*) – juvenile.
Oregon holly grape (*Mahonia aquifolium*).
Privet, common (*Ligustrum vulgare*) – as hedge.
Pyracantha (*Pyracantha*) – against the wall.
Red ribes (*Ribes sanguineum*) – juvenile.
Russian vine (*Polygonum baldschuanicum*) – against the wall.
Silver fir (*Abies alba*) – juvenile.
Snowberry (*Symphoricarpus albus*).
Spruce fir (*Picea excelsa*) – juvenile.
Willow (*Salix*).

Fruits and berries—Which to feed?

Many birds, including, of course, the fruit-eaters, love to eat soft, juicy fruits and berries. Examples are apples, pears, plums, oranges, raisins, currants, bananas, dates, figs, gooseberries, rowan-ash berries, and elderberries (black and red). If you want to feed tropical birds some wild-growing berries, note which types your local wild birds eat; these will also be suitable for your tropical birds.

You can feed dried berries, if you like, but you must soak them for a few hours in cold water before serving.

Poisonous berries

Don't depend on visual attractiveness alone. When gathering berries for your birds, be careful! Remember, the local birds know by instinct which berries to stay away from; but tropical birds have no experience with local wild-growing plants. Use your own knowledge—or get expert advice—to avoid poisoning your birds, not to mention protecting yourself and your family.

Below are a few examples of berries to stay away from:

Holly (*Ilex aquifolium*). In humans, causes serious diarrhea. For an adult, 20 to 30 berries are fatal. For a few birds, like thrushes,

Bushes where birds build nests: upper left, Box (*Buxus sempervirens*); upper right, English ivy (*Hedera helix*); lower left, English holly (*Ilex aquifolium*); lower right, Juniper (*Juniperus communis*).

evidence has shown that a few berries per day are harmless.

Spindle tree (Euonymus europaeus). In humans, causes stomach and intestinal upsets after 8 to 10 hours—as well as fever and rapid pulse. Two berries have proven fatal for a seven-year-old child.

Thorn apple (Datura stramonium). In addition to the berries, other parts of this plant are also poisonous, although not as severely so. In humans, the symptoms include fever, widening of the pupils, racing of the heart, dry mouth, and trouble in swallowing; the skin turns very red. Three berries can kill a child.

Lord and ladies (or cuckoo pint) (Arum maculatum). Berries and leaves are both poisonous. Just a few of the berries or leaves can cause stomach and intestinal upsets, bleeding, and cramps—often fatal.

Blue laburnum (Wisteria sinensis). The seeds and pods can cause serious stomach and intestinal upsets. (The *golden laburnum, Laburnum anagyroides*, causes these symptoms in a more severe form.) Its leaves and bark are also poisonous to birds. Parakeets, for example, which like to gnaw on the branches, can experience fatal results.

Below are more examples of poisonous plants—those with parts other than berries that are nearly all poisonous.

Common Rhamnus (Rhamnus cathartius). Causes prussic acid poisoning, with tightness around the chest and other distress. For a one-year-old child, five to six leaves have proven fatal.

Meadow saffron (Colchicum autumnale). This weed is commonly found along roadsides. It is a very poisonous laxative. It causes acute stomach and intestinal upsets after two to five hours, burning pain in the mouth and throat, tightness in the chest, and racing of the heart. After two to three days, suffocation and death can result.

Lily-of-the-valley (Convallaria majalis). Affects the heart, producing irregular heartbeat. Also, stomach and intestinal upsets, disorientation, convulsions, and possibly death.

Daffodil (Narcissus pseudonarcissus). Only the bulb is poisonous. Causes stomach and intestinal infections, fever, headache, confusion, and suffocation.

Snowdrop (Galanthus nivalis). (Includes both spring and summer snowdrop.) All parts are poisonous. Same symptoms as with the daffodil.

Common monkshood (Aconitum napellus). The bulb, flowers, and leaves are all poisonous. Causes loss of sensation in the mouth, spreading to the rest of the body, as well as nausea, vomiting, cold sensation, restlessness, muscular aches, and then paralysis and suffocation (from paralysis of the respiratory system).

Larkspur (Consolida regalis). Same as with common monkshood, but to a lesser extent.

Purple foxglove (Digitalis purpurea). Affects the heart, producing irregular heartbeat. Also stomach and intestinal upsets, disorientation, and almost certainly death.

Edible berries
Berries with a good, practical use include the following: *Prunus serotina, Rubus odoratus, Polygonum baldschuanicum, Mahonia aquifolium (or hortorum), Viburnum opulus, Rosa canina, Viburnus lantana, Prunus avium*, and *Crataegus oxyacantha (or monogyna)*.

To have berries available out of season, dry them or preserve them in jars. Drying is best done in the oven. When berries begin to look like currants or raisins, take them out of the oven and store them in dry sand. Before serving the dried berries to birds, soak them a few minutes (no more than three) in hot water. This rehydrates them.

Two of the best berries for drying, those of the mountain ash and the elderberry, stain whatever they touch. This is also noticeable in the droppings of birds that eat them and is nothing to be alarmed about.

BREEDING
Breeding cage and aviary birds
As part of a successful breeding program, the aviary should first be located in a quiet place and planted with good, preferably dense plants. Overpopulation must be avoided, so watch for continuous bickering—a sure sign of overly dense stocking. Provide adequate and varied nesting materials and a diet that is balanced as carefully as possible; the latter is very important.

Also important is the composition of the collection. Remember: not all species go well together. In inharmonious aviaries, the number of successful hatches will be considerably reduced—if they occur at all!

Don't start breeding too early; restrict the breeding season to between the end of March or early April to mid-August. Generally, birds should breed three times per season. Additional hatches are not recommended if one wants to avoid egg binding (see page 94), which can be fatal for the female.

Young birds should generally be taken away from their parents as soon as they are independent, or they will inhibit further breeding, and anyway the parents may eventually attack them. For feed, supply seed plus grit, cuttle-fish bone (sepia), and charcoal. Also furnish several drops of cod-liver oil in water or seed to improve the chance of good results, but don't overdose. At the most, put five drops in one kilogram of seed or in one liter of drinking water. The various vitamin preparations should also only be administered with care. Here, too much of a good thing can be bad. If birds are receiving a proper diet, they do not really need extra vitamins anyway. One last piece of advice: store all your vitamin preparations in a dark, cool place (e.g., in a cellar) so that they will retain their quality and strength.

Many fanciers believe that seed-eating birds raise their young exclusively on seed—but that is not the case. Most species feed insects, such as ant larvae, small mealworms, fruitflies, aphids, grasshoppers, spiders, etc. Therefore, insects and spiders should be furnished during the breeding season. You can gather them near home; aphids, for example, can be found on elderberries and roses. During the breeding season, also supply old white bread soaked in milk—as much as your birds use up in one day, two times per week.

It is important to breed only birds that are neither too old nor too young. Check specific age limits for the larger species of birds. For small exotics, I'd recommend 12 months (sometimes 8 months) as the minimum. Breeding females too young causes egg binding in many cases or keeps them from raising their young properly. Birds are too old for breeding in many cases after four to five years.

Breeding birds, of course, should be totally healthy, or else you will get young that will please nobody. Totally healthy young can be produced only by totally healthy parents. And remember, for good fertility, feed and house your birds well.

A greenfinch's nest.

Breeding season

A caution worth repeating because it is often ignored is this: don't start breeding too early in the season. It applies to all cage and aviary birds that are regularly inclined to reproduce. Many birds—zebra finches are one example—even have to be held back somewhat. If left to their own devices, they would be brooding eggs in the heart of winter, and that leads to getting young in the wrong season. Furthermore, early breeding robs strength from the females, which can lead to poor results in later hatches. The young from too-early broods are generally weak, which manifests itself noticeably if you start breeding them at eight months of age.

I recommend keeping birds separated by sex. I know by experience that separating birds by sex is easy if you first band them by sex. Then reform the pairs toward the end of March or early in April. For most species, you will still be able to raise about three to four broods over the course of a breeding season.

If birds can spend the winter building up their reserves for the coming breeding season in peace and quiet, they will express their good health by producing absolutely healthy young. While it is true that you may lose one or even more broods with this system, the young will be of outstanding quality. If you care for them properly, they will be exceptionally pure in color and in superior health. Furthermore, the parent birds will not be worn out and will continue to produce superior young in ensuing seasons. Waiting to breed until the end of the cold, wet weather means you likely will have good weather for the young birds.

Top, a brooding greenfinch. Bottom, female bullfinch feeding her young.

I strongly advise against *extending* the breeding season by using sunlamps or other artificial means. Letting nature follow its course produces the best results. If you start at the end of March, you can continue until mid-August; leave it at that. The young from later broods are weak and poorly feathered. In some cases, a bit of bad weather is enough to cause the young to die. And, once again, an extended breeding season is an excessive strain on the female; among other possible troubles, she can become seriously weakened.

It is advisable to keep males and females apart until shortly before the breeding season. If you use breeding cages housing only a single couple, you won't have any problems in pair formation. If, however, you intend to house several couples together, pair formation may take some effort. I make use of several small exhibit cages. I place the intended pairs inside for about two weeks. I don't give them anything they could possibly use for nesting material, and, of course, I don't give them access to nest boxes. The two birds just spend their time sitting together and eating to their heart's content. (Some extra reserve body fat will do them no harm.) In short, they aren't given the opportunity to start breeding, but they do get a chance to get used to each other's company. It encourages pair formation and mating once they are released into the aviary or colony breeding case. I find that virtually all couples formed in this way stay together the entire breeding season, a big advantage if you want purely inheriting offspring. I use different colored legbands so that I can keep accurate records on the developments that I notice.

To ensure color consistency, I still recommend keeping birds separated by color if you're breeding species such as canaries, budgerigars, or zebra finches. Since the birds you pair may not remain together once they come into contact with other birds of their species, the cagemates should be homozygous for their color: purely inheriting. Birds are not that different from people; they prefer choosing their own mates.

As long as you observe the basic rules, with most species breeding isn't that difficult. Don't force birds to nest if they aren't ready. Exposing them to other breeding may put them in the mood to build nests for themselves. Always wait before taking further actions; generally things will work out all right.

It can happen that two birds just won't fit together. One common sign of this is their continued restarting to build the nest. Or they may produce abnormally large clutches of eggs that are covered by a new nest after several days; this is common with zebra finches, among others. In such cases, it's best to separate the two birds and mate them to others. Generally, these symptoms then disappear.

Another cause of nonbreeding might be the use of birds that are too young. Also, birds that are too old, especially females, may not breed. I have obtained the best results with birds 1–4 years old.

For nest-building materials, I heartily recommend hay and short lengths of sisal from rope. These two basic materials offer birds the opportunity to build a neat nest that is of sound construction. Don't furnish the two types of materials at the same time; first provide hay, then the rope. This is easy to do in housing that contains only one pair and more difficult in colony housing. If you plan well, however, the several breeding pairs won't be very far out of synch. In cases where they are at different stages of nest building, don't panic. Just keep the two building materials available in separate racks; the birds will naturally first use the hay and then the rope.

Most birds don't build very fancy nests, but some species (weavers) do build very artful ones. Generally, they use the hay for the outside, while the inside is carefully lined with rope, short lengths of horse hair, wool, feathers, and such. To avoid problems, unravel the rope thoroughly and be sure not to cut the pieces too long. Pieces of about 6 centimeters are safe. Longer pieces can't be worked into the construction as well, and they pose a real hazard to the birds once they start flying into and out of the nest, because their legs can get caught in the loose strands. If you don't come to their aid quickly in such a situation, the birds can get into serious, even fatal trouble. This is particularly true for species that tend to grow long nails, like spice finches and certain nun species; although problems can also occur with other species, such as quail.

Though hay and sisal are best, other nesting materials need not be avoided. For example, you might supply a little carpet wool, strips of soft (toilet or tissue) paper, hair, thread, or pieces of rags. My smaller exotics, like zebra finches, take to carpet wool in particular, and they also like hemp rope. Natural colors are a runaway favorite. Darker colors, like red, blue, or green, are accepted, but much less so than natural colors.

Most birds are tidy and either eat all droppings the young make in the nest or remove them by carrying them off. Once a parent bird has fed a young, it stops to look attentively for a moment. The young bird that is ready to defecate turns itself slightly before relieving itself. The parent bird then picks up the droppings and carries them off or swallows them. The latter method is frequently used by all members of the thrush family. It looks revolting to us, but it isn't; for one thing, the droppings are neatly packaged in a thin membrane or fecal sac.

Young birds are always incredibly hungry and the demand for feed is tremendous. As their caretaker, you must pay extra attention to feeding during the breeding season. If they are growing rapidly and are in good health, baby birds will eat more than their own body weight in a 24-hour period. The parent birds really hustle to bring them these enormous amounts. Ornithologists have counted the number of feeding flights for several species. The late Dr. Arthur A. Allen of Cornell University recorded on film a female wren that brought feed an amazing 1,217 times between sunrise and sunset. The late Dutch ornithologist Dr. Jacques P. Thijsse counted 1,356 such flights for a blue tit. I have filmed the daylight feeding flights of a zebra finch and counted 1,237.

These extraordinary efforts by the parents may raise questions in your mind: Are all my young birds getting enough feed? Are any of them being forgotten? Do all get their share regularly? Let me reassure you—nature has an infallible system that keeps things right.

When parent birds arrive at the nest with feed, all hungry beaks open wide. All beg and cry for feed. Father or mother then deposit feed in one of the open beaks, at random. If the young bird doesn't swallow it quickly, the parent neatly removes the morsel and puts it in another little beak. Only the young bird that swallows quickly actually gets to eat.

The mechanism at work here is a swallowing reflex that is activated when food is placed in the throat of a young bird. The reflex action works faster and more actively depending on how empty the little crop is. Conversely, the fuller the crop, the slower the reflex works. Therefore the hungrier bird is fed first.

Continuous feeding at this level can't help but produce a large

The embryonic development of a chick, in the following order:
1. soon after incubation starts, the germinal disc can be seen
in the yolk; 2. capillaries extend over the yolk, transporting nutrients
to the embryo; 3. early stages in the development of the eye
and crystalline lens, the four limbs and the encephalon; 4. the embryo
has detached itself from the amnios and moves like a frog; the heart takes

1 2

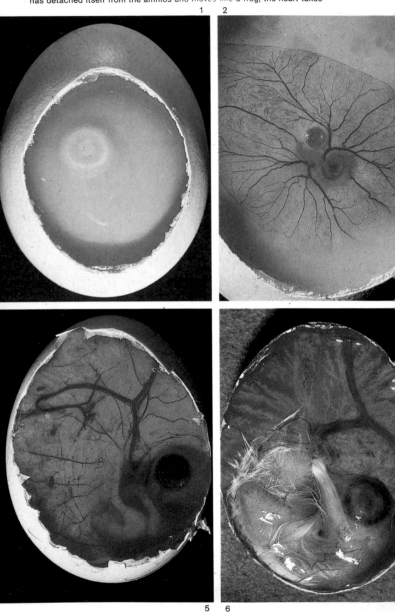

5 6

on its definitive shape and the vascular system is further
developing; 5. the bill hardens and the iris takes on pigment;
6. the head is now fully formed, and the first feathers
can be made out between the feet and wings; the sex organs are formed;
7. the chick pecks out a circle in the shell in order to get out.

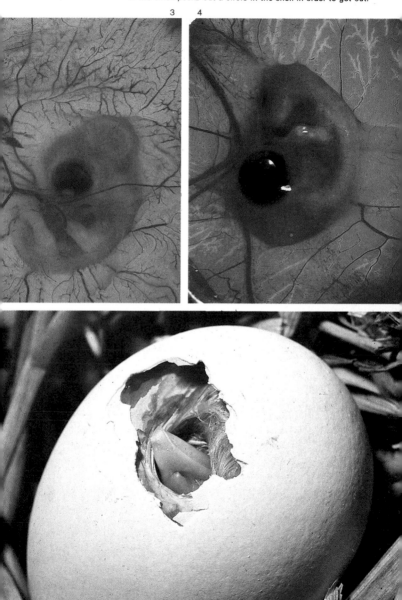

3   4

7

amount of feces. Why one bird is scrupulously tidy about its nest and another—like the zebra finch—isn't so particular will probably remain an open question. The zebra finch doesn't carry off the feces and seldom swallows it. It merely picks the feces from the nestbowl and deposits it neatly on the rim. This is one reason for recommending the type of nest-building materials mentioned above—they provide a certain amount of ventilation. The droppings harden quickly and reduce the likelihood of infection.

Bird fanciers experienced in breeding zebra finches know that these birds are enthusiastic builders. They continue nest building until no more material is available in their quarters. Therefore, it is not advisable to make more nest-building material available than the birds need for one round of breeding. The male does the most work, building the outside wall; the female does the interior decorating. (If she gets too involved in this, she often delays her egg laying.)

Brooding

Brooding is a natural occurrence, an instinctive drive to maintain a species. When this instinct commences to express itself, the breeding season has begun for the birds. Generally, this occurs in spring, but some birds begin earlier or later.

Inside the bird's body, a process develops that is best compared to a fever. Its body temperature rises—but not throughout the whole body. The rise occurs only where it is needed: at the so-called brood spots—locations where a large supply of blood collects—which are pressed against the eggs during brooding. Brood-spot locations differ in various species. You can confirm that observation by comparing several unrelated bird species. The way of sitting on the eggs is influenced—among other factors—by the shape of the nest; the location, size, and heat intensity of the brood spots; and the number of eggs. If you compare a zebra finch with one of the long-legged water birds, for example, you will immediately spot some of these differences.

Fortunately, many tropical birds are known for their excellent brooding abilities. Once they have built their nest, the keeper doesn't have much more to do than to wait patiently.

Many birds build their nest in a nest box. These boxes should be installed fairly high and at differing heights in an aviary. It should be kept away from perches and resting places, or the birds will foul one another. Also don't place the boxes near drinking and feeding stations.

Most tropical birds are generally quite industrious. They will raise brood after brood enthusiastically—especially the domesticated birds like ribbon finches, budgerigars, canaries, Bengalese, and zebra finches. You can see this when these birds build their nests, an activity that primarily involves the male. He diligently searches out a suitable place, often with a big piece of building material in his beak, not resting until he has found a place. This behavior is clearly noticeable with zebra finches. The female remains calmer, as if convinced of the important task awaiting her. Generally, she restricts herself to rearranging and redecorating with materials brought by the male, although I have experienced cases in my aviaries where females also flew back and forth industriously with nesting materials. It can also happen that a female selects certain building materials and deposits it into the beak of the male for him to bring to the developing nest. This type of cooperation is always attractive to watch.

After three or four days, the nest box is completely piled full, with a small hollow left in the center, the so-called nest bowl. The female then starts to pay more attention to the amorous behavior of her mate. She starts to rapidly beat her tail up and down and back and forth, a sign that mating may take place at any moment.

Some other species of birds mate before building nests—using a horizontal branch in a shrub, for example. The couple mate several times, and, about a day later, the female commences to sit on the nest. The first egg can be expected soon after. The clutch of eggs may vary considerably from the standard; fewer eggs need not be cause for alarm, and more eggs are not uncommon in captivity, particularly for the later broods. Feed the birds right and all will be well.

Don't overdo checking on the birds. They can easily be disturbed, and, as a result, they may abandon the nest and the eggs and sometimes even the young. Fortunately, most domesticated birds are not that flighty. I once had to move a zebra finch's nest with a complete clutch of eggs from one birdhouse to another. The birds took no particular notice, continued brooding normally, and raised a first-rate family.

Done properly and with restraint, checking on the birds is justifiable, and sometimes even necessary, although it is preferable not to start until the eggs have been brooded a whole week. Then you can look to determine if all eggs are indeed fertile, removing the infertile ones. You can best avoid breakage by picking up the eggs with a plastic spoon—an operation that's not hard to learn. Don't use your fingers, because the egg shell is too thin and fragile. Hold the egg under a strong light to see if it has been fertilized.

You don't need a light if the eggs have been brooded longer; you don't even have to touch the eggs. The infertile ones at that point have turned a drab red—sometimes called "dirty red." By contrast, fertilized eggs can be distinguished after about five days or so by their purplish brown, shiny look.

My own practice is to look at the eggs after a week to eight days. I take them out of the nest to an egg candler—a box with a 40-watt bulb at the bottom with a net above the bulb to hold the egg. The net is made from soft woolen thread with a moderate mesh—small enough to keep eggs from falling through. A hair net also may be used. Even a cursory look can distinguish fertile from infertile eggs. The strong light lets you see the embryo, the beginning stages of new life; you may even see it move. It is important not to hold the eggs above the light for more than a few seconds; the heat may become too intense, killing the embryo. It is advisable to candle eggs only once. Parent birds usually either throw infertile eggs out of the nest or work them into the edge of the nest.

The most important concern in handling eggs is to be extremely careful. The shells are very fragile and can easily be broken or cracked. The smallest crack is often fatal if it goes unnoticed. If noticed, you can mend it with a piece of transparent tape and save the egg—particularly a larger one.

In general, it is advisable to disturb your birds as little as possible during the breeding season. When you service the feeding and drinking stations, move gently and quietly. Don't make sudden moves or gestures or talk with people who may be watching from outside the aviary. While you are working with your birds, keep any visitors well away from the edge of the aviary. The birds are bound to be uneasy while you are inside, so don't make things worse by unnecessarily heightening their anxiety with visitors hovering nearby.

Once the young are born, they are initially given food that has been predigested in the parents' crops. The parents also eat the smaller pieces of the egg shells left by the young. The bigger pieces are carried off by the parents or worked into the edge of the nest. This instinctive act of preserving the young has been carried over from the wild state; with the pieces of shell discarded, potential predators won't be attracted to the nest.

Depending on the species of birds you are raising, you will hear the begging cries of the young after they are about a week old. The cries stimulate and guide the parents to bring feed to the right place. The parents are also stimulated and guided visually by reflective spots on both sides of the beak of each chick (often the rest of the beak is still black or white). The tip of the chick's tongue may also have small reflective spots, and they may also occur on the inside of the beak and around the inside of the throat. These light spots are called papillae, and ornithologists have identified a number of different ones that can be distinguished by color, light intensity, and location.

It sometimes happens that a parent bird accidentally drags one of the young off the nest as the older bird flies off. The chick apparently gets caught on one of the parent bird's legs. The chick then drops to the floor, but if you can react quickly and put the little one back in the nest, it generally recovers quickly. This type of mishap occurs most frequently when the parent birds fly up too suddenly—another reason to make sure that they aren't startled by sudden noises or movements. Should you pick up a young bird that has fallen from the nest, it may be a good thing to cup it in your (warm) hand for a few minutes, while breathing over it. Usually after a few minutes the young bird will revive; then put it back in the nest.

Occasionally, when the baby birds get older, one of them may flutter from the nest a few days too early—perhaps because it wants to escape from the oppressive warmth and the tight space of the nest bowl (where four or more other young may be pushing each other around). If the weather is warm enough, the precocious young can be left on the aviary floor. The parents will still feed it there. Do return it to the nest if the weather is poor and the little one would be exposed to rain or heavy winds. Gently set the bird inside the nest, and then keep your hand in front of the nest opening until all the little ones inside become completely calm again. If you replace a chick toward evening, it will probably stay in the nest for the night. But it is quite possible that the next day—often early in the morning—it will escape once more. If this happens, don't replace it again. Chicks that leave the nest precociously tend to be disquieting, and—this is undesirable—they also stimulate the rest of the brood to leave the nest early.

The general rule is that young birds may leave the nest once they are fully feathered; but even after that they still like to be fed by the parents. I particularly like to see how young zebra finches beg for food: they beat their wings passionately and turn their heads in the strangest ways. If father and mother don't immediately pay attention to the begging young, the cries for food become increasingly loud and penetrating, and can often be heard at a distance of dozens of meters. One or two weeks after leaving the nest, most young can pretty well care for themselves, but even then they often continue begging for food. They don't just solicit the attention of their parents—they also beg from other birds that are feeding their own young. Even strange birds—other species—are subjected to their pleas. The interesting thing is that virtually the entire aviary population will help the beggars grow up to become independent.

Even when complete independence is reached, young birds are not ready for further breeding. They have not yet attained adult plumage, and their internal organs are still immature. This is especially true for females. Equip the new generation with leg bands and house them separately by sex in a cage or aviary.

The new generation can be considered sexually mature and ready to breed once the birds are eight months to one year of age. Larger species may take longer to reach maturity, and you can find specific recommendations in the entries for the various species.

Finally, one question—rather a side issue—remains to be asked: is it possible to keep a single pet bird?

The answer is a qualified "yes" in the case of canaries, Bengalese, green singing finches, budgerigars, parrots, or mynah birds. You can house one of these in a cage by itself without risking drooping.

Still, most birds are truly "family minded" and therefore are best kept in pairs (although some species, such as weavers and pheasants, have a different family structure, being mainly colony breeders or living in groups). Placing extra males or females in a group is generally not recommended. Also remember: you can put one or three pairs of a species together, but *never* two, as in the latter case the male often shows interest in the female of the other pair. Strangely enough this seldom occurs when there are three or more pairs in the same cage or aviary.

Nest boxes

Nest boxes come in many varieties: in addition to birch nesting logs for Australian parrakeets and budgerigars, there are closed and half-open nest boxes, nest baskets, nest bowls, woven heather nests, and others. No matter which you use, provide more of them than you have bird couples—double the number of nest boxes, if possible—to avoid fights.

After a little experience, every bird breeder seems to develop a preference for certain types and models, even though the birds definitely have no model preference. Birds that brood in hollows will also use an open nest box for one brood and a half-open one for the next brood in the same season.

Disposable nest boxes are being used in the United States, Britain, and to a lesser extent in Germany and Denmark. They are burned after each breeding season to eliminate lice and other small vermin that gather in the corners, cracks, knots, and seams. If you intend to re-use the nest boxes a following season, wash them out thoroughly, using hot water with a detergent and a disinfectant, paying close attention to the hiding places for lice and vermin just mentioned. Rinse with clear water.

Commercial nest boxes should not be hung in shrubs because this would inhibit the birds' urge to build their own free nests. Place commercial nest boxes in the covered part of the aviary, under the roof, along the wall. If you have only parrakeets and their relatives, however, you can place commercial nest boxes in the open flight (run) as well. If you use closed nest boxes drill some ventilation holes in the sides directly under the roof; this prevents the young from suffocating if the parent birds decide to rest by sitting in the nest opening and blocking the fresh-air supply.

Hyacinth macaw chicks and eggs.

Here are some other suggestions for nesting possibilities:

Earthenware bowls lined with commercially made nests of coconut fiber are suitable for canaries bred for song and color; British birds, such as finch, gold finch, linnet; and canary hybrids of these birds. This structure is quite stable, and many breeders fasten a piece of foam rubber between it and the aviary wall, so that the nest can move a little. This is very important, because young birds depend on vibrations to sense that one of the parents has arrived with food.

The wooden Harzer Canary Show Cages can also be used as a nesting place for other canaries and finches. They are more suitable for the outdoor aviary, but the indoor aviary is another possibility.

A closed nest box (or a birch nest log that's not too deep) is best for all the somewhat-larger tropical birds, such as Bengalese, strawberry finch, zebra finch, and other Australian grass finches. The entrance hole should be 3 1/2 centimeters in diameter—no larger or the birds may not accept it. Most birds prefer a nest box that's a little too large than an entrance hole that's too big. They will cover the entrance hole with feathers or some other nesting material if the hole is too large.

The interior dimensions should be about 15 × 15 centimeters of floor space and a height of 15 centimeters as well. It is possible to use smaller boxes (suitable for waxbills, for example), but they are not as satisfactory.

Birch nest logs or roomy, closed nest boxes—preferably with a double floor—are best for budgerigars. The upper floor should be

removable and slightly hollowed with a gouge, so that eggs don't roll away. Budgerigars use very little if any nesting materials. The floor should preferably measure 17 × 15 centimeters, and be 20 centimeters high. The diameter of the entrance hole should be 4 centimeters.

A nest box of wood at least an inch thick is appropriate for lovebirds. The dimensions should be at least 17 × 17 centimeters for the floor and 25 centimeters for the height—preferably several centimeters more. The diameter of the entrance hole should be 5 centimeters. The biggest lovebird, *Agapornis roseicollis* (peach-faced lovebird), should get more space—at least 20 × 20 × 28 centimeters.

Large boxes or logs of at least 27 × 27 centimeters are needed for large birds of the parrot family, such as Bourke's parrakeet, elegant grass parrakeet, red-rumped parrakeet, splendid grass parrakeet, turquoisines, and cockatiels. The entrance hole should measure 7 centimeters in diameter. All nest logs must have a landing platform at the entrance hole. Particularly if you use a rather deep nest log, fasten a strip of screen or mesh on the inside just below the hole to make it easier for the bird to get out. (Make sure that the screen has no sharp points or hooks that could hurt the birds.) Install a double bottom, so the top floor can slide in and out. The top floor should also have a shallow hollow place to keep the eggs from rolling away. On the nest log or box floor deposit some sawdust, wood shaving, moss, peat pulled apart into small pieces, or—best of all—rotted wood. Before placing the nesting material inside, moisten it thoroughly. You don't have to push down the material to make a hollow for the nest; some books advise you to do this, but don't bother; the birds will arrange things to suit themselves anyway.

Even larger boxes, over a meter long, should be provided for members of the parrot family that are larger than the species just mentioned. Although required box size is specified in discussions of the various species, dimensions needed to accommodate a number of well-known species appear below.* If you have birds of about the same size, you can follow the dimensions noted here, although you will still often have to experiment. This makes the hobby that much more interesting.

Type of bird	Floor space	Height	Diameter of entrance
Golden-fronted and tovi parrakeets	22 × 32 cm	32 cm	7 cm
Red-bellied conure, sun conure, thick-billed parrot, nandaya conure	27 × 27 cm	38 cm	8 cm
Amazones	35 × 35 cm	55 cm	15 cm
African gray parrot	30 × 30 cm	50 cm	12 cm
Ring-neck parrakeet	27 × 27 cm	37 cm	8 cm
Alisterus-species	27 × 27 cm	37 cm	8 1/2 cm
Trichoglossus species and Alexandrine parrakeet	32 × 32 cm	47 cm	10 cm
Port Lincoln parrakeet and Barnard's parrakeet	27 × 27 cm	45 cm	12 cm
Rosella species	25 × 25 cm	37 cm	8 cm

When you buy parrakeets or parrots, it is wise either to buy their breeding box as well, or build one that is as much like the old one as possible.

Design a breeding box that allows easy access. A roof with hinges or a hinged door in one of the slides is a useful feature, permitting you to check on the nest if necessary. Again, don't overdo this or you can make your birds shy and flighty, and they may abandon the nest and their eggs or young. Nest control can be accomplished much more easily and more safely with domesticated and tame birds, such as many hookbills.

Homemade boxes should never be built of plywood or similar layered material because hiding places for all kinds of vermin and bacteria are created as soon as the glued-together sheets start separating. At any rate, these materials, if used, should be discarded after one season. (A good nest log—which is more sanitary and lasts longer—is actually more economical than plywood or composition board nests.)

British birds as well as many others also like to build their own nests from scratch in trees and bushes. This presents no problem, provided you are prepared to accommodate them. You must have the right kind of plantings for the birds to build a normal nest—for example, broom, heather, elderberry, ivy, arbor vitae, and juniper. If there aren't enough forks in the plantings, tie a few branches together with a piece of wire and make a nesting place out of it with,

---

* The dimensions given for floor and height refer to inside measurements and must be regarded as minimums. A few centimeters larger will never be a problem.

for example, a canary nest that can be bought ready-made at the store. Most of the planting will be in the open part of the aviary, so construct a temporary roof above the nest if you expect a lot of rain during the breeding season.

Provide birds with a wide variety of nest boxes hung at various heights. Don't hang them too close together; allow at least 60 centimeters between them. Although some squabbling is inevitable, fights will be avoided. Squabbling is bound to occur from time to time, but don't worry about such altercations if they stay mild and occur only occasionally. If a particular nest box engenders too much competition, it is wise to furnish more boxes of the same type. Don't hang the new boxes close to the one that started all the commotion, but spread them around the aviary. And again, homemade nest boxes should be of sturdy wood, like oak or beech, and never plywood or composition board.

Don't paint nest boxes; just let them weather naturally. Unpainted, they can be cleaned and disinfected more thoroughly.

Most nest box models available commercially are too small; that's true in particular for the well-known birch logs. For successful breeding be sure that the dimensions of your nest boxes meet or exceed the minimums noted above. Only then can you ensure that the female will lay her eggs. If you have nest boxes that are too deep for the birds, fill them up with nesting material to just under the entrance hole. This prevents the birds, especially zebra finches, from building nest upon nest to reach the hole. (Breeding birds like to look outside, to see what is going on in the aviary.)

Eggs

A bird's egg has various parts. The round yoke or *ovum* has several layers, alternately yellow and white in color. In the center of the ovum lies the *germinal spot*, the incipient structure for a new life, that of the young bird or chick. The new life comes into being during brooding, and the developing chick is fed from the yolk and the egg white. The yolk is surrounded by a yolk sack and a yolk membrane. The yolk floats and is cushioned in several layers of albumen (egg white), which consists mostly of water, and a little protein. The yolk is held in place by spiral bands of tissue, the *chalazae*. These bands enable the yolk to turn about, it is believed, so that the germinal spot always remains on top, and therefore receives most of the heat provided by the brooding bird.

One specialist, the Dutch zoologist Dr. W. P. J. Hellebrekers, holds that the "chalazae serve to keep the yolk from falling against the inner shell membrane and adhering to it. Also, they serve to prevent the shock-waves that otherwise would occur when an egg is suddenly turned."[*]

The egg white is surrounded by two shell membranes, which form an *air chamber* at the blunt end of the egg. The outer layer, the *shell*, is not solid, but is riddled with numerous tiny pores, making the exchange of gases possible. The shell may be smooth, in some cases, deeply pitted (as in toucan eggs), or rough and corrugated (as in emu eggs). It may be thick or so thin that the yolk can be seen through it. The shell can have widely differing designs, which are typical for the species that lays them. Other ways to identify eggs are by size, form, color, and structure.

Many birds that nest in holes, like parrots and parrakeets,

* *Limosa* supplement, Vol. 26, No. 1-2, p. 6.

woodpeckers, and some ducks, lay white eggs. Those of some species that lay eggs on the ground have designs on the shell that help camouflage the eggs. The size of the egg is not so much dependent on the size of the bird as on the amount of yolk.

The ovaries of an adult female bird look much like a small bunch of grapes. These are the individual ova that ripen in the breeding season, ready to be fertilized. A fertilized yolk or ovum moves from the ovary either by ciliary movement or by peristalsis to a type of long tube, the magnum of the oviduct where, in a couple of hours, it receives the various layers of albumen. The developing egg then acquires the double shell membranes, when it passes to the isthmus. From there it goes to the uterus where it remains for ten or twenty hours, while receiving its shell and pigment (color). Then the completed egg passes through the muscular vagina and is laid.

When brooding or incubation is completed, the chick frees itself with the aid of its egg tooth, a little hook on its upper mandible that drops off soon after the chick hatches.

Legbands

To differentiate between young birds, by sex, they must be banded, which many people, especially those who are inexperienced, consider a nerve-racking job. If you proceed calmly, however, it isn't so bad. You can obtain bands through your bird club or from the pet store. They are engraved with the current year and a serial number, which number enables you to identify the young's parents. If you keep accurate records, you will be able to see that, for example, 6, 7, 8 came from two birds with the designation 1983, serial number 2 and 3.

To fit leg bands, hold the bird loosely in your right hand in a way that allows you to grasp one of the legs easily between your thumb and index finger. With your left hand, daub some petroleum jelly (Vaseline) on the toes. "Glue" the three long toes together with the Vaseline and lay them forward. Lay the short toe back, and "glue" it to the leg. Everything is now arranged in a straight line, permitting you to push the legband into place easily.

Parrots' and parrakeets' feet (zygodactyl feet) are exceptionally well equipped for climbing: the first and the fourth toe point backwards forming a big X with the second and third. The technique for banding a zygodactylic bird is basically the same. Just put the two front toes through the band first and "glue" both back toes to the leg. With small exotics, you can even hold the toes together with saliva.

Band birds when they are seven to eight days old. Canaries are usually banded when the droppings start to show up on the edge of the nest, which means that the parents are no longer carrying off the feces. Therefore, the problem of one parent bird mistaking the shiny band for dirt and trying to remove it from the nest is avoided. For the same reason, blacken newly placed bands with a felt-tip pen. It is also advisable to do the banding toward evening, when the birds are not so actively cleaning up anymore.

If you want to band older birds, use a band that can be clamped shut with the fingernails or fingertips. Be gentle, however; a bird's leg is very fragile and can easily be broken or injured. Special clamp-on color bands are particularly useful for older birds whose hatching dates are unknown. These color bands are made of light metal or hard plastic, while the above-mentioned identification bands are usually of copper or aluminum and are spiral-shaped.

Color bands, however, are useful only when there are no other characteristics by which birds can be identified. If, for example, you own only a single unbanded pair of fawn zebra finches, it isn't necessary to band them. The young from this couple would receive the normal, closed leg bands.

Color bands are often handy to distinguish several birds of the same variety kept in the same aviary or breeding cage; pair A gets a green band, B gets yellow, C red, etc.

If during an extra busy breeding season you neglect to band the young, you can do so later provided you know who the parents are. You can use the normal leg bands, which is more trouble, but generally workable. If you don't know who the parents are (this can happen in large group aviaries containing several pairs of birds of the same species and color), it doesn't pay to band with a closed band. If at all possible, the best procedure remains to band birds when they are seven or eight days old.

After banding the birds, clean their legs and toes thoroughly with a bit of cotton. When you place the young birds back in the nest, watch the parent birds closely, since many of the females will do all they can to remove the rings from their chicks' feet. This can result in some very unfortunate consequences, such as a chick falling out of the nest. If not killed by the fall, a chick could sustain a serious injury—a broken or badly wounded leg. If one week after the ringing procedure nothing has happened, we can safely assume that the parents have not been bothered by them, and that in all likelihood they will not unwittingly endanger their chicks in a last attempt to remove them. Blackening the rings by holding them in the flame of a candle will often help to avoid parental intervention for it is particularly the bright, shiny (and strange) nature of the object that so annoys the parents.

GENETICS

The inexperienced bird fancier will soon get to know the needs of his birds for housing, feeding, and general care, and will learn what steps to take if any get sick. Next comes the question of breeding them, and successful breeding demands a working knowledge of genetics. This is not as difficult as it often sounds.

At this stage in your hobby, you are determined to get a better grasp of heredity and purposeful breeding. Perhaps you once had a pair of white zebra finches and fully expected to raise a bunch of white offspring. Instead, you were surprised to discover that your birds produced two gray and three white young. How did that happen, when other breeders seem to know exactly what to expect from mating a certain pair of birds?

The answer lies in the rules of heredity. Let us discuss its chief aspects by taking a well-known example; the zebra finch. (The same basic principles apply to other birds.)

Most living creatures (including humans) develop from the union of an egg cell, contributed by the female, and a sperm cell, contributed by the male. The union produces a new cell, called a zygote. After a period of development, the zygote is formed into a new organism. All higher plant and animal life, including humans, contain millions of cells, all derived from the zygote.

The enormously large number of cells develop through cell division. The original zygote divides and, after a period of development, the two daughter cells also divide, and so on. Bird eggs also develop from a single cell—with a calcified shell around it

Structure of a bird's egg.

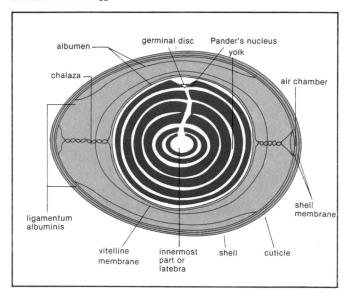

germinal disc   Pander's nucleus

albumen

yolk

chalaza

air chamber

ligamentum
albuminis

shell
membrane

vitelline
membrane

innermost
part or
latebra

shell

cuticle

for protection. After being brooded by a mother bird or both parents, a new young bird is produced. After hatching, the young continue to grow through cell division. Once the bird is fully grown, continued cell division doesn't result in further growth, but rather in replacing worn-out cells.

Let us return our attention to the very first cell, the zygote, initiated by the union of the egg cell and the sperm cell contributed by the mother and father bird. In the nucleus of these reproductive cells—called gametes—are chromosomes, small bodies that carry genes. Genes are chemical units which determine various hereditary traits.

Chromosomes come in pairs, and each is composed of two chromatids; in other words, two chromatids form one chromosome. The chromosomes determine the expressed characteristics of a living organism.

When a cell divides, the chromosomes are divided also, so that each daughter cell receives the same number of chromosomes (as the mother cell). In actuality, the chromosomes split up into chromatids, each of which has the ability to grow into a complete chromosome.

A major exception in cell division affects the reproductive cells only and causes sperm and egg to have only half the usual number of chromosomes. If this were not so, the union of two gametes would produce a cell with double the normal number of chromosomes.

Let me illustrate with this example. If the body cells of a species have 18 chromosomes, the egg cell of the female and the sperm cell of the male each have nine chromosomes. Unite these two cells, and you get a zygote with 18 chromosomes. This 18-chromosome zygote undergoes regular cell division, as discussed earlier. In the course of time, there will be 2, 4, 8, 16, 32, 64, 128, 256, 512, 1024, 2048, 4096 cells, and so on, and each of these cells maintains 18 chromosomes.

A zebra finch chick receives hereditary factors from both the male and the female parent—half from each. However, this does not mean that a cross of two different colors will produce a combination of these two colors. That is because one has to take account of visible and invisible factors, also called recessive (or "shy") and dominant (or "bossy"). Both genes (factors) are important in understanding the heredity of birds like zebra finches. One color can strongly dominate another.

For example, with a white bird and a gray bird that both inherit purely, each is homozygous (that is, pure) for its color. That means that the white bird has parents that were white, and these also had white parents, and so on. The parallel situation was true for the gray bird. If we now cross the white and gray birds together, we will get all gray young that are "split" for the factor white—meaning that they carry an invisible white factor. We won't get the gray young with white patches, because the gray factor is dominant—it bosses the white factor; conversely, the white factor is recessive—it makes way for the gray.

To denote this situation, breeders designate such birds as normal/white zebra finches; the slash denotes that the birds are split for a trait, in this case for "white." One can also say that the birds are gray, split for white, or gray split white or gray/white.

The young carry a gene for white. If two birds that are split for white are crossed, the rules of heredity indicate that we should get some pure white birds—theoretically, 25 percent. The white present in both parents thus had the opportunity to express itself in this percentage of the offspring, despite the presence of the gray factor.

We now know that if a bird has a certain expressed color, this color is not always expressed by the young. As stated earlier, a cross of gray × white definitely produces no gray-white or white-gray offspring nor any combination of the two colors. (There are nonbird cases where a mix *can* occur, for example, in the snapdragon. A red flower × white flower produces pink flowers, and such a factor is called "intermediate.") In the case of gray and white zebra finches, however, the color factor is either recessive or dominant, and only the dominant factor is expressed visibly.

Birds of "impure heredity" are called "heterozygous." Let us see what this implies in practice. A cross of white × gray produces entirely gray young that carry a hidden potential for white and are called split for white. A cross of white × gray/white produces 50 percent homozygous, pure white birds; that's because as in this cross, the white factor had a strong presence. The male was totally white and the female was split (that is, gray/white). The other half of the offspring are gray in color *but* split for white.

If, however, we breed a couple that is gray and split for white, then gray will once again dominate white and most of the young will appear gray; however, some 50 percent are gray, split for white (and thus heterozygous); 25 percent are purely inheriting grays (homozygous); and 25 percent are purely inheriting whites (homozygous).

This example illustrates how strongly a certain color may dominate, so that apparently purely colored birds turn out to be heterozygous once they are bred. Conversely, homozygous birds are absolutely true breeding for the factor involved.

The point is that impurely inheriting birds and those purely inheriting ones may sometimes be outwardly indistinguishable from one another. In the cross of white × gray/white, we saw that 50 percent of the young would be gray/white, but with the external appearance of a homozygous gray zebra finch. Only further crosses will reveal that they carry the hidden color white, which will be expressed in a certain percentage of their young.

If, however, we mate two homozygous birds, we are guaranteed to have young with pure heredity for color. The parent birds cannot pass on a color trait that they themselves don't carry. Of absolutely pure breeding, they cannot pass on gray, white, or cream color. Their young are 100 percent pure breeding and they also will produce purebreeding young.

In practice, it isn't all that easy to get one's hands on a pair of homozygous birds. Most breeders still allow too many types of color variants to breed with one another, too often without forethought. Eventually, it becomes practically impossible to determine the hereditary background of the young, and therefore difficult to tell which expressed color will be inherited purely. Assurance on this score is possible only if it is possible to follow carefully the progeny of a breeding pair and note the results, case by case. This is difficult, if not impossible, in a colony breeding cage or aviary; the only way would be to populate group quarters with homozygous pairs of a single color. For the rest you would need single breeding cages.

Heredity follows the so-called Mendelian laws. Gregor Mendel (1822–1884), a monk and botanist, worked principally with garden plants, particularly peas. Very briefly, the Mendelian laws hold the following:

1. Male and female reproductive cells have the same influence in passing on heritable traits. In other words, it doesn't matter at all if a certain trait is passed on by the father or by the mother.

2. Gametes are purely inheriting and therefore can never have a bastardizing effect. In other words, the sex cells never contain *pairs* of chromosomes because they only contain one chromosome of every pair. Because the number of chromosomes is halved, a reproductive cell can only pass on one trait from each pair of chromosomes.

3. Heredity involves many tendencies that work independently of each other. It was the Danish naturalist, Wilhelm Johannsen (1857–1927), who named these basic hereditary units, "genes."

An important conclusion to be drawn from the study of genetics is that when any color, like white or fawn, is being discussed, the reference is to totally *pure* white and *pure* fawn. Applied to birds, this means that the color with which they are designated is homozygous, or purely inheriting. If the bird is heterozygous (not purely inheriting) for a color, then this is designated by noting the invisible color after the visible one. As mentioned earlier, a heterozygous white bird that carries a hidden factor for gray is designated as white/gray.

Another key word often used in genetics is inbreeding and the associated key question is whether inbreeding is useful or dangerous. Many breeders have come to associate the word with bad breeding; they consider it a mistake, a very serious mistake, that leads to "sick, weak and defective" birds.

Genetic phenomena: left, an albino blackbird, a mutation. The bird on the right was born of a male serin and a female yellow canary.

It is quite true that certain defects in birds show up as a result of inbreeding, but it is important to understand the underlying cause. We have seen that parent birds can pass on certain traits, including shape, color, and singing ability, to their young. As a consequence, if a bird with an undesirable trait is bred to another bird with the same undesirable trait (hidden or expressed), the tendency to inherit that trait is strong. This effect occurs frequently by breeding birds that are close relatives. Their young tend quite strongly to have this undesirable trait—not because close relatives were mated (which is called inbreeding), but because both parents had the same undesirable trait and passed it on to their young. Close relatives in inbreeding include father and daughter, mother and son, brother and sister, and cousins. More distant relatives are not considered; in fact, many people don't include cousins.

Inbreeding itself should not be feared, provided that we breed good birds—birds that have been well fed, properly selected, without defects, and of the desired color and hidden (split) trait. Inbreeding can even be quite useful and necessary: useful to reach a breeding goal by a shorter, surer route, as with a certain color variation; and necessary to be able to retain a certain mutation.

Say, for example, that you want to breed to obtain a pair of white zebra finches. And assume that you start with a white zebra finch and a gray one, both purely inheriting. In this simple example, all young are gray split for white (gray/white). Now inbreeding begins. The original white male is mated to a gray/white daughter, resulting in 50 percent pure white young and 50 percent that are gray split for white. So in just two matings, you will have achieved your goal of getting a pure white couple when you originally had only one pure white bird—the original male parent. Just mating him with a pure white granddaughter produces 100 percent white offspring.

This was a rather hypothetical example. In fact, the young from a white × white mating with the background we assumed would not be good birds to breed; too much inbreeding would have occurred. In practice, it is wiser to breed toward the desired goal with two parallel lines of birds. Then you don't have to inbreed repeatedly because you can form couples by taking white males and white females from two different lines.

Now a word about *mutations*. By a mutation we mean the sudden appearance of a color or form in a plant or animal that can't be explained by the rules of genetics. An event (usually of an unknown nature) takes place causing the genetic composition of the chromosomes to change. Such changes in color or form can be brought about intentionally, but with amateur breeders they usually occur spontaneously.

Mutations shouldn't be confused with *modifications*. Color, for example, can be affected by special feeds which lack certain ingredients such as vitamins, or contain certain additives, such as carrot juice used to bring about a deeper red in red canaries. These changes disappear when regular feeding—without the special color modifiers—is resumed. Modifications cannot be passed on.

It is possible to use inbreeding to establish a mutation. Let us assume, for example, that during normal breeding a mutation is discovered: a fawn zebra finch with a red tail. Let us further assume that the parent birds are homozygous for all color factors, so that they aren't split for any color. The mutant is a female and the male parent was the source of the mutation. In this case, you could mate the male to the mutant daughter and expect 50 percent of the offspring to carry the mutant trait; fawn with a red tail.

In a less fortunate example, the male is *not* the source of the mutation. In this case, the road to success is longer by one round of breeding. Mating the mutant daughter to the male parent would produce all normal-looking fawn offspring; but half of them would be split for the mutation and thus be able to pass on the trait. Mating one of the young to the original mutant could then produce more mutant birds.

These two fairly lengthy discussions on the productive use of inbreeding should have rehabilitated this strange word in your vocabulary. In our hobby, inbreeding can often be useful and necessary.

Sex

The sex or gender of a bird also is determined by chromosomes and the hereditary factors carried in their genes. Sex is determined by a single pair of chromosomes, one of which is the X (male)-chromosome and the other is a Y (female)-chromosome. (To be completely accurate, the Y-chromosome is really a *missing* chromosome, but we will use it here because most discussions of genetics refer to X- and Y-chromosomes as if they really existed.

A male zebra finch has two X (or male)-chromosomes. The female has one X (or male)-chromosome and one Y (or female)-chromosome. That one seemingly simple difference is all that stands between the sexes. Males are determined when a female contributes her X-chromosome to a new life and the male contributes one of his two

X-chromosomes. Females are determined when the female parent contributes a Y-chromosome to the male's X-chromosome (all the male can contribute is X-chromosome). In other words, unlike with man and many other mammals, the *female*, not the male, determines the sex of the offspring.

This relationship can be expressed schematically. The symbol ♂, representing the Roman god Mars, stands for male (the plural is ♂♂). The symbol ♀, representing Venus, represents female (the plural ♀♀). The formula showing the determination of a male is: (♂) X-chromosome × (♀) X-chromosome = 2 X-chromosomes = male.

This provides the basis for understanding another term important in breeding: *sex-linked heredity*. This refers to instances where color factors are located on the sex chromosomes, producing a situation where sex and color remain in a fixed relationship. As a result, sex is connected with certain externally observable traits of a living creature such as a zebra finch. Technically, sex is linked to the trait or traits in question.

Not every bird carries observable sex-linked traits. In the case of zebra finches, only the black mask, black back, fawn-brown and cream colors are sex linked. In the female, the factors for black mask, black back, fawn-brown and cream are missing. Therefore, females cannot inherit black mask, black back, fawn-brown or cream as a split factor; only males are split for these colors.

In budgerigars, cinnamon, opaline, and slate blue are sex-linked traits, while there can be sex-linked as well as non-sex-linked lutinos and albinos. A cross between cinnamon and noncinnamon produces females that are cinnamon and males that are split for cinnamon; the males don't express the cinnamon color although they possess the hidden potential for cinnamon. This is true for *all* males produced by this cross.

In canaries, melanine is a sex-linked inherited color; melanine is composed of brown and black pigment, and both brown and black are inherited in a sex-linked fashion. This brings about a number of complications.

In order for a male canary to express the brown color, he will have to inherit the gene for brown *double* (a double quantity of the brown character). If a male has only one gene for brown, then his appearance is not brown, but he does possess (split) the brown color in his genes and he can pass the brown trait on. Such a male canary can be called brown-inheriting. By contrast, it is sufficient for a female to have a single gene for brown to express brown externally. This means, however, that there are no brown-inheriting females that don't look brown. The same can be said for other pigments. Females can only pass on their visible colors, but males can pass on not only their externally visible color but also an invisible color. In other words, pigmented females are always homozygous for their pigmented color, while canary males also can be heterozygous for their pigmented color.

Pigmented color refers to the pigment possessed by the original green canary in some form—including agate, brown, isabel (cinnamon) and pastel (colors listed according to their relative dominance). Green, the natural color, is dominant over agate; agate dominates brown; brown dominates isabel, and isabel dominates pastel. This relationship is important to keep in mind. Mating a brown homozygous male with an isabel female, for example, produces brown females, because brown dominates isabel; and

An example of sexual dimorphism; in this species of parrot
(*Eclectus roratus*) the male is green and the female is red.

these brown females are all homozygous because heterozygous
brown females don't exist. The males are brown, but can pass on the
isabel trait and are thus heterozygous.

Finding and Selecting Good Birds

If you go to a bird show, you will notice that birds are judged not
only by color but also by shape and condition. A breeder who works
sloppily will not get far. He won't have any ribbons in his trophy case
and the quality of his birds will degenerate. A breeder who
concentrates on breeding as many birds as possible, without
attention to color, shape, or condition will gradually see his birds
become unmarketable. Even an inexperienced beginner will shy
away from such birds. The person who has his heart in his work will
not rest until he has real competition-class birds. And he will have
every right to ask a good price for his breeding stock.

The best way to achieve such a goal is to conduct a rigidly
executed yearly selection among your birds. You should start off
with good parent stock that is in first-rate condition (see
Acquisition). If you have sickly birds, you may be able to nurse them
back to health; but color and form, for example, are difficult to
change. Such birds should be kept only if they are strictly for
enjoyment, without the intention to enter any exhibits with them or
to breed them for profit. I suggest that for the first four years you
devote yourself to breeding for condition; breeding for color can
come later.

Another way to insure quality is to breed birds that inherit traits precisely as you have anticipated, meanwhile keeping close watch on health and quality. Don't begin, however, before you have developed a good routine. This routine, or breeding program, depends very much on a single issue that can plague an old experienced hand in the bird business as much as a newcomer: how can you tell by looking at good, healthy birds which laws of inheritance they follow? Generally, this is a question of good luck since it isn't easy to acquire a purely inheriting (homozygous) pair of birds (see *Genetics*). You may think you have a pair and still find, after several rounds of breeding, that birds appear with strange coloration that was noticeable neither in the father nor in the mother. If you do have impurely inheriting (heterozygous) birds, however, you don't have an unsolved problem, and it certainly is no reason to give up the bird fancy.

For example, to get zebra finches that inherit as purely as possible, you need to work with a single color or with several colors, each of which is *separately* housed in an aviary or cage; fawn with fawn and so on. Conversely, people who breed blindly and mate color variants and mutants without thought, will get an odd collection of colors, many of them awful looking, with which nothing further can be attained.

You must determine which color variants and mutants in your aviary or breeding cage are pure (homozygous). If their heritage is not pure—and you won't be able to tell this by looking at them—they will have some *hidden* traits, meaning that they are *split* or homozygous for these factors. This condition often only becomes apparent after mating the birds and looking at the young. It is therefore important to acquire this information in advance of breeding.

If you know that your white zebra finches pass on the white trait purely, then the rules of heredity will insure that mating white with white will produce pure white. If you then use leg bands of certain colors, you will be able to easily distinguish old birds from young ones. This is important for further breeding and equally so for attaining other color variations and mutations.

For example, say that you want to breed purely inheriting gray into your zebra finches, which is sometimes necessary. If you know that the gray birds you are mating with your stock are purely inheriting for the gray factor, then the procedure is fairly simple. If, however, you introduce *impurely* inheriting gray zebra finches, colors other than the desired color variation or mutation may appear.

To breed a pure line, you must keep color with color. Any impure young that appear out of the matings (for example, white zebra finch young with gray in their feathers) should be removed. After a while, you will come up with a homozygous white line, provided you also remove from breeding any parent birds that produce young indicating that the parents are not purely inheriting for white. You will then have a line that is pure white "inside and out." You should understand that this goal cannot be reached in a short time, certainly not if you have to search on your own for those birds in your stock that are homozygous. You bypass this problem if you purchase homozygous birds from a trusted source.

Still, it is interesting to try doing it yourself. Just realize that it may be a long time before you have birds with the same hereditary factors so that you are able to establish a breeding line. Buying such birds will cost more; on the other hand, you will soon have purely inheriting young to sell for which you can ask a good price. But don't overtax your birds; leave it to someone else to determine the absolute maximum number of young that can be produced to make money.

Records and Recordkeeping

When you breed young birds or have many birds of the same species, it is of utmost importance for you to keep good records on the condition of your stock. Together with the use of leg bands, discussed earlier, your records will help establish who's who in the aviary. You don't need anything fancy; a loose-leaf notebook will do the job.

Every bird should have its own page in your notebook. As time passes, the ensuing record will be of immeasurable value if you are a hobbyist who wants to accomplish something in the world of bird breeding. It will reflect your good management, which will make a favorable impression on any future purchaser.

It is of the greatest value that you maintain good breeding records. If you update them regularly, you will eventually be able to characterize your bird pairs as to traits they possess in visible or invisible form. You will also be able to determine whether they breed well or poorly, eat heavily or sparingly, tend to fight or are peace loving, and so on. It may take several breeding seasons before you know everything there is to know about your birds.

Let me show you an example of the records I keep by taking a page out of my own notebook on zebra finches. (In your own notebook, you can make any changes, improvements, or additions that seem useful to you.)

Location: Breeding cage No. 67
I.D. No. of male: 72-1984
I.D. No. of female: 38-1984
Expressed coloration of male: Gray
Expressed coloration of female: Gray
Color of leg band (male and female): Blue
Notation: To differentiate them from any young they may produce, this pair of adult zebra finches have their colored legbands on the right leg.
Birth date of young: May 17, 1984
Leg bands of young: I.D. No.: 14-1984; 15-1984; 17-1984; 18-1984 (No. 16-1984 died in an accident one week after fledging)
Color of leg bands (all young): Blue (on left leg)
Coloration of young:
14 (male): Gray (= normal)
15 (male): Gray
16 (male): Gray (deceased)
17 (female): Fawn
18 (female): Gray
Special remarks:
1. Expressed coloration is that of normal gray zebra finches.
2. Not homozygous, as evident from coloration of young (gray and fawn).
3. Male parent bird passes down a fawn trait (No. 17 is a fawn female).
4. Female parent is a good breeder.

This recorded information forms the basis of a number of conclusions. Since fawn is a so-called sex-linked trait, it seems from the breeding record that the male is not pure gray (or, technically, he is not homozygous); rather, he passes down a trait for fawn, as shown by the first brood in the fawn female, No. 17.

My conclusion regarding the fawn color trait was confirmed in the second round of breeding, which, according to my further records, produced two fawn females. If I now want to produce fawn males, I have to mate the male parent (No. 72) with one of his fawn daughters. This is an example of purposeful inbreeding. According to the rules of heredity (see the section on *Genetics* pages 57–62), such a mating will produce fawn males as well, even if they don't appear in the first round of breeding. This cross also will produce fawn females and gray (normal) males, as well as females that are split (/) for fawn and gray. My intention is to produce the fawn males with which I will be able to breed homozygous fawn birds, ones that will inherit purely. How that is achieved was discussed in the section on genetics. If only for breeding purposes, keeping good records is of the utmost importance; in fact, you can't do without them.

You may also set up a card file, a good, but more time-consuming method of recordkeeping. Each bird gets its own card, which notes its description, vital information, events, and the like. You can keep the cards in a ring binder or in a file box. An office supply store or printer can furnish blank perforated cards of any desired dimension or color. For a small fee, a printer can even cut cards for you to any specified size.

The file cards can be set up in much the same way as the pages of a notebook. A typical card can record the following points, one beneath the other:

```
Color:
Date of birth:
Color of Mother:
Ring No.:
Color of Father:
Ring No.:
Sex:
Ring No.:
Heredity line:
Color of Grandmother:
Ring No.:
Color of Grandfather:
Ring No.:
Special Observations:
```

The more details you furnish on the file card, the better the information you will accrue on the quality of the bird involved.

With a proper record, when you are ready to sell the bird, the buyer will have a complete picture from the wealth of detail you can provide. In a real way, the buyer receives a bonus, which will remain useful to him and can provide information on future developments.

A really well kept file card can sometimes reveal a surprisingly accurate picture of a bird. It indicates not only the genetic traits, but also such aspects as its behavior to birds of the same and other species and its breeding record. The record provides the means to differentiate birds of good quality from those of lesser quality. Good records will enable you to sell the really good birds to a true, enthusiastic breeder, reserving the other birds for the impulse buyer. It is also now possible to keep records of your birds on a personal computer.

DIET
Water
As with all living creatures, water is absolutely essential for birds. They should never go for more than a couple of hours without water. Tests show that a canary will die within two days if water is withheld. Budgerigars, by contrast, seem to be able to extract enough water from seed and green feed, and can therefore go without water considerably longer. Don't put this ability to the test! More than half of a bird's body is made up of water. (Adult birds require less water than young ones.)

Water can be regarded as the carrier for food in the digestive system. It is used to soak seeds in the crop which enables enzymes to digest them. A good deal of the blood is made up of water (the plasma or blood serum) and so is lymph. Water regulates body temperature. Holsheimer explained this as follows: "Birds have no sweat glands, which differentiates them from most mammals. They rid themselves of excess heat via the lungs and air sacs. The excess heat is given off by the lungs and air sacs through panting (which can also be a sign of oxygen deficiency). They also shake their feathers to rid themselves of heat trapped between skin and feathers."* He further states: "Practically all types of feed contain water. Water is also produced, along with carbon dioxide, when the body generates heat through combustion of substances such as protein, fat, and carbohydrates. The bird can make use of part of the moisture from the feed; but it still has a need for extra moisture that must be taken in as drinking water. The higher the percentage of moisture in the feed, the lower the feeding value of the feed."**

This information clearly shows that birds must have water available all year long—even if the weather is freezing outside. Never provide warm water, not even in the winter, or you run the risk that the birds will take a bath in it. As a result, the feathers, including the wing feathers, will freeze, with death as a direct consequence. To keep drinking water from freezing, add three tablespoons of glucose to every half liter of water. (Vitamin-enriched glucose in sold in most pet stores.) It not only keeps the water from freezing, it is also a good fortification for the birds. If you do add glucose, however, be sure to put something over the bowl (mesh, for instance) to prevent the birds from bathing in the water, or the glucose will foul their plumage. You can also purchase water bowls with built-in heaters and thermostats, and these are especially useful to the bird fancier.

Feeding
Let us begin with some seed mixes that I have worked with, and had good results with for many years. Apart from the seeds described below, seed-eating birds must have access to a rich variety of weed seeds. As a matter of fact, they will not only eat the seeds but often the greens as well.

---

* J.P. Holsheimer, *Voeding van Vogels* (Zutphen, Netherlands: Thieme, 1980), p. 55.
** *Ibid.*, p. 55.

A portion of mixed seed for *canaries* can be composed as follows:

white seed	2 oz	⎫
broken oats	1½ oz	⎬ 50 percent starch
millet varieties	1½ oz	⎭
rape and cole seed	2 oz	⎫
niger seed	1 oz	⎪
sesame seed	½ oz	⎬ 50 percent oil bearing
linseed	½ oz	⎪
plantain seed	¼ oz	⎪
hemp seed	¼ oz	⎭

Treat for *canaries:*

5 percent blue poppyseed 20 percent niger seed
5 percent grass seeds 10 percent white lettuce seed
5 percent hemp seed 20 percent black lettuce seed
5 percent white poppyseed 20 percent sesame seed
10 percent thistle seed (*Sesamum indicum*)

Seed mix for *British birds* and a *mixed group of aviary seed-eating birds*

white seed	5 oz	⎫
La Plata and red or white millet	1 oz	⎬ 75 percent starch
broken oats	1½ oz	⎭
rape seed	½ oz	⎫
cole seed	½ oz	⎪
niger seed	0.8 oz	⎬ 25 percent oil bearing
sesame seed	0.3 oz	⎪
linseed	0.3 oz	⎪
hemp seed	0.1 oz	⎭

Seed mix for *small finches*:

55 percent Senegal setaria ½ percent sesame seeds
15 percent panicum millet ½ percent poppyseed
15 percent white pearl millet ½ percent plantain seed
10 percent white seed ½ percent niger seed
 3 percent mulled oats

Seed mix for *larger tropical birds*:

40 percent white seed 10 percent panicum millet
30 percent white pearl millet 5 percent hulled oats
15 percent Japanese millet

Seed mix for *budgerigars, lovebirds, and small parrakeets*:
60-70 percent Japanese millet, plate millet, red millet, and/or white millet
20-25 percent white seed (canary seed)
10-15 percent whole and/or hulled oats

Seed mix for *large parrakeets and parrots*:
25-35 percent white seed
10-15 percent whole and/or hulled oats
15-20 percent white pearl millet, Japanese millet, etc.
30-40 percent sunflower seed

One of the most important seeds for tropical and subtropical birds are the various millet varieties: La Plata millet, red millet, and white millet, among others.

Many texts just refer to the general term "millet," but every bird fancier ought to know that there is a real difference between the large- and the small-grain millets. Most fanciers of tropical birds believe that spray millet (*Setaria italica* or *S. viride*) is the most suitable seed for their small birds, such as the red-billed firefinch or the golden-breasted waxbill. *Setaria* is especially suited to "little wee ones," like the red-eared waxbill, strawberry finch, and similar species. The larger seed-eaters, such as the cardinals, parrakeets, and indigo bunting like to eat white seed (*Phalaris canariensis*) in addition to millet. White seed is sometimes called "canary seed"; but be sure that you distinguish between this name for a specific seed and the seed *mixes* for canaries, which are available in all kinds of packing and under different trademarks.

The true canary seed, or white seed, comes in different varieties. Generally birds prefer the so-called Moroccan canary seed, which has a high nutritive value (protein 14 percent; fat 5 percent; carbohydrates about 50 percent; and minerals 2 percent). Note carefully that this seed is definitely not limited to feeding canaries—and this is reflected clearly in the seed mixes given above. Many other types of birds just love white seed.

Large- and small-grain millet and canary seed are best fed separately in an automatic feeder. Naturally, one also would provide other seed; but those just named constitute the main dish. To keep your birds 100 percent healthy and vivacious, there is more to the art of feeding them. Some forget that seeds don't contain all the nutriments needed to keep a bird's body totally healthy. That's why it is absolutely necessary that these birds get animal protein and other supplements to their seed diet, such as ant pupae, enchytrae (white worms), small mealworms, flies, beetles, spiders, aphids (look for them in the summer on rose and elder), universal feed, rearing foods, old white bread soaked in milk, and—of course—cuttlefish bone, the shell of the cuttlefish (genus *Sepia*). The birds should also be given green feed, fruit, berries, and grit.

Don't overlook weed seed that can be freely gathered in the fields, although make sure that it is not a kind that will harm your birds. Thistle seed, for example, is enjoyed not only by the European goldfinch, but also by many tropical songbirds. Also think of dandelion that has gone to seed and, especially, chickweed! Everywhere you will be able to find an abundance of excellent, highly nutritious seed in open fields.

We have referred to the key ingredients you are likely to find in various seeds; this assumes, of course, that the quality of the seed is up to par. It must be emphasized that all seed should be bought from a dependable dealer. Seed that stands around too long loses its food value.

You can conduct a small test to see if the seed you buy is fresh enough. Fill a small dish with water and sprinkle the seed on it. Set the dish in a light, not too cold location, for example in front of the living-room window. If you replace the existing water daily with fresh water that's not too cold, the seed should sprout after about three days. If the seed doesn't sprout in three days or so, then you know it isn't fresh. If you get a negative result several times, change suppliers.

Let's take a closer look at the ingredients of seed. If we leave out

Varieties of birdseed. From left to right and from top to bottom;
coleseed (*Brassica*), hempseed (*Cannabis*), hulled oats, white millet,
linseed, pannicum, sunflower seed, Niger seed.
Their actual size has been doubled in the photographs.

water, we get: fats, carbohydrates, protein, and minerals. The fats are especially essential in the fall and winter months because they help the birds keep warm. Of course, they are also needed during the rest of the year because they provide energy for flying, walking, and other physical activity. The same is true in even greater measure for the carbohydrates; they also provide warmth and energy after being digested. In a sense, they are being "burned" in the body. Protein is essential for growth, building up the tissues, and preventing deterioration. Minerals are especially essential for young birds because they help build a strong frame and provide the glands, blood, and intestines with material that helps them function properly. Seeds that have all of these constituents in more than adequate quantities are: white seed, large- and small-grain millet, sunflower seeds (especially for large parrakeets and parrots), hemp seed, black seed, blue poppyseed, wheat, rape seed, linseed, barley, and corn (preferably cracked).

Always be sure you have enough seed and other feed at home. Set up an emergency supply, so that you won't be caught short. Running out of seed on the weekend could create fatal consequences in the aviary. However, since seed should be as fresh as possible, a large supply is neither necessary nor desirable.

Why Feed a Variety of Seed?

Birds need a wide variety of feed to give them the opportunity to build and maintain their bodies—feed that is rich in protein, fats, and carbohydrates plus the very important minerals. Calcium, potassium, sodium, magnesium, manganese, phosphorus, sulphur, iron, fluorine, and chlorine are among the essential elements for the building and maintenance of the human and avian body.

Potassium, sodium, calcium, and iron, among others, are preventatives against some parasites. Sodium combines with chlorine to produce common salt. It is found mainly in the blood and lymph of the body. The sodium content helps to keep the body from becoming too acid. Calcium and magnesium are essential for the formation of bones and certain tissues. Calcium is also necessary to the formation of healthy blood.

Iron and magnesium in the blood help the lungs absorb oxygen from the air, thereby creating and promoting good blood circulation. Sulphur promotes the normal development of the feathers, while chlorine (sodium chloride, or table salt) promotes a firm construction of the tissues.

A varied diet is essential. The most important seeds for this diet are rape seed, white seed, hemp seed, hulled oats, millet, lettuce seed, poppyseed, and niger seed. Rape seed is best provided in a separate feed dish so that the birds can regulate their own consumption. The other seeds can be fed in a mix if desired, as long as the proportions that were mentioned earlier are followed. To put together a mix of the key seeds that is appropriate for just about all birds, preferably keep the following proportions: 4 parts poppyseed, 4 parts white seed, 6 parts hulled oats, 2 parts rape seed, 1 part hemp seed, 1 part millet, and 1 part niger seed.

Although exotics really like it, canaries won't eat white pearl millet. For that reason it is better not to include it in a mix for singing and color canaries, although some breeders are of a different opinion.

It has been said that it doesn't matter if a bird overeats on seed; the excess will be eliminated naturally. But that is not the case.

Every seed that is consumed by a bird is worked on by the various internal organs. An excess overtaxes the organs and cuts their effectiveness by half. It also causes fermentation in the intestines, especially if an overload of protein is involved. This results in certain poisons being produced that are taken up by the blood and have a poor effect not only on the condition but also the body functions of the bird.

Look at the situation biologically. Proteins are converted into glucose by the liver. This conversion produces urea as a byproduct, which is poisonous. Urea, in turn, is filtered out and removed by the kidneys. If there is overfeeding, liver and kidneys can't handle the load. An excess of waste and half-processed material develops and searches for a way out via the blood. The result is poisoning.

Fortunately, nature is our ally. Birds generally follow their instincts. They eat just enough seed and select what they need for their good health. It is the breeder's job to see that the quality of the feed is good!

In order for you to appreciate the uses of various seeds and the importance of a balanced composition, let's discuss some of the major seeds in some detail:

Rape seed (*Brassica rapa*)

Rape seed is the most important in a seed mix for canaries. Its high fat content keeps the birds in good condition and promotes good health. The same is true, of course, for exotics; but rape seed also contributes towards the beauty of the feathers and makes the throat supple and soft. A sweet, melodious birdsong without rape seed is almost impossible.

There are certain dangers connected with feeding rape seed. It spoils easily and, if it isn't kept dry during storage, its nutritive value is nil. Good rape seed has approximately the following composition: 12 percent water; 3.7 percent protein; 80 percent fats and carbohydrates; and the rest, minerals.

Good rape seed must taste like walnuts. If it doesn't, don't use it. Canary breeders often talk about sweet summer rape seed, which can easily be mistaken for cole seed. Trying to distinguish them by color is difficult. Cole seed is often given a color rinse and therefore takes on the same color as sweet summer rape seed. A Dutch expert, A. Bartels, has said: "Under the microscope, rape seed has a structure that differs from cole seed, but this is not visible to the naked eye. The clear evidence that distinguishes rape seed is the taste. It has a mild, walnutty flavor without being bitter. Cole seed, which generally is also somewhat bigger in the grain, definitely doesn't have that flavor."[*]

Despite the fact that rape seed leads the list of essential seeds in the bird diet, particularly for singing canaries, oddly enough the birds eat it the least of all the seeds. This is good and natural. If birds were to eat a greater amount of rape seed, the excess would cause the birds to become fat. That's why it is recommended that you furnish rape seed in a separate dish, so that your birds can regulate their own consumption. This method also reduces waste. If you furnish rape seed as part of the mix and your birds crave only rape at any point, they will spill the rest to get at it.

---

[*] A. Bartels, *Kanarievogels* (Amsterdam: Kosmos, 1967), p. 15.

Below, chickweed (right) and dandelion (left). Opposite page, a seed-eating bird.

Canary seed (*Phalaris canariensis*)

The primary ingredient in most seed mixes is canary seed, also known as white seed or, popularly, as bird seed. It is yellow, shiny, and pointed.

The proportion it takes in the mix is indicated earlier in this chapter. Canary seed contains a lot of starch, and experience indicates that an excess has a negative influence on the song of birds. Some breeders provide this seed generously because they believe that their canaries derive their exquisite colors and shape from the seed.

Canary seed contains about 14 parts water, 3.5 parts minerals, 11 parts protein, 51 parts carbohydrates, and 1 part fat. It is available commercially in two principal varieties—Moroccan, a large-kerneled variety, and Turkish, with a small kernel. The seeds come from an annual plant that flowers from June into the fall.

Hemp seed (*Cannabis sativa*)

Hemp, when properly ripened, has white grains. If they are green, the seed is not ripe. Hemp has a hard hull that can be broken only by older, adult birds. Before feeding it to your birds, it's best to roll or flatten the seed with a rolling pin or bottle. But don't roll more than you need for one feeding, because rolled seed spoils very quickly and then is quite harmful to the birds. Hemp contains about 12.3 parts water, 4.5 parts minerals, 12.2 parts protein, 16.2 parts carbohydrates, and 30.2 parts fat.

The seed is quite useful for overwintering females in cold rooms,

in order to keep up their strength. In this case it can be fed in somewhat larger quantities without danger. It is also a good means to help a weakened bird get back into good condition. The seed tends to constipate a little, so be sure to provide adequate amounts of green feed.

Hemp comes from an annual plant that flowers in July and August, although it is now illegal to grow it in many countries.

Broken oats (*Avena sativa*)
Oat seed is whitish yellow and is marketed as debittered whole or broken oats. It is easy to digest and increases metabolism. Generally, it is fed in broken form, but I recommend that you feed it unbroken in the winter. Hulling the grain gives the birds a pleasant occupation and also strengthens their beaks.

Broken oats contains about 14 parts water, 3.3 parts minerals, 8.9 parts protein, 4.5 parts carbohydrates, and 3.2 parts fat.

Oats comes from an annual plant that flowers in July and August.

Lettuce seed (*Lactuca sp.*)
This seed is relatively expensive. It has a slight loosening effect on the stools and a favorable influence on the colors of the feathers. It is therefore a first-rate feed. The composition of an absolutely fresh seed is about 94.3 parts water, 1 part minerals, 1.4 parts protein, 2.2 parts carbohydrates, and 0.3 part fat.

Lettuce seed comes from lettuce plants that flower from July to October.

Linseed (*Linum usitatissimum*)

Linseed is known by its flat, brown kernel. Some people say that it promotes moulting, especially with canaries, but with few exceptions this seed isn't eaten by most birds anyway. It contains 12.3 parts water, 3.4 parts minerals, 17.2 parts protein, 18.9 parts carbohydrates, and 35.2 parts fat.

Linseed comes from an annual plant, the common flax, that flowers from June to October.

Poppyseed (*Papaver somniferum*)

Poppyseed is available in white and blue varieties; birds prefer the blue. It has a constipating effect and thus can serve you well when birds run a little loose in their digestion.

Some believe that the proportion of poppyseed in the commercially available seed mixes is too high, and generally one sees the recommendations of two parts of poppyseed instead of four. This leads me to the following explanation. The body temperature of birds, because of their rapid metabolism, runs quite high, about 41 degrees Centigrade. This metabolism is stimulated by broken oats, lettuce seed, and green feed provided on a regular basis. My recommendation is to hold things back a bit with a somewhat higher percentage of poppyseed. Many leading feed specialists agree that this is to the benefit of the body functions. It contains 14.7 parts water, 5.3 parts minerals, 14.7 parts protein, 15.3 parts carbohydrates, and 39 parts fat.

Poppyseed comes from the opium poppy, which flowers in June and August. It is now illegal to grow it in many countries.

Niger seed or black seed (*Guizotia abyssinica*)

This seed somewhat resembles black, shiny sticks. Birds, especially canaries, like to eat it. It contains 18 parts protein, 16 parts carbohydrates, and 43 parts fat.

This seed comes from the Guizotia plant, and is imported from East Africa.

Sunflower seed (*Helianthus annuus*)

This seed is available in white, striped, and black. It is rich in albumen (about 15 percent), minerals, and vitamin E.
· The seed comes from the sunflower, that flowers from July to October.

Along with millet (discussed in detail under *Feeding*), these are the most important seeds for a good mix. They contain the essential nutrients to guarantee the maintenance and proper development of birds.

Insects as Food

Many species of birds eat insects, including, of course, the "insect-eaters," so called to distinguish them from seed-eaters. It is generally known that insect-eating birds regularly ingest different types of indigestible material which is later regurgitated in small lumps. The ingested material stimulates the production of digestive juices, but is not itself digested. To stimulate the formation of these lumps, provide some small cut-up feathers in the feed, preferably twice a week. And if you see the birds regurgitate, don't worry. It is a completely normal and natural phenomenon.

Good commercial feed for insect-eating birds is available. I have used Universal Food, made by Bogena, Sluis Befkin and Sluis Universal Food, among others. These are appropriate for all insect-eating birds, including Indian white eyes, Pekin robins, cardinal species, and shamas. The attraction of this feed is that dried insects have been mixed into it. Other feeds are available commercially—even for birds with small beaks and those with somewhat larger beaks, such as mynah birds and thrushes.

In addition to commercial brands, it is essential some live food be supplied. Consider using several of the live foods listed here, because variety is extremely important for the health of your birds. In addition to those foods on the list, one variation you can try is beef hearts; they should be ground and can be served cooked or raw—in small amounts. Mix them with cracker crumbs or bran. You can also add to the mix some roughly ground meal or shrimp, beetle, or silkworm. Offer small quantities at a time and supply fresh material twice daily. Before serving, you can moisten the tidbits with carrot juice, grated apple, or even water. (Carrot juice is my favorite.) Whatever you use, keep in mind that the mix should be just damp, never too moist or wet. The same is true if you serve a pure commercial mix and want to moisten it slightly. If the weather is warm, serve small portions several times per day.

White worms (*Enchytraes*)
You can get a starter supply of these thin, white insects under rotting wood or leaf piles. A box 35 x 35 x 25 centimeters, filled with good humus and leaf mold, is an excellent medium for raising white worms. The material should be loose and slightly moist; definitely not packed down or too dry. Using a small spade, make a hole with a diameter of about 15 centimeters in the middle of the contents. Put a slice of white bread soaked in milk or water on the bottom of the hole and place the starter colony of worms on top of it. Cover the top of the box with a tightly fitting piece of glass, and then cover the glass with newspaper to keep the breeding area dark. Check regularly to see that the soil doesn't dry out and that the worms still have enough food. The ideal temperature for raising a good batch of worms is about 12 degrees Centigrade. After several weeks you can literally harvest the worms. Wash them off under running water and the birds have one of the best types of live feed available. White worms are especially good to have when the birds are brooding and feeding their young.

Maggots
Raising maggots is hardly an attractive activity, and few breeders do it. But if you want to try and have enough room, hang a piece of meat from a tree somewhere outdoors. Flies will lay their eggs in the meat. After several days, take down the meat and put it in a cookie tin with a tight-fitting lid. Store the tin out of the sun. After another several days, you can harvest a large collection of maggots.

Another simpler and neater way to raise maggots is to fill a canning jar with boiled potatoes and sour milk, then set it outside without the lid. After several days, put the lid on, and a few days later you will have a supply of maggots.

Maggots require some preparation before you can serve them to your birds. You need to rinse them under a fairly strong stream of running water for at least fifteen minutes. Holding them under the tap causes the maggots to release the contents of their intestines.

Mealworms

These worms should be available year round to all species of birds, but especially so when the breeding season starts. Do not give birds too many mealworms. They will get too fat and, as a result, less able—or totally unable—to breed.

Mealworms are best raised in a wooden box measuring about 50 × 25 × 25 centimeters. Drill three holes of about 3 centimeters in diameter in each of the sides, 2 centimeters above the bottom. Attach some screening to the inside of the walls to prevent escapes. To prevent decay, line the box first with plastic or zinc—but be sure not to block the holes you drilled in the sides. Cover the box with a tight-fitting lid, both to prevent escapes and to minimize odors. Drill several ventilation openings into the lid (they can be larger than 3 centimeters). Put screening over the inside, as you did with the walls, and again, cover the rest with plastic or zinc.

When the box is ready to use, fill it with a 5-centimeter layer of chopped straw. Cover that with an old towel and add a layer of bran, about 4 centimeters thick. Again put an old towel on top of the bran, and add another layer of bran, and so on until you have filled the box to 3 centimeters from the top. Cover everything with a piece of cloth and then a strip of sturdy strawboard. Place food on top of the strawboard, in the form of soaked white bread, pieces of fruit, or green feed. After the contents are in place, check that the lid can still fit tightly.

You will need several beetles of the mealworm—available at your local pet store—to start the breeding process. You will be able to harvest new mealworms once per week, located on or near the board.

Before feeding mealworms to your birds, wash them under running water. If you have young or small birds in your quarters, cut the heads off the worms before feeding them. Otherwise it is possible for a live mealworm to gnaw its way through the crop wall of the bird that eats it. Many true insect-eating birds either bite the worm heads to pieces before swallowing the worms, or pull the worms quickly through their beaks, thus freeing the "insides" of the worms and swallowing them. The outside or "hull" of the worm is discarded.

Ant pupae

A true bird fancier won't let his birds do without "ant eggs" as the pupae are sometimes popularly called. You can find them in ant hills in some countries and also under stones, behind the bark of tree stumps (the sunny side), in sod, and in many other places.

The grass ant (*Tetramonium caespitum*) that lives in lawns has its egg storage so near the surface that you can easily scoop out the pupae even though you will probably harvest only a small amount, just enough to feed a few birds one time.

For larger quantities you will have to go to the nest of the red forest or wood ant (*Formica rufa*) or other species of similar size, which has large ant pupae, and lots of them! If you go about it right, you can keep harvesting a single nest for years.

Study this large structure to see where the storage places are, and then carefully remove any sticks, needles, and other debris, until one of the storage chambers is laid bare. Wear gloves and tie your sleeves down for protection; it is also wise to wear boots. Spread out a piece of cloth next to the nest—an old sheet will do fine. Fold the four corners toward the middle until an appropriate space remains in which to deposit the pupae that you scoop out of the nest. Place some small sticks under the flipped up corners of the sheet.

Larvae inside the pupae die quickly if they are exposed to the sun. The ants sense this. If you put the pupae in the sun-exposed center of the sheet, the ants will come and drag them to the nearest shady spots, namely the folds of your sheet. You don't have to stand by while they work; depending on the amount of work you gave the ants, you can go away and enjoy nature for a half hour or an hour. The ants will neatly separate the pupae from the nest debris and deposit them under the folds of your sheet. You may scoop up some ants when you empty the corners of the sheet, but that doesn't matter.

Remember that the key to having the ants separate their larvae is sunlight, so collect "ant eggs" only on sunny days. Never completely empty out an ant nest, or you will ruin the colony. The colony may move out or die if its nest is severely disturbed, and you won't be able to use all that many pupae anyway since they lose their food value in storage. After harvesting, help the ants restore the damage by returning any nest material left on your sheet; do this by putting it back neatly in the hollow that you created by scooping up one or more storage places. In three or four days, the hollows will be closed and everything inside the nest will be restored. No trace will remain of the ravages you visited on the nest. (You should have disturbed the nest as little as possible. As a friend of nature, it is not your intent to do serious damage.) Now the ant colony can maintain itself and remain a supplier of good bird feed for many years.

When you get home, open the lid of the tin with the pupae just a crack and set it in the aviary. The adult ants will crawl out and your birds will probably eat them immediately. You can keep a supply of pupae in your refrigerator, after having given your birds a treat of fresh "ant eggs."

Earthworms

Dig for earthworms only in soil where no agricultural chemicals have been sprayed or spread since earthworms have a lot of soil in their bodies; a bird that eats earthworms therefore also eats poisons from any contaminated soil. This could be fatal or at least cause problems, such as making egg shells brittle or egg membranes tough—both causes of poor reproduction.

When digging for earthworms, push your shovel into the ground and then beat against the handle. The earthworms will come to the surface and you can just pick them up.

I am not the greatest promoter of earthworms because they can be an intermediate host (and thus carriers) of tracheal worms. Other bird breeders, however, have had good results with earthworms, so the decision to use them is yours.

Water shrimps

There are several species of birds that love to eat little water shrimps, and by experimentation, you can soon find out which are the true gourmets. The problems of pollution affect the water fully as much as the soil, and unfortunately it becomes increasingly more difficult to find pure water. Yet there are still places with clean ponds, brooks, fens, rivers, and lakes in which to gather water fleas (*Daphnia*) and the smaller kinds of crustaceans. These are extremely good food, especially for birds with red in their feathers, for which they are really essential. The positive effect of water fleas on birds with red in their feathers was proven many years ago, when a group of ibises only developed red in their plumage when they were put in a pond where a rich population of water fleas was present. Aphids on elderberry and roses, among other sources, also have the same effect, so you can regularly give your birds a branch with aphids on it. The birds will respond enthusiastically. If you gather water shrimps, use a scoopnet; you can make your own from a nylon stocking or pantyhose.

Egg Foods or Rearing Foods

Experienced breeders know that the many brands of egg foods available are not uniform in quality. It often takes long searching through various brands until one is found that satisfies the requirements for brooding and health. Sometimes birds don't do well until the right brand is found.

The bird fancier usually doesn't know the composition of most egg foods because, in nine out of ten cases, ingredients are not given on the package. With experience, it is possible to tell rather quickly whether the nutritional value of the brands used is adequate and whether the various components have a favorable influence on your birds. Unfortunately, many beginners buy a large quantity, perhaps 1 kilogram, of some unknown concoction. After a few months, their birds often become fat and listless, sit sleepily on the seedbin, and, in short, are unable to start breeding, to sing, to fly deftly, or even to walk. The reason is that some feeds contain too many vitamins or too many minerals, but not a proper balance.

Of course, there are also excellent feeds that can be fed to birds confidently. These manufacturers have long experience that guarantees absolutely first-rate nutritional value. And some experienced fanciers make up their own rearing foods, which if properly done, works out well. But beware of amateurish efforts. The majority of bird breeders prepare feed that is too unbalanced; the nutritional value is too high, and the birds receive an excess of vitamins, carbohydrates, fats, or minerals.

It is a well-known fact that more adult and young birds die from being fed feed that was too rich than from being exposed to cold. It is therefore worth repeating with emphasis: don't begin creating your own feed until you are well aware of its proper composition. When you buy commercially, buy a well-established, trustworthy brand.

Additionally, homemade rearing food can spoil rather quickly, particularly in the summer when we need it the most. Every year, many birds die from intestinal upsets caused by misplaced economy—the feeding of spoiled or half-spoiled feed that teems with harmful bacteria. Homemade egg food or rearing food also generally costs more than the commercial products, which, in comparison, are safe to use for a longer time. Furthermore, home preparation is a lot of work, and one needs to have the refrigerator space handy to prevent rapid spoilage.

A recipe for rearing food

For those who are willing to brave all the disadvantages, here is a recipe that I have found satisfactory through many years of use. Take and beat one chicken egg and bake it into an omelette with as little butter as possible. Take four slices of light toast (I use Dutch rusk) and pulverize these with a roller, a bottle, or simply with your hands. Then cut up the omelette into the smallest possible pieces and stir into the pulverized toast or rusk. To this mixture add a finely grated fresh summer carrot as well as a finely grated sweet apple.

(You could use a pear if necessary, but I greatly prefer a sweet apple.) Be sure everything is mixed thoroughly, preferably with an electric mixer. Then add the juice of half an orange, an ounce of finely rolled hemp seed, a dash of blue poppyseed or lettuce seed.

This mixture doesn't keep well in warm weather and must always be stored in a refrigerator. Put out small quantities at a time, and that feed which the birds don't eat before going to roost must be removed and discarded.

Grit

Grit, consisting of finely ground shells, is obtainable in every bird store in several brands, and I would only buy known brands. It must be available to your birds every day, as it plays an important role in digesting seeds. Birds kept in a decorative cage could be given shell sand and river sand; washed aquarium sand is very appropriate for this use. I particularly like oyster grit and shell sand available in canisters and plastic bags. Small stones dug or hoed up in an aviary where that is possible will provide your birds the help they need to grind up feed in their gizzard. I don't recommend furnishing beach or dune sand, because this is too fine and too salty; birds will continually run to the water dish, which can cause intestinal upsets and other disturbances.

Lime

Birds also must have daily access to lime. They especially need a daily ration of cuttlefish bone, the shell of the cuttlefish, which is available in pet stores, and which can also be found on some beaches. Whether you gather cuttlefish bones from the beach or get it directly from the store, you should soak it several days in pure tap water, changing the water three times per day.

Another good source of lime is dicalcium phosphate, ground into small pieces. Lime is especially important for birds just before and during brooding and during molting. During the so-called youth molt (for example with canaries), lime is essential. "Youth molt" refers to the time when the young birds lose their down but not their wing or tail feathers. In most cases, if feed and housing are in order, and the birds are not exposed to wide swings in temperature, this molt takes place without problems.

Minerals

A good metabolism requires inorganic materials in the form of minerals. They are also needed for the proper development of the frame or skeleton, the replacement and overall growth of tissues, the regulation of the osmotic blood pressure and the acid/base balance (pH), the transport of oxygen, the manufacture of red blood corpuscles, and other body functions. Deficiencies, therefore, can cause all types of illnesses.

Calcium

Calcium is needed for the development and maintenance of the skeleton (frame), to encourage the blood to clot, for the proper function of the heart and nerves, and for the manufacture of the egg shell. Calcium (Ca) is found in, among other sources, cuttlefish bone, grit, dicalcium phosphate, and chalk.

Phosphorus

Together with calcium, phosphorus (P) constitutes the building block for the bones. There is mineral, vegetable, and animal phosphate. Dicalcium phosphate is recommended, along with green feed and animal protein.

Sodium and chlorine
Among its other uses, sodium (Na) is important for the development of the frame as well as for regulation of the pH of the blood. Chlorine (Cl) is available, along with sodium, in table salt. But never feed too much.

Potassium
This mineral is important for the formation of the bones and for the acid/base balance in the body. Large loss of body fluids, as in diarrhea, quickly causes a shortage of potassium (K), which inhibits growth, particularly in young birds. Dairy products (a little cheese, milk-soaked bread, etc.) and fruit provide enough potassium for the birds.

Magnesium
This mineral is important for the metabolism of carbohydrates. It is present in bones, in tissues, and also in the egg shell. A deficiency of magnesium (Mg) inhibits growth and results in medium to poor feathers; it may even lead to convulsion. Wheat and nuts contain an ample amount of magnesium.

Iron
This mineral is important for the production of hemoglobin (the red "pigment" of the blood) and countless enzymes. Too much iron disrupts bone growth because it interferes with the utilization of vitamin D. There is adequate iron (Fe) in legumes and egg white (and therefore in egg foods and rearing foods).

Zinc
Zinc activates and constitutes part of some enzymes. It also functions in the formation of the bones and the egg shell. Birds need zinc (Zn) for early development and growth. A deficiency causes poor development and a diminishing of feather pigment. Zinc is present in any good vitamin and mineral supplement.

Copper
Essential for the production of blood, copper also activates absorption of iron in the intestines and plays a role in the production of hemoglobin. A deficiency of copper (Cu) results in anemia and therefore a discoloration of the feathers. Copper is supplied in most commercial diets and supplements as trace mineral salts.

Sulphur
This mineral is probably of little importance for birds. Sulphur (S) is found in dairy products, meat, and, to a lesser extent, in fruit.

Iodine
A deficiency in iodine (I) occurs if there is too little of this element in the drinking water. It produces problems with the thyroid gland, causing respiratory problems and often vomiting as well. Parrakeets and doves sometimes experience this problem. Seeds are generally low in iodine, so it is best to compensate for this by providing cod-liver oil, mixed through the seed.

Manganese

This element is of great importance in the formation of feathers, bone structure, and other aspects of growth in young birds. It also is involved with enzyme production. Adequate absorption of manganese is inhibited by excess absorption of calcium and phosphorus. This results in a more breakable eggshell, and the young inside the egg develop very slowly. Fruit, green feed, and especially berries are rich in manganese (Mn).

Fats, Proteins, and Carbohydrates

Fats and carbohydrates have similar roles, namely, to deliver the calories needed for adequate warmth and energy. They also contain vitamins A, D, and E. In the winter, birds should have extra fat as a precautionary measure, and, since fat takes longer to digest than carbohydrates, it is important that fats should be available daily. Special fat balls (made of fat and a mixture of bird seeds) are available for birds that overwinter out of doors. In severe cold, birds really devour these. Fat is found in hemp seed (32.2 percent), linseed (40.8 percent), niger seed (32.5 percent), rape seed (40.2 percent), millet (5 percent), and white seed (5 percent).

Proteins are essential for the building and maintenance of the body and for providing warmth and energy. Remember in this connection that a bird egg is made up almost completely of proteins. Proteins are needed for muscles, blood, feathers, and skin. In fact, with the exception of the bones, the whole body demands proteins. Most cage and aviary bird deaths are caused by protein deficiencies.

About 12 percent of the bird's diet should consist of proteins, with the percentage for young birds considerably higher. Proteins are chemical molecules made up on the average of carbon (53 percent), hydrogen (16 percent), oxygen (22 percent), and sulphur (2 percent). Proteins can also contain phosphorus, iron, copper, zinc, and manganese. Proteins can be poor or rich in certain amino acids that are taken up by the blood; birds should therefore have daily access to egg food, green feed, mealworms, and other insects to get adequate proteins. Insect-eating birds are particularly dependent on proteins.

Carbohydrates are chemical molecules of carbon, hydrogen, and oxygen. A very well-known one is glucose ($C_6H_{12}O_6$), which occurs through the photosynthesis of plants. Carbohydrates come in the form of sugar and starch. Starch in seeds is not directly absorbed by the body, but is first broken down into smaller molecules. This is done by ptyalin in saliva and secretions of the pancreas. Digested starch is then taken up by the blood from the small intestine and carried to the body tissues. There it maintains the combustion that produces warmth and energy.

An excess of starch can bring about the accumulation of fat in the body, especially if the body doesn't use up the carbohydrates that are taken in—perhaps through a slowdown in activity. An excess of carbohydrates in the form of sugar is stored in the liver; from there it is sent to the places in the body which demand it. To achieve a proper use of carbohydrates, it is important that birds get enough exercise. That is why bird fanciers should house their birds in roomy cages and aviaries where they will be able to move about freely and burn carbohydrates generously.

Not all carbohydrates are digestible. A poorly digestible one is cellulose, the chief building material of plants, and the chitin of animal cell bodies (the skin and exoskeleton of insects.) Even though cellulose is made up of starches, it leaves the bird's body practically unchanged after its feed is digested.

Since birds depend on carbohydrates for combustion, bird feed must contain a good supply of them. Fortunately, they are richly available in seeds, fruits, green feed, and animal protein. Some common bird seeds have the following percentages of carbohydrates: hemp seed, 15.8; linseed, 17.5; millet, 60.4; niger seed, 17; rape seed, 10.4; white seed, 50.8.

Most sicknesses in birds are caused by deficiencies in their food. Poor nutrition causes deficiency diseases, which bring about debilities in the body, providing an opportunity for additional illnesses to become established. Very few captive birds receive too little food; rather, many of them don't get the *proper* food!

All feed must contain proteins, carbohydrates, fats, minerals, vitamins, and water. Not every food source contains each of these, certainly not in sufficient amounts. Hence the recommendation of variety in the menu, and seed mixes that contain a variety of seeds. Together, they provide all essential nutrients in the necessary amounts.

Feeding can be difficult when the aviculturist has a varied collection of birds, including seed-eating, fruit-eating, and insect-eating species. For that reason, it is absolutely necessary that the bird fancier be well acquainted with the requirements of a proper modern feeding program.

Vitamins

The concept of deficiency-caused diseases originates with Dr. G. Grijns and Dr. C. Eyckman, who discovered a substance in rice hulls that protected people against beriberi. The substance that protects against this disease was called a vitamin (vitamin B). Later studies of vitamins produced several very interesting results. For example, when Hopkins fed young rats on casein, salt, and sugar, the animals remained alive but didn't grow. When he added fat (milk, egg yolk or butter), the animals did grow. He therefore correctly concluded that fat must contain some growth stimulant that was essential for the body. This substance was later called vitamin A.

Several other vitamins were discovered over the years, and each was designated with its own letter. Since then, the chemical composition of the vitamins has been established, so that a large number of them are manufactured synthetically. In many cases, synthetically produced vitamins also were given scientific names indicating their makeup; vitamin C, for example, is known as ascorbic acid.

Studies also indicated that several vitamins, which originally were considered to be a single substance, really consisted of several components. One example of this is vitamin B, which is composed of no less than 12 substances; vitamin B_1, B_2, B_6, and B_{12} are the best known of these. In such a case we speak of a vitamin-B complex.

Vitamins are made up of the elements carbon (C), hydrogen (H), and oxygen (O), and often also of nitrogen (N), sometimes sulphur (S), and phosphorus (P). The sole mineral in vitamin B_{12} is cobalt (Co).

The most important task of vitamins is to maintain body cells and to permit the functioning of the various organs. Vitamins are distinguished by whether they are fat- or water-soluble. Vitamins A, D, E, and K are fat-soluble and are also found in fatty substances. People and animals can generally store these vitamins, and they can't be removed via the urine. Vitamins B_1, B_2, B_6, and B_{12} plus biotin, choline, folic acid, nicotinic acid, pantothenic acid and vitamin C are water-soluble. They cannot be stored in the body and so must continually be supplied in the food. An excess of water-soluble vitamins can be removed via the urine.

Avitaminosis is the name for a condition in which one or more vitamins are missing. Hypovitaminosis is when one or more vitamins are in short supply. Hypervitaminosis is when there is an excess of one or more vitamins. All three conditions must be avoided.

Vitamin A

This is best supplied through a vitamin additive (and so can all the other vitamins). A deficiency of vitamin A in birds can be diagnosed by among other symptoms, flaking off of the epithelium (upper layer of the skin) when you touch it. Mucous membranes, throat, gullet, air passages, and urinary ducts can also be affected. If you look into the beak of a bird so affected, you will see white spots that extend far into the crop. This is most noticeable in doves. The kidneys are no longer able to carry off ureic acid, bringing about gout. Resistance to infection is lowered, productivity of the reproductive organs is sharply reduced in both sexes, and young birds either grow slowly or die.

Provide vitamin A/D drops in the seed. Guard against an overdose, which could cause discoloration of the feathers. Vitamin A occurs naturally in milk, so provide a slice of bread soaked in milk, especially at brooding time. This will prevent much trouble and discomfort. Also provide milk-soaked bread to newly acquired birds; their eye infections and other problems often clear up miraculously. Vitamin A is also supplied by cod-liver oil. And carotin, the substance from which vitamin A is produced, can be found in sprouted corn, rye, wheat, parsley, carrots, Brussels sprouts, and kale.

Vitamin B$_1$

A deficiency in vitamin B$_1$ (thiamine) disturbs the carbohydrate metabolism; B$_1$ is especially important for the muscles and nerves. Symptoms of deficiency include a weakness in the legs and tail, slimy droppings, and, shortly thereafter, lameness in the wings.

If you suspect vitamin B$_1$ deficiency, change the diet drastically and include a regular supply of green feed and sprouted seed.

Vitamin B$_2$

Also called lactoflavin, riboflavin, or vitamin G. It is required in small quantities, only 0.0035 mg per kilogram of feed, but it is nevertheless important, especially for young birds, as it helps promote normal appetite, good digestion, and healthy skin. It is present in sprouted seed, milk, and many bird seeds, and if you feed normally, no deficiency should occur.

Vitamin B$_3$

Also called pantothenic acid. It is absolutely essential for the skin and for normal breeding. Vitamin B$_3$ is found in green feed, sprouted seeds, cod-liver oil, grains, and many bird seeds. A deficiency causes poor or rough feathering, bald heads, inflamed eyes, rough legs, and crusty scales at the corners of the beak.

Vitamin B$_4$

Also called vitamin P and nicotinic acid, it occurs in both animal and vegetable products. It is essential for carbohydrate metabolism and the production of fatty acids. It also influences growth and feathering. Protect against deficiency by providing green feed daily.

Vitamin B_6 and B_{10}
Vitamin B_6 (pyridoxine) regulates the metabolism in the nerves and liver. It is also important for growth. It occurs in all kinds of grains, yeast, and bran. Vitamin B_{10} (folic acid) prevents anemia and is also found in grains and yeast, as well as in green feed. Birds that are deficient have leg cramps, weaken quickly, and sit on the ground, exhausted.

Vitamin B_{12}
Also called cobalamine or cyanocobalamine. It is very important for proper metabolism and growth. The so-called intestinal flora, bacteria that grow in the intestines and are necessary for proper digestion, also require B_{12} to function properly. It is present in bird droppings, and that's why you see birds peck regularly at their own or other birds' droppings. Young birds and the parents of nestlings also ingest droppings frequently. Vitamin B_{12} contains the metal cobalt (Co). It occurs in penicillin, aureomycin, streptomycin, and terramycin. It can be supplied to birds in powder form, mixed into the feed. Don't overdose—that could kill off the intestinal flora. It could also result in reduced fertility caused by inhibiting the absorption of vitamin E, the fertility vitamin.

Vitamin C
Most animals can synthesize this vitamin on their own, and deficiencies should not occur if normal housing, care, and feeding are provided. Green feed and fruit help assure adequate supplies. Research has shown, however, that the red-eared bulbul cannot synthesize vitamin C, and it must, therefore, be provided in the feed.

Vitamin D
This is really a vitamin complex, like the B-group. It is produced in the body when exposed to sunlight. It occurs in milk and cod-liver oil. Birds don't synthesize vitamin D directly; rather, a so-called provitamin is converted into the true vitamin D by the ultraviolet light from sunlight.

Almost all birds have glands that secrete a substance with which they grease their feathers. This substance contains the provitamin, and this provitamin is converted into vitamin D by the ultraviolet rays of the sun, and then absorbed into the skin.

It is important that birds of prey eat their catch "complete" with skin and feathers, because they absorb vitamin D into their bodies this way. Jays, pittas, and other meat-eating cage and aviary birds, therefore, must be provided dead birds and mice with feathers and skin intact.

Conversion of the provitamin into vitamin D requires, as we have seen, exposure to sunlight. For this reason, cage and aviary birds must be in sunny locations.

Deficiency of vitamin D causes rickets; its symptoms are eggs produced without shells; birds that grow poorly and look dazed; and all kinds of paralysis, misshapen bones, and other problems. You can provide vitamin D by adding cod-liver oil to the seed mix, and by supplying dicalcium phosphate, green feed, and milk (preferably by soaking a slice of old bread in the milk).

Vitamin E

This is important for fertility, growth, and metabolism. It can be supplied in wheat germ oil, and should be—particularly for birds that lay large clutches, such as quail, zebra finches, and Bengalese.

Netting Birds

Catch birds with great care. First of all, the net should not have so large a mesh that the birds become entangled. Wrap foam rubber or medicinal cotton around the edge, because birds can be injured if they take a solid blow from the net. You'll enjoy the best results if you can scoop them up in flight or when they are hanging against the wire. A short-handled net is best.

The best procedure is to move your collection into the inside aviary in stages. Do it gently; you'll get good results only if you move calmly and control your movements. This way, you will catch these birds without making the others in the outside aviary tired and flighty. Catching birds in stages has never cost me any casualties. Be sure to remove all nest boxes, perches, and the like from the inside aviary (or sleeping shelter, if you want to use that for the purpose). Places on which birds can perch interfere with good, rapid catch.

A complete catch should be accomplished early in the morning. Generally, the purpose of a complete catch is to move the birds to their winter quarters; if you start early, the birds will have a chance to rest completely and to find their feed and drinking bowls in the box cages. This job should naturally be done in the fall before frost and snow is expected. And remember, it is better to be a few weeks early than one night too late!

Washing Birds

If you provide fresh bathwater daily—with some nontoxic disinfectant added if you like—birds keep themselves pretty clean. It can still happen, however, that their feathers get a little gray and dingy, which is particularly noticeable in white and yellow birds. If you intend to exhibit such birds, you will have to wash them, or the judges will deduct some points.

Washing birds is a very delicate job. A bird's body is very sensitive and may never be held too tightly. Larger birds, like doves, quail, and pheasants, are a bit sturdier, but you should always be careful as each bird has its tender spots.

Prepare a container of lukewarm water with a bit of baby soap dissolved in it. Hold the bird carefully and correctly in the palm of your hand, with your thumb and index finger around the shoulders, the bird's back to the inside of your fingers. Use a natural—not plastic—sponge or a softhaired brush (a shaving brush with soft bristles works quite well). Wipe gently in a single direction, that is, lay it on its back in your palm. Most birds find this position somewhat uncomfortable and often try to turn around (tame canaries will usually lie quietly in this position, without movement; but if you are working with birds other than canaries that are tame and trusting, be extra careful). Don't squeeze the birds too tight, while continuing to wipe in the direction of the tail. Keep all your movements very controlled.

After washing a bird in soapy water, rinse it with pure, lukewarm water. Again, use a sponge or brush and carefully wipe in the direction of the tail. Then pat it dry with a clean handkerchief; this will absorb most of the water.

Place the bird in a warm cage, for example, in the living room. Withhold sand and seed; seed can be furnished again after a half hour. When the bird has dried completely, you can slowly move it to a more lightly heated location and finally to its usual place. Three days before a show, stop furnishing bathwater and discontinue bathing the birds. This will encourage the return of the shine that comes from natural oils to the feathers. (See also *Molt*.)

Bird Shows

Various bird societies and clubs ordinarily organize competitions and shows between the end of October and early February. Often, they offer considerable prize money. The bird with the most judging points becomes a champion of its breed, and the best breeder takes home the top prizes and trophies. The championship of a species is based on official judging; every bird that is entered in competition is judged and awarded a certain number of points.

Enter competitions not just for the prizes, but much more importantly to find out how your birds are evaluated by experts and the judges and what the potential of your birds might be.

In various countries bird clubs have well-organized classes for judges, who have to pass an examination. The course is serious business. The basic prerequisite for candidates is to have kept and cared for birds at least five years. After passing an entry exam, you can become an official candidate; the course for judges usually takes two years.

The candidate must learn a great deal about birds in general and also about genetics. He then specializes in birds in which he has a particular interest. In this way, there are judges for water birds, color canaries, singing canaries, canaries bred for form and posture, budgerigars, large members of the parrakeet family, zebra finches, Bengalese, and tropical birds.

Birds entered in competition are judged according to set standards, which, unfortunately, are not uniform for all of the existing clubs. After being judged, the birds are placed in exhibit cages that also must conform to dimensions set by regulation for prescribed bird species. Singing canaries are judged solely for their song and must be trained to sing for the judge.

Color canaries shouldn't be nervous so that they damage or break feathers while they are in the cage. Budgerigars, and tropical birds to a lesser extent, should be trained not to cower in the corner of their cage so that they can't be inspected carefully. One way to keep the birds from hiding in this way is to take a piece of linoleum that is slightly larger than the cage floor and put it in the exhibit cage, angled toward the front. This will force the bird inside to slide toward the trellis in front. After trying to get away for a while, the bird will give up and sit quietly on a perch, so that it can be inspected easily. You should, of course, do this type of training several weeks *ahead* of the competition.

If you belong to a bird club, ask the appropriate commission to send you the standards and rules for competition. Even if you keep birds only for your own pleasure and don't belong to a bird club, you should still attend the annual exhibits and shows—either local or nationwide. The experience will prove fascinating and invaluable.

Talking Birds

Talking in birds is nothing more than mere imitation of sounds. Several birds—including mynahs, parrakeets, and parrots—are

Top, outline of the vocal apparatus of a songbird: the vocal organ
is the syrinx and it is located where the two bronchi meet to form
the trachea. Bottom, sonograms of the same species of bird's song,
taken in different regions. The differences in the sonograms
lead to the belief that different "dialects" exist even in birdsong.

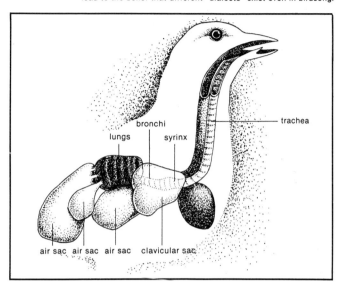

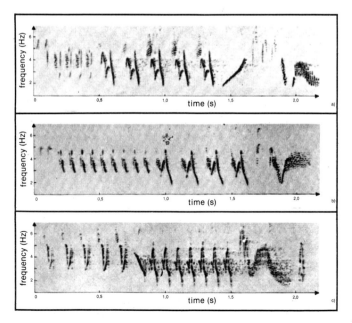

experts in this, even though not all individuals learn to talk and imitate sounds with equal facility.

Your best opportunities to develop talkers are with young birds that are completely made part of the household—birds that are tame and hand-fed, preferably by a woman, because they respond better to women. The birds should be allowed to fly around the room for several hours a day and interact with the woman who takes care of them. They should receive daily lessons in the words that they should learn, using a tape recorder as an aid, if you like. Teach short words with many vowels, like "Polly," "Coco," and "Jacob." Once the birds know simple words, they can graduate to more difficult ones.

Male and female birds have the same basic aptitude for talking, but obtaining results takes a great deal of patience. Often the birds remain silent for weeks and even months, and then suddenly start speaking several words or phrases. Noon and in the afternoon are the best times for lessons; these are natural times of rest for the birds. Don't teach more than one bird at a time; each should receive individual lessons, away from other birds.

ILLNESS AND DEBILITY

According to the cliché, an ounce of prevention is worth a pound of cure. So, if you keep birds, make sure their quarters are scrupulously clean. Water for drinking and bathing should be put out fresh at least once—and often more than once—daily. Troughs, bowls, and other eating and drinking utensils should be washed. Leftover food must be removed.

Keep floors sanitary. Have clean paper in the bottom of the cages. Since soft-billed bird droppings are somewhat moister, be sure to cover the bottom of their quarters with sand. This is necessary to keep them healthy and comfortable.

Plantings and roosts should also be cleaned regularly. Especially if you keep fruit- and insect-eating birds, roosts should get your special attention. Many of these birds have the habit of wiping their beaks on roosts, and if bits of insects, berries, etc. are caked on the roosts, they become reservoirs of infection. Hose down plants regularly, with special attention to the natural roostings places. To clean them effectively, you must keep plants trim, especially in the larger bird quarters.

Recently acquired birds should be quarantined in a roomy box cage and observed carefully while becoming acclimatized and accustomed to their new food. Don't place them with the rest of the collection until the newcomers are clearly in perfect health and used to any change in temperature. Then, introduce them to the aviary *inside* the quarantine cage. In this way, the newcomers and those established can become acquainted without territorial claim disputes. In order to ensure that newcomers don't harbor infectious diseases, they should be quarantined for two weeks as an absolute minimum. These two weeks are also of importance in providing you and your new birds the opportunity to become familiar.

Buy only those birds with whose dietary requirements you are familiar. If you don't want the disappointment of having birds become sick and die, don't experiment. It is not necessary, however, to know the exact scientific name of every attractive bird you see in the store and want to acquire. You or the proprietor will know enough to class it as a thrush, parrakeet, finch, weaver, etc. If you know the general norms for the care and feeding of these families, you won't go far wrong. Also a good bird dealer should be aware of the proper feed and feeding procedures; these he can then pass on to you. This feed is probably somewhat monotonous, but if you provide the feed to which the bird has been accustomed and slowly mix it into the proper diet, it will become familiar with its new food. For example, you can top off fruits with mealworms, egg food or universal food can be crumbled on top of an orange sliced in two—as can ant's eggs and enchytrae (white worms).

Always provide water for new birds in flat, earthen dishes placed on the floor. Don't expect them to use the standard glass drinking fountains that can be fitted through the trellis; they just won't know what to do with such equipment. Only when newcomers have become completely used to their new surroundings and their new cagemates can they be expected to learn about drinking fountains. Then and only then you can place their old dishes near the fountains for a while. Offer newly arrived birds as many of their favorite foods as you can. If they don't eat because the feed is strange to them, they become hungry and weak, sicken and die. This is especially true for soft-billed birds. And since their natural foods are digested rapidly, they are very poor at fasting for any length of time.

Newly arrived birds are generally shy and suspicious because they have usually been hauled around in small cages. Once you get a new bird home, it will remain nervous and flighty for some time. Provide it with as much rest as possible. A good quieting technique is to cover the cage with a cloth. The first evenings and nights be sure to keep a night light burning so that the bird won't injure itself when it suddenly hears or sees something and reacts by nervously jumping or flying about its quarters. Such a bird should have enough light to be able to find its food and drinking dishes without trouble, even after you have covered the cage with a cloth. Keep other people away from new birds even if you would like them to be admired. Concentrate on the new bird. The faster you calm it down, the greater the chance it will survive its new experience.

Despite all the good care and preventive measures you take, even birds that are long-standing residents in your collection as well as new arrivals can become sick. Determining that birds is generally not difficult. The stricken birds sit drawn together with puffed up feathers. They are listless, with dull eyes, and tend to sit near the feeding trough, where they spill more feed than they eat. When they eat, they eat very slowly. Or they may sit quietly, hidden in a dark corner of the aviary, with their head tucked away in their puffed up feathers.

In this short space, we can't deal with all the common ills of birds. At some time you may have to consult a veterinarian, especially if valuable birds get sick or if the illness is contagious and could wipe out your whole stock. But don't let the possibility of illness frighten you away from the bird fancy. If you take proper care, calamities are unlikely to overtake you.

When you notice a sick bird in your aviary or cage catch it immediately—but very gently. Since the bird could have a very contagious disease that would be a potential danger for the entire bird population, immediately disinfect the entire aviary (or other quarters) where the sick bird was housed; then mix some preventive medicine into the drinking water. As with every medication, read carefully what is stated on the label and follow the instructions implicitly.

Place the patient in a separate, medium-sized cage, preferably one with the back and sides closed, having wire only in the front. If necessary, the front can be covered with a cloth to help maintain a constant temperature. Locate an infrared lamp between 30 and 50 centimeters from the cage. If you place your hand in front of the lamp, you can readily determine whether or not it is too hot for the sick bird. There should be no perches in the cage, and the cage should have a wire bottom so that the bird's droppings can fall out, eliminating the danger of the bird soiling itself with its own (perhaps infected) feces. The temperature should be maintained at 40°C. As soon as the bird has recovered, the temperature can be gradually dropped to room temperature. To be sure the patient does not catch a cold, watch out for any drafts.

Internal, difficult-to-diagnose illnesses are generally also difficult to treat with the established readily available medicines. Particularly where an expensive species is concerned, it is wise to consult a veterinarian who will very likely prescribe dissolving an antibiotic in the bird's drinking water. (If he does not, you could suggest it yourself—perhaps Aureomycin or another such drug which can only be obtained by prescription.) If our patient dies anyway, it is a good idea to ship the body to a university which has a veterinary science department so that in the case of a contagious disease drastic and timely measures can be taken by an authority.

There are so-called hospital cages available on the market, but with a little skill you can put one together yourself. The best way to go about this is to make a small box cage 70 cm high, 40 cm wide and 50 cm deep. In the approximate center of this cage install a small window of bars or a well-fitting piece of wire screen. Beneath this wire install a few light bulbs—ideally, 60 watts—in such a way that they work independently of each other (to achieve a correct temperature no matter what the season). At the back wall attach an easy-to-read thermometer. The cage should also be equipped with a "sand drawer" bottom that will slide out. Replace the sand at least twice a day; dangerous bacteria and viruses often hide in the droppings of sick birds. Make a little door of glass at one of the sides through which you can offer the bird its food and especially its water. We say "especially" because the bird will become very thirsty due to the high temperature and will therefore drink quite a lot. Naturally, a bird that is placed in such a warm cage also needs some fresh air; to provide this, drill a few air holes above the little door. Although it is not entirely essential, it is definitely convenient to attach the roof of the cage with hinges to provide easy access to everything inside. Convenient access to the inside of the cage will be important when your patient has recovered and you wish to disinfect the cage.

Let's discuss a few diseases, discomforts, and a couple of troublesome insects, even though we hope you will not have too much need for this advice and instruction.

Abnormal Nail Growth
Many birds, especially the smaller species, can experience excessive nail growth. They can become snagged on all sorts of things, and if you can't rescue them quickly, they may just hang there and die. (Another reason why you should furnish nesting material—particularly rope—in short pieces.)

Some species, especially nuns and buntings, require a constant check on their nail length. Nail growth can be kept in check by furnishing a few stones such as flagstones in the aviary, some reeds, etc. If they don't do the job, cut the nails with an extremely sharp pair of nail clippers. Cut just short of the red blood capillaries, which should be easy to see through the nail if the light is right. Grasp the bird's leg between your index and middle finger while holding the bird on its back in the palm of your hand. Sometimes a capillary grows along with the nail and you'll get some light bleeding when you cut the nail, so have some styptic cotton at hand to deal with this minor mishap.

Anemia
Anemia is caused by poor housing and feeding, although insects could also be a cause. The color of the skin, legs, and beak lightens, and the bird loses weight rapidly. Correct the problem by improved feeding and housing.

Calcified Legs and Feet
Old birds, especially parrots, parrakeets, and canaries, may suffer from calcification of the legs and feet. One of the causes may be mite infection. If that's the case, disinfect the housing. Gallinaceous birds generally get a calcified appearance of the legs from a mite (*Cnemidocoptes mutans*). Apply a mixture of salad oil and iodine to the affected parts and bathe the legs in baking soda; follow with an application of petroleum jelly. Other alternatives are to treat the area with Bayer's Odylen, a 0.15 percent solution of Neguvon, or a 4 percent solution of Lysol.

Treat all cases with vitamin A, which aids recovery. Do not use contact insecticides in an oil base.

Colds
Inadequate housing, exposure of the birds to draft, and dampness can all lead to a cold. It is one of the most common ailments that confronts birds. The symptoms pretty well parallel those of intestinal disturbances. Here, too, the bird will be sitting in the shape of a ball, asleep with its head tucked into its feathers. Or it might be on top of or under the feeding dish, rather listlessly pecking at some seed, though hardly eating any, with its wings hanging down and almost touching the ground. The feces will remain normal for a time. Respiration is difficult, with the poor bird making squeaking sounds; it may even sneeze.

When birds spend a great deal of time in an outside aviary, they may occasionally fall victim to a cold, which may be contagious to humans. It is mostly those birds that live in a damp and often dark and drafty cage that become sick—and little wonder! It is our responsibility, therefore, to see that the birds are housed in light and draft-free facilities. They also need a good and varied menu (we cannot emphasize this enough) because the lack of basic nutrition also helps a cold take hold; after all, without proper fuel there is nothing to keep the motor running. Here also the patient needs to be isolated immediately in the hospital cage with the temperature brought up to 42°C. If you do not have the equipment to create this environment, place the sick bird in a draft-free and warm location in a vacant indoor cage. A little honey placed in the throat with a small artist's brush can do wonders. Good food and six drops of creoline on a slice of white bread—which has been well soaked in boiled milk—can also help bring about the cure. After a week, gradually allow the temperature to drop back to normal. Wait a little longer for some nice weather, and the bird can once again be returned to his friends.

Birds kept in cages should have daily access to bathing water. When they have bathed, however, they can easily catch a cold, so keep an eye out for open doors or windows which can cause a draft. Bathing facilities should be offered only at predetermined times so that your bird will have ample opportunity to dry off before it retreats to its perch at night.

Diarrhea
Correct the problem by supplying blue poppyseed and other seeds that have a constipating effect. Give small bird species vitamin-B complex supplements. All birds, including the small ones, should be given Tetracycline-HCl, Terramycin, and/or Aureomycin. Supronalum, a sulfonamide, made by Bayer, also works well; put four drops of it in 30 cc of water. Under no circumstances should birds suffering from diarrhea have access to green feed.

When the affected birds have been isolated in a warm place, regularly clean their feathers, especially along the lower part of the body. The bath water should not be too cold—about body temperature. Add a bactericide solution to the drinking water.

Egg Binding
Egg binding occurs when the female cannot expel her egg. The bird invariably leaves her nest and sits on the floor fluffed up and in pain. She can seldom fly more than a few feet and may crouch in a corner. Egg binding generally occurs among birds that are either too young for breeding or are breeding too intensively, raising more than the advisable number of clutches (two or three) per season. Never exploit your birds by allowing them to continue breeding throughout summer and winter; don't think of them as egg-laying machines!

Birds that are housed in aviaries where the flight is too small can also suffer from egg binding, as can those that are regularly exposed to extreme temperature variations. When housing and feeding are up to par, egg binding is not likely to happen. Should it happen anyway, the laying of the egg can be helped along by smearing some salad oil under the bird's tail or by dunking just the under part of the bird's body in alternating cold and warm baths. Be very careful that the egg shell is never broken inside the bird's body.

French Molt
French molt occurs now and then only in budgerigars, especially in fledglings. The pin feathers of the tail and wings fall out, and show a constriction in the shaft a few centimeters above the inferior umbilicus (the "beginning" of the quill). Without pin feathers, the birds are unable to fly, and crawl along the floor of the aviary (hence they are called "runners" or "hikers"). If the young are otherwise healthy, new feathers will grow in approximately two months.

The cause of French molt lies in a genetic defect that also occurs in the wild. It can be prevented by restricting the parents to just one brood per year. Research is continuing intensively to solve French molt in budgies, a problem that is not completely understood at present. There are some remedies available, but they don't solve the problem completely.

Dr. H. S. Raethel has remarked in this connection: "Genetic research into the problem of French molt has proven that it is caused by a single gene of incomplete dominance. Still, there appear to be other contributing factors, as shown by Enehjelm and other researchers. When they removed recently hatched birds from parents with French molt in their system, and placed the hatchlings with normal couples, the young initially appeared normal. However the young eventually showed French molt when they were 11 to 12 days old. Mr. Enehjelm concluded that there is a critical period for young budgerigars that are fed by carrier parents and that this critical period falls within the first 10 days of life."[*]

The cause of this unusual development seems to lie in poor crop milk (a protein-rich milky substance from the crop) of the carrier parents, and this can be confirmed experimentally. The inability of many budgerigars to secrete much protein-rich crop milk may be dependent on hereditary factors; some couples may have a predisposition to produce young with French molt.

Enehjelm recommends providing all breeding budgerigars with the best possible living conditions until such time as the cause of the problem can be completely clarified.

He therefore recommends reducing breeding pressure by restricting breeding to two broods per year with three to five young each. A rearing food rich in protein and vitamins should be provided. Weak and degenerated birds should be destroyed, and birds with French molt should be used for breeding only in exceptional cases. (Practical considerations may dictate not immediately destroying valuable breeding birds that have occasionally produced young with French molt.)

Frozen Toes
This particularly afflicts lovebirds and Australian grass parrakeets; in fact, their toes become frozen at a mere −2°C. For this reason they must be kept either indoors or in a heated night shelter during the winter. These very interesting birds are also enthusiastic bathers, even during the winter, so that any bathing water must be removed if freezing temperatures are forecasted.

The toes become whitish in color and a little swollen after about a week. At that time the bird will constantly pick at the toes, because they apparently are very itchy. This nibbling at the toes of course leads to bleeding, but strangely enough, the pain seems to stimulate the bird to even more intense picking, with the result that the toes are often gnawed to the bone, causing excruciating pain. Plum-headed parrakeets frequently suffer from this ailment as well, but they generally do not attack the toes with their beaks; after a period of time, the toes rot away. According to Dr. H. S. Raethel, the frozen toes of the red-winged parrot of Australia become mummified.

When frozen toes occur, move the bird(s) to a frostfree (but not too warm) room. The chances of the toes healing are almost nil, but we must still do all we can to help the afflicted bird(s). Occasionally if the problem has been caught in time, a massage using Vaseline can help to restore the blood circulation and thus regenerate the tissues.

If you have parrakeets that are housed in an outdoor aviary, make sure that their aviary has a good night shelter that is wind- and draft-free, and in which there are some weather-secure nesting boxes for use as sleeping quarters. You can also hang a few boxes (without nesting material, of course, to prevent winter breeding) in the outer aviary. As long as they are wind-free they are ideal shelter for birds.

[*] Dr. H. S. Raethel, *Krankheiten der Vögel* (Stuttgart: 1965).

Inflamed Eyes

This problem usually occurs in winter or while transporting birds. The gray-singing or white-winged finch and the yellow-eyed canary or green-singing finch are particularly susceptible. It is principally caused by a vitamin deficiency. Provide lettuce and oil-rich seeds and add some cod-liver oil to the seed, and also apply a proprietary eye ointment.

Inflamed Fat Glands

Inflamed fat or oil glands can trouble birds tremendously. The oil gland is located at the base of the tail. It can become inflamed if the bird has insufficient flight space, or is unable to wash regularly. A little salad oil smeared under the tail is a good remedy.

Jaundice

Jaundice is characterized by a pale, yellow-colored skin and frequently occurs after diarrhea. This problem can be corrected by improved feeding and housing.

Leg Fractures

Some leg fractures can be set, others can't be or needn't be. The femur, tibia, and fibula can't be set; the toes needn't be, especially with small birds, as they heal spontaneously within several days. The toes may heal a little crookedly at times, but that doesn't seem to interfere with effective breeding. Birds missing toes, however, rarely mate successfully.

The tarsus ("leg") bone, in most cases, can be set without difficulty. For the splint use a chicken quill cut open lengthwise or a sturdy plastic straw. We are referring here to a simple fracture, not a total break. If the broken leg is merely hanging from a piece of skin, the leg can't be saved and amputation is the only answer. Setting the leg works well only if muscles, tendons, and blood vessels are still intact.

Setting a leg fracture is performed by first pushing the leg bone back into its normal position. Then apply the splint from the toes to far above the fracture. Wind some woolen yarn or surgical tape around the leg and splint from top to bottom. Then cover the splinted area with plaster of Paris.

The splint can be removed after about two weeks. You can dissolve the plaster with ether and/or acetone, but be careful not to anesthetize the bird (or yourself) with the fumes.

Molt

When housing and feeding standards are up to snuff, the molt should take place every year without hitch. When birds do not molt at all, a far more serious situation than when the birds go through an occasional heavy molt is indicated. Improper nutrition or not enough free movement is usually the cause, and animal protein is the only solution, or "medicine." Abundant live insects should be given to our birds, and we must not forget to give our birds the opportunity to bathe daily. Certain birds simply refuse to take a bath unless the bathing water is placed in the direct rays of the sun. So before taking other steps, try moving the bath water a few times if you have birds that will not bathe. If they still refuse, you will have to use an atomizer (misting device), which obviously should not have been used for anything else, such as spraying fertilizer on indoor plants. Fill this with lukewarm water and give the birds a shower, after which they should be placed under an infrared lamp for about half an hour. Birds that stop in the middle of a molt are usually the victims of a cold, change in food, radical temperature difference, or bad food. In these instances, medicines that contain vitamin H (Biotin) should be provided.

Newcastle Disease
This dreaded, highly infectious disease is characterized by a general listless appearance of the bird, and the green, slimy droppings it produces. It is the ultimate disaster of the aviary and means the end of your bird collection. Your whole stock may have to be destroyed and incinerated.

Pasteurella Infection
The basic sign of a pasteurella infection is that the bird appears fluffed up and the droppings are thin. The infection is hard to cure. Immediately isolate the affected bird and add 1 percent salicylic acid to the drinking water of both sick and healthy birds. Disinfect the aviary thoroughly, treating the floor with quick lime. After treating the aviary floor, turn the soil with a spade before returning the birds to their housing.

Pox and Diphtheria
These illnesses are caused by a virus (*Borreliota avium*). There are several forms, such as pigeon pox, chicken pox, canary pox, etc. The course of the illness can have a very varied nature.

Dr. H. S. Raethel says: ". . . it is not so strange that such greatly diverging symptoms were once held to indicate two separate illnesses. There can be skin changes that look like warts and were called skin pox, and infection of the mucous membranes that was called diphtheria. Only later did research results show that the pox virus was the common causative agent."[*]

In some cases of pox and diphtheria, septicemia (or blood poisoning) can occur and progress so rapidly that the bird dies within several hours.

Canary pox is unfortunately all too prevalent among canaries. With canary pox, there is sluggishness in the blood circulation; acute breathlessness results. Initially it will appear as though the bird hopes to free itself from some obstruction in its crop or beak by shaking its head a great deal; others make peeping sounds and have difficulty with breathing, which is dry and raspy. Canaries that have contracted canary pox will never live longer than four days, although it can also occur in a less serious strain, in which case it does not take a great deal of doctoring to nurse the patient back to health and motivate it to raise its young properly.

There is also a chronic version, where pox appear in the corners of the beak, on the eyelids, around the chest area and on the "hinges" of the wings. The pox are small, resembling pin heads, and are yellow in color. When they burst open, a bloody fluid oozes out. The pox on the eyelids look more like blisters filled with a watery fluid.

Diphtheria, the mucous membrane form of this disease, may appear together with skin pox; diphtheria shows itself as a whitish, somewhat fatty substance that adheres to part of the mucous membrane in the mouth and throat cavities. Of course the coating must be removed, since it will obstruct breathing, and the bird will

[*] Op. cit., p. XX.

Some bird diseases. From left to right and from top to bottom: macaw with his left wing fractured; parrakeet or budgerigar with fleshy excrescences around the eyes caused by chronic *Cnemidocoptes* infestation (Scaly Face); an asmatic canary; pigmy dove with a molted belly (a disease often self-inflicted and psychosomatic).

choke to death. When this is removed (particularly when it is not skillfully done) a rather bloody wound remains. Sometimes, small particles break off from this matter (due to the bird's huffing and puffing) and enter the windpipe; it follows that the bird is in grave danger of choking when this happens. Because the bird is contagious, it must immediately be separated from the other birds, and all healthy birds should be inoculated with a vaccine. In chronic cases, we will need to treat the skin creases and the coating on the mucous membranes ourselves. The pox on the skin can be treated with a solution of one part iodine and two parts glycerine. Generally, 24 to 48 hours after such treatment, the pox can be removed with a sterile pair of tweezers. The coating on the mucous membrane can be peeled off very carefully, and the wound or wounds that result can be treated with the same iodine-glycerine solution. Infected and closed eyes can be treated with a 2-percent boric-acid solution.

Psittacosis and Ornithosis

Psittacosis, or parrot fever, which only occurs in parrots and parrakeets, is not caused by the virus *Miyagawanella psittaci*, as was originally thought, but by a rickettsia-like organism called *Chlamydia*. Ornithosis can infect all other bird species. Both rickettsia-like organisms are variations of a single infectious agent.

Sick parrots sit withdrawn on a perch or in a corner and look like they have a bad cold. They continually shiver and the feathers are fluffed.

Healthy birds can be carriers, and the symptoms appear only if care and feeding are improper. The disease is transmittable to humans. Symptoms in humans begin with a bad headache and a fever up to 40°C followed by shivering, mild diarrhea, and coughing. In serious cases, pleuritis may occur.

Birds infected with psittacosis or ornithosis have a runny nose and lose much saliva, causing their feathers to become smudged and shivering increases. Isolate the sick birds and treat them with antibiotics (Tetracycline-HCl, Aureomycin, or Terramycin). Disinfect the housing with a 0.5 percent phenol solution, diluted Lysol, or 1 to 3 percent Delegol-T (made by Bayer).

To avoid infection yourself, do not kiss your parrot or let him take food from your lips.

Red Bird Mite

This grayish, agile and long-legged mite is the scourge of all birds. This blood-sucking parasite (*Dermanyssus gallinae*) emerges during the evening and night from its various dark hiding places, such as cracks and seams in housing, and attacks sleeping birds. If the birds are attacked by these mites in force, you may even be able to spot them on your birds during the day. You cannot simply cure the problem by moving birds to new, clean, thoroughly disinfected quarters. You also cannot get rid of an infestation by letting the housing lie unused for a while, even though I heard a bird fancier claim differently with strong conviction. In fact, the red bird mite can survive without food for at least five months.

It is easy to determine if your birds are infested. They sit restlessly on their sleeping perches, pecking and scratching themselves incessantly. If you shine a strong flashlight on the roosts or on the birds, you will usually be able to see the red parasites. Be careful, however, not to get the mites on yourself. They can cause an irritating, burning skin rash and a serious infestation can cause anemia in humans.

To guard against the red bird mite, you should check your birds regularly. I do this during the day by sticking the blade of my pocket knife into cracks and seams. If I don't get bird blood on the blade, there are no mites. If you place a white cloth in the night shelter, you will be able to see the parasites on it during the day.

Red bird mites can spread quickly. A single female mite can lay up to 2,600 eggs in her two-month life span.

As soon as you notice mites, catch all the birds in the affected quarters and treat the aviary with a contact insecticide. Remember to treat absolutely everything in the aviary. Cover all holes, cracks, seams, perches, wire, nest boxes, and all furnishings of the quarters. Be especially careful to do the undersides and outsides of feed and drinking dishes.

Remove all old and fresh nesting material before spraying. After the insecticide has worked for several days, wash nest boxes, feed and drinking dishes, etc. with soapy water. Rinse cages with boiling water. Check storage areas to be sure no mites are hiding there, or the aviary will soon be reinfested.

Treat the birds by applying an insecticide powder spray or one containing pyrethrin. A 0.15 solution of Neguvon generally obtains good results. Be sure none of this is taken internally by the bird. Shield their heads with your hand; for larger birds, use a headcover. You can make this from any smooth material or soft leather, such as chamois. This headcover is recommended for birds such as thrushes and toucans. Inhaling the powder or spray can cause clogging of the respiratory system. Don't use DDT under any circumstances.

Scab Mite
In contrast to the red bird mite, the scab mite can also be found on the birds during the day. This parasite buries itself under the skin, lays its eggs there, and feeds on lymph and skin substances. The mite belongs to the genus *Cnemidocoptes*. To cure an infestation, consult a veterinarian immediately, rather than trying to treat the problem yourself.

Sweating Sickness
This remarkable name came into being because the lower parts of an infected canary hen's body are wet, sticky, and rather dirty. Any young in the nest also look anything but healthy. What makes this sickness conspicuous is that a bird cannot perspire, for the simple reason that it has no sweat glands. The lower parts of the body become dirty and wet because droppings are no longer being removed from the nest. Spoiled and wet food can cause this. Sweating sickness can also appear if the birds are too cold, too damp, or too dirty. Insufficient greens or drinking and bathing water that is too cold can be the villains. Provide them with good food, drinking water that is room temperature with a non-toxic disinfectant dissolved in it, and bathing water that is also of room temperature and refreshed daily. An infected female should be placed with her young in a separate cage and washed regularly. The nest must be replaced. Contaminated birds should have as little access as possible to laxative foods, so seeds rich in oil are not appropriate. With the proper feeding the illness can be cured rapidly.

Wing Fractures
Wing fractures usually occur when a bird flies against some object with force. If the impact also causes a concussion, it will be difficult to save the bird.

Setting a wing fracture is not easy, because you cannot actually splint it. All you can do is to move the wing back into its natural position and tie it to the body with surgical gauze. Wind the gauze across the back and both wings, and cross it between the legs. Protect the breast by placing a piece of cotton under the bandage there.

Wing fractures heal more slowly than leg fractures; the recovery generally takes 22 to 25 days. Larger birds will take considerably longer. And only in rare cases will the injured bird recover its full flying ability.

Lower a perch for birds with a broken wing so they won't have trouble finding a place to sleep or rest. They should be able to reach their perch with an easy hop.

Wounds
Small wounds—such as wounds on the head, legs, or body caused by flying against obstructions or by fighting with another bird—usually heal without aid. Larger wounds, particularly head wounds, should be treated with medicinal powder such as penicillin powder like Marfanil Prontalbine by Bayer. If torn skin is still attached, place it over the wound with a pair of tweezers.

Without treatment, even large head wounds will generally heal, although they will leave a permanent bald spot, which is undesirable, especially on large birds. In the case of large wounds to the body, such as injuries from a splinter or nail, take the bird to a veterinarian for stitches.

Injured birds should be isolated to prevent other birds from pecking at the wounds, which practically all species of birds will do when given the opportunity.

During the breeding season, particularly during actual mating, many species will hold onto the hen's neck feathers during copulation (doves, for example). Naturally, after a few matings, it is not unusual for such a hen to develop some bald spots. Feathers in these areas will soon grow back, however, and are no cause for alarm. If you wish to promote the growth of these feathers, you can use a solution of alcohol-based Peruvian balsam.

Small exotic birds often have bald heads and necks. There are several reasons for this phenomenon, among them improper nutrition (lack of vitamin A), feather plucking among the birds, or a location that is too dark. Another reason is mutual feather picking from boredom. You can relieve the boredom by supplying some toys, like flax rope, a string of peanuts, a bacon rind, or something similar.

Destroying Birds Quickly and Painlessly
When you see that a sick bird will not (or cannot) improve, you will want to put it to sleep permanently to prevent unnecessary misery. I prefer the "Thijssen method," which uses ethylchloride, a freezing anesthetic. Put several drops on a piece of cotton and press it against the head where the forehead and beak meet. If ethylchloride is not available, you can make do with anesthetic ether, which is cheaper. Don't use chloroform, as it is too dangerous to work; guard against fire with all anesthetics.

Should you discover a disease not discussed in this book, consult a veterinarian.

Don't be overly concerned by all this somber discussion of diseases! If feeding, maintenance, bathing facilities, temperature, etc. are in order, you will rarely experience these discomforts and accidents with your birds.

Today many aviculturists play an important role in the conservation of bird species. With increasing pollution, deforestation, and the drainage of swamps, ponds, rivers and lakes, the environment is being slowly destroyed, with little consideration for the many forms of life which are thus threatened with extinction. Zoos have saved many species from extinction; aviculturists have preserved many birds for future generations to study and enjoy.

Sympathy for caged birds, when they are properly looked after and kept in the right surroundings, is entirely misplaced. The great number of nests full of chicks which appear every year in cages and aviaries show that aviary birds cannot be suffering unduly from being in captivity. They have many enemies and predators (humans included) in the wild, and their natural habitats are slowly being encroached upon by civilization. Naturalists have studied how birds which at one time were found only in the forests have moved to parks and later into towns. Some species—if they are not able to move on when their habitat is encroached upon—totally vanish.

1 EMBERIZA TAHAPISI
Cinnamon-breasted rock bunting

Classification Order Passeriformes, Family Emberizidae.
Characteristics Length: 16.5-18 cm (6½-7 in). Cinnamon: seven white-gray and black stripes on the head. Females are duller and have darker heads. In the winter the sexes are alike in coloration. Eyes brown, upper mandible brown-black, lower mandible yellowish, legs yellowish-brown.
Habitat Scrubs and rocky regions. They often build their nest on the ground, in tall grass.
Distribution Abyssinia to the Cape and up to western Africa.
Captivity Excellent aviary bird, not aggressive, and willing to breed. Supply milk-soaked bread (especially in the breeding season), mealworms and ant's eggs, weed seeds and the usual canary menu. Place rocks and flagstones in the aviary, and plant tall grass among them to make the birds feel "at home." The female lays 3-5 brown-spotted, white eggs. Incubation time is 12 days. Although they build free nests in low bushes and on the ground, they occupy canary nest pans and half-open nest boxes as well.

2 EMBERIZA HORTULANA
Ortolan bunting

Classification Order Passeriformes, Family Emberizidae.
Characteristics Length: 16.5 cm (6½ in). In the summer the male has a gray head with a greenish tinge. Neck greenish-brown; back darker with black stripes. White throat and eye ring (becoming more yellowish as the birds grow older). Olive-gray breast. Upperparts brown. In the winter, the bird is considerably duller and lighter. Females are duller than males. Eyes dark brown, beak light brown, legs brownish-yellow.
Habitat Open country, scrubs, cultivated areas (meadows, farmland), mountainous regions, and savannahs.
Distribution Europe (occasionally Britain) and Asia, east to Mongolia and west to Central Africa, Arabia, and Iran. Not in northwestern Germany!
Captivity Quiet and excellent aviary birds; in the breeding period, however, males can become quite aggressive, even towards large birds. The species build their nest on the ground from grass, hay, leaves, and such, but occupy nest pans and half-open nest boxes as well. The female lays 4-5 red-grayish eggs with dark spots. For more details see *E. tahapisi*.

3 SICALIS FLAVEOLA
Saffron, or Brazilian saffron, finch

Classification Order Passeriformes, Family Emberizidae.
Characteristics Length: 15 cm (6 in). Forehead and crown bright orange. Yellow head. Greenish-yellow above, with dusky streaks on the mantle; underparts bright yellow. The female is duller above and considerably paler beneath. The older the birds become, the more the yellow and green colors intensify. Eyes dark brown, beak brownish-gray (lower mandible paler), legs deep pink.

Habitat Scrubs, gardens, parks, forests, palm groves, etc.
Distribution Peru, Ecuador, Colombia, Venezuela, and into the Guianas. Introduced to Jamaica (about 1923).

Captivity These friendly birds usually build their nest in a tree hollow, which is why they should be supplied with the closed type nesting boxes in the roomy aviary. Their clutch consists of 3-4 white eggs with just a few sparse black or gray markings. It is not unusual for them to have a few squabbles with other birds during the breeding season, and they may well inspect the nests of these birds, too. This is why only one pair should be kept in an aviary, along with some of the sturdier finches that can look after themselves. If you wish the birds to breed, it will be absolutely necessary to supply a great many insects. Greens must not be forgotten either.

4 SICALIS LUTEOLA
Yellow grass, or little saffron, finch

Classification Order Passeriformes, Family Emberizidae.
Characteristics Length: 11.5-12.5 cm (4½-5 in). As *S. flaveola*, with a pale olive head and upperparts, streaked with brown-black. The female is duller in coloration. Eyes dark brown, beak light gray, legs gray.

Habitat Grassland, cliffs, and marsh borders.
Distribution Mexico to Argentina. Introduced to the Lesser Antilles.
Captivity Excellent aviary birds. Their behavior resembles that of the gray singing finch. The female lays and incubates 3-4 white eggs with dark brown spots. Incubation time 12-13 days. After 2 weeks the young leave the nest. Both parents feed the youngsters. After 14 months they have the adult plumage. Next to a good canary menu, insects and greens are essential.

5 TIARIS CANORA
Cuban grassquit or Cuban finch

Classification Order Passeriformes, Family Emberizidae.
Characteristics Length: 10 cm (4 in). Olive-green; forehead, chin, face and throat black, bordered with yellow; lower throat yellow. Underparts dark gray. The female has a brown "face"; her crown is brownish-gray. Eyes brown, beak black, legs gray-brown.
Habitat Scrubbery and woodland.
Distribution Cuba; this well-known, sometimes quite aggressive finch is also seen in Florida on occasion.
Captivity When kept as a pair, they are peaceful aviary birds; if the cock is kept without a mate, however, he can terrorize the other aviary inhabitants. Strangely, at times—particularly in the wild— either the cock or the female suddenly decides to pull the nest apart, desert the eggs, or throw certain young out of the nest. This does not mean that this couple is unsuitable for breeding; you can look forward to a good brood of perhaps 4-5 young if conditions (food, weather) are right. The parents also sometimes throw out just the young males or just the young hens, and then continue to rear those left in the nest as if nothing ever happened (natural sex limitation?). They frequently reuse an old nest. The hen alone incubates the eggs (11-13 days), but the young are fed by both parents. After 12-17 days, the young leave the nest; but the cock will continue to feed them on his own, sometimes for more than a month. The hen generally begins a new brood.

6 TIARIS OLIVACEA
Yellow-faced grassquit or olive finch

Classification Order Passeriformes, Family Emberizidae.
Characteristics Length: 11.5 cm (4½ in). Olive-green with yellow on wings and tail. Forehead and breast black. Yellow line from beak, over the eyes, to the ear coverts. Yellowish-orange throat. Underside gray. Eyes brown, beak black, legs dark gray. The female is duller and lacks the black face.
Habitat Grassland and cultivations. The natives consider this species to be a bit of a pest, because the birds damage their sugar cane crops by drawing the marrow from the drying sugar cane.
Distribution Cuba, Jamaica, Haiti, the Atlantic slope of Mexico, Greater Antilles, and Central America to western Venezuela.
Captivity To keep these "sweet tooths" really satisfied, you will have to offer them a piece of honeycomb regularly. The care required parallels the previous species; in other words, they must have universal food, egg food, ant eggs, hard-boiled egg, insects, mealworms, leaf lice (to be found on the elder tree and on roses), little spiders, greens (chickweed and the like), supplementing a good mix of tropical seed varieties. The female lays 2-3 blue-white eggs with brown or black-brown dots which often form attractive little circles. The breeding period takes place in the spring although some clutches are bred later in the year. It is possible to crossbreed them with the Cuban grassquit.

7 LOPHOSPINGUS PUSILLUS
Black-crested finch or pygmy cardinal

Classification Order Passeriformes, Family Emberizidae.
Characteristics Length: 12.5 cm (5 in). Gray. Black crest, white superciliaries. Black line on either side of the eyes. Black on wings and tail. Underparts white; black spot on throat. The female has a gray crest and lacks the black spot on the throat. Eyes dark brown, beak light gray-brown, legs dark gray.
Habitat Open, shrubby plains.
Distribution South Bolivia, West Paraguay, and northern Argentina.
Captivity Usually quite aggressive towards other aviary birds, but if they are housed in roomy, well-planted surroundings, they won't present too many problems. Live food is essential during the breeding season, as they feed this to their young. The male is very active in feeding his offspring, even after they have left the nest. But it is nevertheless important to remove the young from their parents as soon as they are independent; this is about 3 weeks after they have left the nest. The female lays 3-4 white eggs with gray-brown markings. Incubation time 12-13 days. Half-open nest boxes and canary nest pans are needed.

8 SPOROPHILA LINEOLA
Lined seedeater

Classification Order Passeriformes, Family Emberizidae.
Characteristics Length: 10 cm (4 in). Glossy blue back, usually with a white stripe on the crown. White cheeks, breast, and underparts. Eyes brown, beak black, legs brownish-gray. The female is grayish olive above with bright ear coverts; paler underside.
Habitat Scrubbery, grassland, near forests and villages; in small groups.
Distribution East Brazil, the Guianas, and Venezuela.
Captivity Can be kept in a roomy cage or community aviary. The male sings nicely. In a well-planted aviary, the birds come to brood regularly. The female builds the nest from grass, leaves, moss, etc. She lays 3-4 pale blue-colored eggs, with a green-yellowish sheen and dark markings. For more details see *S. albigularis*.

9 SPOROPHILA ALBIGULARIS
White-throated seedeater

Classification Order Passeriformes, Family Emberizidae.
Characteristics Length: 10 cm (4 in). Gray; black head and ear coverts; white bib, underside, and breast; the last with a black band. Thighs black on the inside and white on the outside. Eyes dark brown, beak horn-colored yellowish, legs gray. The female is duller with a black beak.
Habitat Scrubs, tall grass, and along forests.
Distribution Northeastern Brazil.
Captivity The male has a nice voice (the female sings, too, although not as well as the male and considerably softer). Particularly during the breeding season, especially pugnacious towards his own kind. The species must be housed in a well-planted, large aviary. The female lays and incubates 3-4 gray-brown eggs, with brown markings. Incubation time: 12 days. After the young leave the nest, they are taken care of for about another 3 weeks. Universal food, supplementing a good canary menu; greens; small mealworms; and fruits (apple, banana) are essential. They use canary nests, but also build flimsy nests themselves; they only work on their nests during the morning hours.

10 VOLATINIA JACARINA
Blue-back grassquit or jacarina finch

Classification Order Passeriformes, Family Emberizidae.
Characteristics Length: 10-11.4 cm (4-4¹/₂ in). Blue back, with purple reflection. Wing coverts and shoulders white. Eyes dark brown, beak brown-black, legs light brown. The female is brownish; grayish on the crown. Back with black streaks.
Habitat Shrubs, gardens, parks, and near villages.
Distribution Lowlands of Mexico, Central America, and South America to Chile and northern Argentina.
Captivity Males are often available, especially in Europe. Lively but somewhat shy in the aviary. Good company with small waxbills and similar birds. The male performs an interesting nuptial dance with quivering tail and wings. They like to breed in a thick bush or in a half-open nest box. The female lays and incubates 2-3 greenish-white eggs with red-brown markings; incubation time 12 days. Later, during the breeding, the male often assists his mate; when the young hatch both parents are active in feeding them. When the chicks are about 10 days old, they leave the nest. After 7 months, they have the adult plumage.

11 RHODOSPINGUS CRUENTUS
Crimson, or rhodospingus, finch

Classification Order Passeriformes, Family Emberizidae.
Characteristics Length: 10-11.5 cm (4-4½ in). Upperparts dark blue-black; underparts reddish-pink, fading to orange on the abdomen. Bright red crest. The female lacks all red and is gray and brown in coloring, resembling a hen sparrow.
Habitat Scrub and bushy areas. Likes to hide in thick cover.
Distribution Ecuador and Peru.
Captivity In the wild as well as in captivity, the breeding season is exceptionally short. The species breeds in open "hives" and in half-open nest boxes; they will also use old nests left by weavers. The hen hatches and builds the nest alone. The clutch consists of 3-4 blue-whitish eggs. The incubation period is (only) 11-12 days. The young leave the nest after 8-9 days. In a large, well-planted aviary, these birds are very tolerant by nature. Although this might be less true during the breeding period, serious irregularities are unlikely to occur. There are usually 3-4 breedings per season, but I prefer 2 per year in order to prevent egg binding, among other things.

12 GUBERNATRIX CRISTATA
Yellow, or green, cardinal

Classification Order Passeriformes, Family Fringillidae.
Characteristics Length: 19 cm (7½ in). Olive green upperparts with black streak on the mantle. Yellow tail with two black central feathers. Crest, chin, and throat black; breast green-yellowish, brighter on the abdomen and undertail coverts. The male has a black, and the female a white, streak over the eye. Sides of the throat and supercilium deep yellow. The hen is duller and has a white color on the side of the throat; the breast is brown-grayish. Eyes brown, beak gold yellow, and legs blackish-brown.
Habitat Shrubbery.
Distribution Southeast Brazil, Uruguay, and north and east Argentina.
Captivity Although they are considerably less agressive than other cardinal species, they can defend themselves sufficiently well during the breeding period so that they can be kept with other cardinal species. The nest is usually built in a half-open nest box or even in a bush (cup-shaped). The hen does most of the building; the male usually sits and sings in the immediate vicinity. The hen also incubates the 3-4 greenish or bluish eggs, with brown and/or black spots, which takes about 12 days. Live food is often appreciated. As soon as the young are independent, they must be housed in a separate aviary; that means about 1 month after they leave the nest.

13 PAROARIA CORONATA
Red-crested cardinal

Classification Order Passeriformes, Family Fringillidae.
Characteristics Length: 19 cm (7½ in). Like *P. dominicana*, but with an even gray back and a bright scarlet head. Both sexes have a small crest. Eyes dark brown, beak pinkish white with a blackish tip, legs black.
Habitat Wet scrubs and shrubbery near woods, farmland, and orchards; solitary or in pairs.
Distribution Southern Brazil, east Bolivia, Paraguay, Uruguay, and northern Argentina.
Captivity This species prefer to build their nest in dense bushes, putting it together with twigs, blades of grass and leaf veins, and lining the interior with horsehair. They naturaly like to be "higher up," so that low aviaries do not suit them very well. Their nest is usually 2 to 4 meters from the ground. Their clutch consists of 3-4 white eggs which are spotted gray at the blunt end. Although individual birds are peaceful, a couple might cause a little trouble with other birds during the breeding season. The birds make grateful use of any woven nest baskets or half-open nest boxes hung at least 1½ meters from the ground. Cock and hen take turns sitting on the eggs (2 weeks), and both will also feed the young which leave the nest after 14 days. They will be fed by the cock for at least another 2 weeks.

14 PAROARIA DOMINICANA
Red-cowled, Dominican, or pope cardinal

Classification Order Passeriformes, Family Emberizidae.
Characteristics Length: 16.5-20 cm (6½-8 in). Head and throat red. Wings and tail gray-black. Black markings on the grayish upperparts. Underside white. Eyes brown, beak gray-brown, legs dark brown. The sexes are alike. Sometimes the males are slightly larger; the red throat is more extensive than in the female, and the white on the scapulars (mantle) is brighter.
Habitat Forest clearings, gardens, parks, and scrub.
Distribution Northeastern Brazil.
Captivity Extremely popular in Brazil. The male has a clear, cheerful voice, but not as nice as the song of a red cardinal (*Cardinalis cardinalis*). Primarily it is the male that sings, especially during the breeding season. They are sometimes aggressive during the breeding season, but in general are very peaceful and friendly birds. They must be housed in a well-planted, large aviary. There they might come to brood, although it is usually difficult to purchase a pair. The species uses all types of nest boxes and baskets, but will also build a free nest in thick bushes. Live food is essential, as are multivitamins, in order to prevent leg disfigurements (something many cardinal-like birds suffer from). The female lays 2-3 eggs; incubation time 13 days.

15 PAROARIA CAPITATA
Yellow-billed cardinal

Classification Order Passeriformes, Family Emberizidae.
Characteristics Length: 16.5 cm (6½ in). Head carmine-red; chin and throat black. Dark gray to black upperparts; white nape and underparts. No crest. The female is duller and the upperparts are grayish. Eyes brown, beak and legs yellow.
Habitat Shrubbery in humid areas.
Distribution Southeastern Bolivia and Mato Grosso south to northern Argentina.
Captivity Excellent, peaceful, and a good breeder; these three qualities make this species one of the best birds for a community aviary. It is essential to feed live food and the proper substitutes; not all birds, however, are familiar with this, and refuse to eat all but seeds. Those birds usually die within two years. Therefore: feed the birds fruits (berries, apples, oranges), greens (chickweed, lettuce), universal and egg foods, small mealworms, ant eggs, and a good canary seed mixture. For more details see *P. coronata*.

---

16 PASSERINA LELANCHERI
Orange-breasted, or rainbow, bunting

Classification Order Passeriformes, Family Emberizidae.
Characteristics Length: 12.5-14 cm (5-5½ in). Tur-quoise-green crown, sky-blue upperparts and tail; orange breast, yellow underparts. Greenish-blue on the scapulars (mantle). Female olive-green with yellow sheen on the un-derparts. Eyes dark brown, beak pale horn-colored, legs brownish-gray.
Habitat Bush, grass and scrub.
Distribution Southwestern Mexico.
Captivity Must be acclimatized with the utmost care. As long as the birds are unfamiliar with universal, rearing and egg foods, and insects, breeding attempts are not, or seldom, made; the same applies for the other *Passerina* species. The indigo bunting (*P. cyanea*) — from Canada and eastern USA to North and South Carolina and western Arizona — is for many European aviculturists the ideal bird due to its beautiful song and blue colors. All *Passerina* species must be treated with extra care, and not be kept with the cardinal species. In the wild, these finches eat seeds as well as great quantities of insects. In captivity provide pine and spruce twigs with plenty of resin on them. They will peck at this, which will be very beneficial for their red, yellow, blue, green, and other bright colors. There are also good canary color foods available on the market. Color finches are very peace-loving in community aviaries.

17 FRINGILLA COELEBS
Chaffinch

Classification Order Passeriformes, Family Fringillidae.
Characteristics Length: 15 cm (6 in). Black forehead, grayish-blue crown and nape. Chestnut back with white. Yellowish rump. Reddish sides of the head; throat and underside are red, too. Undertail coverts whitish. The female is greenish gray-brown; underparts brownish-gray. Eyes brown, beak dark horn-colored, legs dark gray.
Habitat Gardens, parks, near woods and cultivated areas.
Distribution Britain and Europe, western Asia, northwestern Africa, the Azores and the Canary Islands.
Captivity Excellent bird in a well-planted, large aviary, although only one pair can be kept per aviary. They build their cup-shaped nest in thick bushes or in canary nest pans. However, the young are usually hard to rear, as the parents must have a large supply of live insects, supplementing soft-billed commercial foods, sprouted seeds (of rape, turnip, radish, among others), and a good canary-seed mixture. During the breeding season, males may be aggressive towards other birds. Good breeding results are obtained in`canary-breeding cages. The female lays 4-5 (sometimes 2-8) eggs; incubation time 11-13 days. The young leave the nest after 12-15 days. This species has hybridized with the canary, among other finches. Can be kept in Britain only if aviary bred and close-rung.

18 SERINUS SERINUS
European serin

Classification Order Passeriformes, Family Fringillidae.
Characteristics Length: 11.5 cm (4½ in). Yellowish-brown, with black-brownish stripes. Yellow back; rump and underparts greenish-yellow. Underparts with brown stripes. Whitish belly. The female is duller, with more stripes on head and breast; rump paler. Eyes dark brown, the short beak and the legs are dark gray.
Habitat Park, gardens, and open woodland.
Distribution Southern Europe, occasionally north to Britain, western Asia Minor, and northwestern Africa.
Captivity Excellent, but somewhat delicate aviary birds; especially when they are molting. They must be housed in a well-planted aviary. Their mating behavior, during which they fly around like butterflies, is extremely interesting to watch. They love small seeds, like lettuce seed, millet spray, and such. The cup-shaped nest of all kinds of plant materials is built in thick bushes. The female lays and incubates 3-5, but usually 4, whitish eggs with red-brown markings. Incubation time 13-14 days. The nestlings are fed by both parents; they leave the nest at about 2 weeks, but will continue to be fed for 7-10 days. Can be kept in Britain only if aviary bred and close-rung, and officially registered.

19 SERINUS ALARIO
Black-headed canary or alario finch

Classification Order Passeriformes, Family Fringillidae.
Characteristics Length: 14 cm (5½ in). Head, nape, and throat black. Black stripe on each side of the breast. White collar. Upperparts cinnamon-red; underside white. Dark wing primaries. The female is paler brownish-gray without black; underparts light brown. Eyes dark brown, beak blackish, legs dark gray.
Habitat Dry and open bush country.
Distribution South Africa. The male of the subspecies *S. a. leucolaema*, from southwestern Africa, has a white throat and face.
Captivity This bird must be housed in a large, well-planted aviary. They are not always friendly towards small finches. The female lays 2-3, sometimes 5, dull blue eggs that have reddish-brown markings. Their nest is built close to the ground; is cup-shaped; and constructed of grass, wool, and occasionally small feathers. In the aviary, they will often use half-open nest boxes, but I would recommend dense vegetation, since they enjoy building a free-standing nest. A large variety of seeds needs to be supplied if they are to be coaxed to breed. Because of their close relationship to the canary, and because they have a pleasant song, they are sometimes crossed with the canary. I do not feel that the song is improved by this. Both parents incubate the clutch for about 2 weeks.

---

20 SERINUS MOZAMBICUS
Yellow-eyed canary or green singing finch

Classification Order Passeriformes, Family Fringillidae.
Characteristics Length: 12.5 cm (5 in). Greenish-gray upperparts; yellowish rump and yellow underpart. Lemon-yellow eyebrow streak, throat, and chin. The females are somewhat duller and have black spots on the neck. Eyes dark brown, beak light horn-colored, legs dark brown.
Habitat Gardens, parks, and open woodland.
Distribution Africa, south of the Sahara.
Captivity This species has much to recommend it: long life; hardiness; bright appearance; a clear and hearty, if choppy, song (only the male sings, and this only during the breeding season); and minimal care. They can be kept in a large, well-planted aviary, but are usually aggressive towards small finches and waxbills. Their mating behavior—lasting about 7 days—is rather rough, sometimes resulting in the loss of many of the hen's feathers. They build a cup-shaped nest or use half-open nest boxes. The female lays and incubates 3-4 pale blue eggs, for 13-14 days. The male feeds her on the nest. Hybrids with the canary are possible; small border or roller canary hens are recommended for this purpose.

21 SERINUS ATROGULARIS
Yellow-rumped serin, seedeater, or black-throated canary

Classification Order Passeriformes, Family Fringillidae.
Characteristics Length: 11.5 cm (4¹/₂ in). Upperparts grayish-brown with dusky streaks. Chin white, throat with brown streaks. Bright lemon-yellow rump. Uppertail coverts grayish with pale yellow edges. Underparts buff with brownish-black streaks. Eyes dark brown, beak and legs gray-brown.
Habitat Bush and light woodland, near water.
Distribution South Arabia, east and south Africa, from Ethiopia to Angola and the Cape; in 7 subspecies.
Captivity Their clutch consists of 3-4 bright blue eggs with red-brown markings. An artfully woven nest is built high in a small tree or bush. This species is often kept both as an aviary and cage bird. While its singing abilities are quite good, they do not match those of its cousin, the gray singing finch; for additional details see this species.

---

22 SERINUS LEUCOPYGIA
White-rumped, Layard's seedeater, or gray singing finch

Classification Order Passeriformes, Family Fringillidae.
Characteristics Length: 11.5 cm (4¹/₂ in). Gray upperparts with dusky streaks. White rump. Gray chin, throat, and breast. White underparts. Eyes brown, beak light horn-colored, legs pinkish-brown. Sexes are alike.
Habitat Open dry bush, gardens and parks, near villages and farms.
Distribution Africa; Senegal across to the Sudan.
Captivity The males are probably the finest songsters of all *Serinus* species (and of many more species besides); especially in the breeding season they compete while chasing each other through trees and thick bushes without actually harming themselves or others. The clutch usually consists of 3-4 white or very pale green eggs with black markings. The hen builds a beautifully woven, canarylike nest high in a small tree or thick bush. When feeding and housing are up to par, a couple may have 3-4 broods per season. The incubation period is approximately 2 weeks. After about 2-3 weeks, the young leave the nest but will continue to be fed by both parents for quite some time; in fact, the male will even continue feeding them for a few days after the hen has started a new cycle. The species is often crossed with canaries. Imported finches often suffer from infected eyes, which can be cured with a proprietary eye-ointment.

23 SERINUS CANARIA
Wild canary

Classification Order Passeriformes, Family Fringillidae.
Characteristics Length: 12.5 cm (5 in). Green. Cheeks, nape, and neck with grayish shine. Throat and breast yellowish-green, whitish on the underparts. Sides with some small, brownish-black streaks. Rump yellow-green. Wings and tail brownish-green, with lighter edges. The female is darker with gray streaks on the sides of the breast; the wings are lighter edged. Eyes brown, beak and legs dark gray.
Habitat Woods, gardens, and parks.
Distribution Canary Islands, Madeira, and the Azores; introduced into Bermuda; almost ubiquitous.
Captivity Wild birds were imported to Europe by the Spanish conquistadors in 1478. From then on intensive breeding and rearing followed. Today there are song, color, and form and posture canaries the world over. The female wild canary lays 4-5 greenish or light reddish eggs with pale green markings. Their nest is cup-shaped. They will use half-open nest boxes as well. Incubation time 13 days. After about 14 days, the young leave the nest but will be fed by the male for quite some time.

24 CARDUELIS CARDUELIS
European goldfinch

Classification Order Passeriformes, Family Fringillidae.
Characteristics Length: 12.5 cm (5 in). Upperparts tawny-brown; rump white. Head with red mask, followed by white and black. Lower part chestnut. Wings black, barred with yellow. Eyes dark brown, beak whitish-gray, legs gray.
Habitat Scrubs, parks, gardens, farms, and forests.
Distribution Britain and Europe, northern Africa, the Azores, the Canary Islands, and Madeira; Asia, east to Lake Baikal and south to the Himalayas and Baluchistan; introduced into Australia, Uruguay, and Argentina.
Captivity An excellent aviary bird. A male that is kept alone is usually willing to mate with different finches, e.g. canaries. A true pair will come to brood in a large well-planted aviary. The female lays and incubates 3-7 eggs, which hatch after about 14 days. The male feeds his mate on the nest. Thistle seeds are essential, among other seeds, as are insects and invertebrates. The courtship behavior of the male is quite interesting to watch: he sways his body before the hen, holding his wings open while beating them quickly. The sexes can be determined by checking the bird's rectal bristles on either side of the gape: they are light in the female, black in the male. Also, the red in a male's face extends beyond the eyes, but stops halfway in a female's (Restall). Can be kept in Britain only if aviary bred and close-rung.

25 CARDUELIS CUCULLATA
Red, or hooded, siskin

Classification Order Passeriformes, Family Fringillidae.
Characteristics Length: 11.5 cm (4³/₄ in). Upperparts and sides of the neck vermilion; a bright sheen on the lower back. Head black; wings and tail red and black. The female is duller with orange and gray wings; the breast is orange-red. Eyes dark brown, beak horn-colored, legs light brown-gray.
Habitat Dry scrub and open country.
Distribution Northeastern Colombia, northern Venezuela, and Trinidad. Introduced into Cuba and Puerto Rico.
Captivity Imported to the United States and Europe for over seventy years, but the price remains very high. New birds must be placed in a roomy, indoor aviary and kept at a temperature of about 25°C, day and night, for at least a week; later gradually reduce this to room temperature. Once properly acclimatized they are hardy and lively birds. Thanks to this siskin the red factor was brought into the canary by pairing a male with a female canary. The males of the resulting offspring are, for the most part, fertile. These hybrids inherit the red from their father and are then crossed back with canaries. After the fourth generation, the birds are again identical to canaries. But a real pair of siskins is worth keeping, too! When they are housed in a roomy, well-planted aviary, they will breed quite readily. The clutch consists of 3-4 bluish-white eggs that have red-brown markings. The hen incubates them.

26 CARDUELIS NOTATA
Neotropical black-headed siskin

Classification Order Passeriformes, Family Fringillidae.
Characteristics Length: 12.7 cm (5 in). Head black; olive-green upperparts; yellow rump. Yellow tail base and black tip. Black wings with greenish-yellow band across the base of the flight feathers. Eyes dark brown, beak gray-black, legs dark brown. The females are duller in coloration and miss the black head, which is olive-gray, as is the rest of the body.
Habitat Farmland, cultivated areas; usually in flocks.
Distribution Mexico, Honduras, Belize, El Salvador, and north Nicaragua.
Captivity There is a tendency to import more males than females, as they can be used to hybridize with the canary. The male has a sweet, goldfinchlike song. These extremely lively birds must be acclimatized with the utmost care, as they are quite delicate. For more details see the other *Carduelis* species.

27 CARDUELIS (CHLORIS) CHLORIS
Greenfinch

Classification Order Passeriformes, Family Fringillidae.
Characteristics Length: 14-15 cm (6 in). Upperparts brownish olive-green; underparts yellowish-green with grayish shades. Yellow outer tail feathers and bar on the wings. The female is darker and duller in coloration. Eyes dark brown, beak horn-colored, legs light brown-gray.
Habitat Parks, gardens, orchards, and woods; sometimes in small flocks; in 3 subspecies.
Distribution Britain and Europe, Mediterranean, northern Africa, and southwestern Asia to Afghanistan. Introduced into the Azores and Australia.
Captivity Able to hybridize with the canary. Lively, hardy bird, even suitable for a large cage. In an aviary, sometimes aggressive towards small birds. A canary seed mixture, rape seed, small sunflower seed, some hemp, linseed, teasel, and greens are essential. The female lays and incubates 3-8 eggs. The male feeds his mate on the nest. Incubation time 13-14 days. After 13-16 days the young leave the nest and are fed on regurgitated food, as are all other *Carduelis* species. Can be kept in Britain only if aviary bred and close-rung.

28 LOXIA CURVIROSTRA
Red crossbill or crossbill

Classification Order Passeriformes, Family Fringillidae.
Characteristics Length: 16 cm (6½ in). Very variable plumage, depending on sex and age. Head, belly, and rump purplish-red. Tail and wings brownish-gray. The female is somewhat smaller and has a gray-green upperside; the lower parts are yellowish-green. The young have much white in the lower parts, but resemble, on the whole, the female. Eyes dark brown, beak (of which the points of the mandibles are crossed) dark gray-black, legs dark gray.
Habitat Coniferous woods and orchards; in the latter, it bores holes in apples to eat the pips.
Distribution North America, North Africa, Britain and Europe, and north Asia; in 5 subspecies.
Captivity Becomes very tame. It is interesting to watch them opening almond nuts and shelling small seeds. This hardy bird requires a large, well-planted (conifers) aviary, and is gentle towards other birds. Breeding results are rather rare; nevertheless a pair must have a choice of wild berries, a good canary-seed mixture, and fresh whole fir cones (on the branch); some birds like mealworms. The female lays one annual clutch of 3-4 eggs, usually in the winter (when conifers bear fruit). Incubation time 13-16 days. Both parents feed the young, which leave the nest after 17-22 days. Can be kept in Britain only if aviary bred and close-rung, and officially registered.

29 COCCOTHRAUSTES COCCOTHRAUSTES
Hawfinch

Classification Order Passeriformes, Family Fringillidae.
Characteristics Length 17.5 cm (7 in). Throat, lores, and base around the strong and highset beak black. Crown and cheeks reddish-brown. Grayish nape; brown back. Black wings with white greater coverts. Rump and tail tip white. Eyes brown, beak gray, legs light-brown. The female is duller in coloration.

Habitat Coniferous and broadleaf woodland and scrubs, gardens, parks, farmland, and orchards; in small flocks.
Distribution Britain and Europe, Asia, and northwestern Africa.

Captivity Peaceful bird and ideal in a large, well-planted outdoor aviary, where they often come to brood; for nesting material supply grass blades, thin twigs, dried grass, and some wet earth and spider webs, with which they hold the nest together. The clutch consists of 3-5 eggs; color is bright gray to light green-gray, with gray and dark brown circles, spots, and stripes. The female alone incubates the eggs. After 11 days the young hatch, and spend some 12 days in the nest, during which time the cock will feed them. The young will be independent after about 20 days. Daily mealworms, sunflower seeds, weeds, fruit tree prunings, and green peas are essential. Both male and female sing very well, though the hen's voice is softer in tone and timbre. Can be kept in Britain only if aviary bred and close-rung.

30 PYRRHULA PYRRHULA
Common bullfinch

Classification Order Passeriformes, Family Fringillidae.
Characteristics Length: 14.5 cm (5¾ in). Bluish-black head; lower parts pink; belly and undertail coverts white. Upperparts blue-gray; rump white. Eyes dark brown, beak blackish-gray, legs dark gray. The female is duller in coloration with brown on the lower parts, belly, and undertail.

Habitat Gardens, parks, woods, farmland, and orchards; generally in pairs.
Distribution Britain, Europe, and Asia.

Captivity Amiable and peaceful birds; ideal to hybridize with the canary; especially the female is willing to mate with any typical finch. This species can be taught to pipe a tune. For this purpose handreared young of about 10 days are taken from the nest. As soon as the birds are about 1 month old, they must be caged separately. Tunes should be played or whistled to them in slow time, approximately 15-20 times per day. This instruction lasts about 9 months; tunes of 6 lines in the keys F, G, and A are mastered best. Not all birds are excellent performers, some birds learn only two or three lines (the so-called broken pipers). Any well-trained bird starts to pipe when told to perform by its owner. The female lays and, occasionally assisted by the cock, incubates 4-5, sometimes 6-7 eggs; incubation time 12-14 days. The young leave the nest after 12-18 days. Can be kept in Britain only if aviary bred and close-rung.

31 AMADINA FASCIATA
Cut-throat, or ribbon, finch

Classification   Order Passeriformes, Family Estrildidae.
Characteristics   Length: 12-13 cm (5 in). Both sexes are light fawn. Each feather is marked with a small black bar. Underside chocolate colored; tail gray; throat whitish. The hen lacks the red throat band and the chocolate abdomen. Eyes brown, beak and legs flesh-colored.
Habitat   Savannah, bush, farmland, and near villages. They brood in trees or in deserted weaver and sparrow nests. During the breeding season, they live in pairs; outside the breeding season, in sometimes very large flocks.
Distribution   Africa, south of the Sahara; in 3 subspecies.
Captivity   Suitable for both large cages and aviaries. They are good breeders, but should not be allowed more than 3 broods per season. Many birds are real troublemakers during the breeding period. They like to inspect other nests, and will often destroy the nests and the young of smaller birds. For this reason, only species of the same size should be allowed in a well-planted, large aviary with the cut-throat. This species uses half-open nest boxes. Preferred building materials are dry grass, feathers, hay, wool, etc. The female lays 4-9 eggs. Incubation time: 12 days; both sexes share the task of incubating and rearing the clutch. The young become independent after about 20 days.

---

32 AMADINA ERYTHROCEPHALA
Red-headed finch or paradise sparrow

Classification   Order Passeriformes, Family Estrildidae.
Characteristics   Length: 13 cm (5¼ in). Somewhat resembles the cut-throat finch, but the male's entire head is crimson; the collar is missing. The female has a gray-brown head, and the underside is less intense. Eyes brown, beak light horn-colored, legs flesh-colored.
Habitat   Especially open country; bush and thorn veldt. They brood in tree holes; deserted weaver or sparrow nests; or in buildings, like the house sparrow *Passer domesticus*. Colony breeders.
Distribution   South Africa, north to Angola and Zimbabwe.
Captivity   This species seldom builds its own nest in an aviary, preferring to occupy old weavers' nests, but will sometimes also use half-open nest boxes. The hen usually lays 3-6 eggs. Incubation time: 12-13 days. Both sexes sit on the eggs; during the day the male sits longer than the female; during the night both parents are on the nest, although the male sometimes sleeps in another nest, or close by on a branch. Don't disturb the parents, as they will otherwise start a nest somewhere else, leaving the young to die. After 2 weeks the young males already have red on their heads. After 23-24 days the young will leave the nest. They are able to reproduce after six months, but breeding should be restricted until the birds are at least 1 year old. This species has hybridized with the cut-throat finch, and the hybrids are fertile.

33 PYTILIA PHOENICOPTERA
Red-winged, or crimson-winged, pytilia; aurora finch; or crimson-winged waxbill

Classification Order Passeriformes, Family Estrildidae.
Characteristics Length: 12 cm (5 in). Ashy gray above. The light gray head has dark gray streaks. Rump, wings, and upper tail coverts are crimson; central tail feathers crimson also; rest of the tail blackish. Underside gray with white bars. The hen is browner and has many more markings on belly and breast than the male. Eyes brown, beak black, legs light red-brown.
Habitat Especially in bushes and tall grass, sometimes close to small villages. They live on insects and seeds.
Distribution From west to east Africa; in 3 subspecies.
Captivity These birds are suitable for cages and aviaries, although the temperature must not fall below 20°C. Therefore, a pair can best be kept in an indoor, well-planted aviary with other finches. During the breeding season, they protect their nest very aggressively. The small, untidy nest is built free in a bush or in a box, from grass, hay, small feathers, etc. Feathers are usually used for lining the inside of the nest. A pair breeds well, although they do not like to be disturbed. The male sings a soft, pleasant song practically all day long. In the breeding season, the cock dances round his hen with a beautiful raised tail and bowing head. The hen lays 3-4 eggs; incubation time 12 days. After about 20 days, the young leave the nest; after 8 weeks, they will have their first molt.

---

34 PYTILIA MELBA
Melba finch or crimson-faced waxbill

Classification Order Passeriformes, Family Estrildidae.
Characteristics Length: 12 cm (5 in). Throat, chin, and forehead scarlet; rest of head gray. Wings and back olive-green; tail blackish. Chest olive. Underside gray with white streaks and spots. Eyes are brown, beak scarlet, legs brown. The hen is duller, lacks all crimson, and has a gray head.
Habitat Thorny thickets. The birds live on seeds and, during the breeding season, on insects.
Distribution Africa, south of the Sahara.
Captivity After acclimatization (at a temperature of about 25°C, and no green foods for at least 3 weeks), the birds can be housed in an indoor, well-planted, and sunny aviary. An outside aviary is suitable only during the hot summer months. This species is usually quite aggressive towards other birds, so it is advisable to keep only one pair in a community aviary. The male has a soft, sweet song. These finches spend a lot of time on the ground looking for small insects, spiders, seeds, and such. They build a little domed nest in a small bush; seldom do they use a commercial wooden nest box. The hen lays 3-4 eggs; both parents incubate the clutch for about 12 days and rear the youngsters. However, quite often after 2-3 days the parents throw their young out of the nest, even when the food is right. The only way to prevent this is to give a rich variety of insects and small seeds, and hope for the best.

35 ESTRILDA MELANOTIS
Dufresne's, or yellow-bellied, waxbill

Classification Order Passeriformes, Family Estrildidae.
Characteristics Length: 9 cm (3½ in). The male has a black mask (lacking in the female); back and wings gray-olive; crown gray; rump and uppertail coverts scarlet; breast white. Tail black. Eyes brown, upper mandible black, lower mandible red; legs dark brown.
Habitat Open forest.

Distribution East and south Africa, from Ethiopia to Angola and the Cape; in 4 subspecies; they all have a gray chest and abdomen in different shades of yellow.

Captivity These lively birds cannot live without all kinds of small insects; especially in the breeding period insects are essential. They must be kept in indoor flights, together with other small finches, as they are extremely sociable and peaceful. They don't like disturbances during the breeding season. Incubation time: 12-14 days. They build nests high in the aviary, although they use nest boxes also. The hen lays 3-4 eggs; the young leave the nest after 21 days. At that time they still have black bills; after 3 months they come into their adult plumage.

36 ESTRILDA MELPODA
Orange-cheeked waxbill

Classification Order Passeriformes, Family Estrildidae.
Characteristics Length: 10 cm (4 in). Mainly mouse-brown with a light gray crown and whitish underparts. The rump is orange-red; the tail black; cheeks orange; eyes brown, beak red, and legs pinkish. The cheeks of the hen are often somewhat smaller; she is also duller in coloration. Only the male sings.
Habitat Grassland.

Distribution West and central Africa, in 3 subspecies; some years ago, escaped aviary birds established themselves in the Caribbean.

Captivity Suitable for cage and aviary. They are known to be fairly prolific breeders. Two males or two hens may act as a couple. During the breeding season, the birds must be housed in a well-planted aviary, with low bushes and high grass, as they like to construct their nests about 1.5 meters from the ground. They also often use half-open nest boxes. The hen lays 3-4, sometimes up to 7 eggs. Incubation time: 11-12 days. After about 2 weeks, the young leave the nest. Both male and hen sit on the eggs and feed the young. A plentiful supply of small insects (aphids, ant eggs, small mealworms, etc.) and egg food is necessary. The young birds assume their full plumage after the first molt (after about 7 weeks). This species is often given a free run from the aviary during the day; in the garden the parents will look for live insects for their young.

37 ESTRILDA RHODOPYGA
Crimson, or rosy-rumped, waxbill

Classification Order Passeriformes, Family Estrildidae.
Characteristics Length: 10 cm (4 in). Very similar to *E. troglodytes*; rump and uppertail coverts are crimson. Central tail feathers with crimson edges as well as the inner secondaries. Underside buff with vague little stripes on the flanks and on the undertail coverts. The red eye stripe of the hen is smaller, and the throat patch less extensive.
Habitat Grassland, farmland, and near small villages.
Distribution East Africa; in 2 subspecies.
Captivity Once acclimatized these birds are very suitable for a community aviary. The hens apparently have more difficulty getting used to climate and captivity than males, and suffer from egg binding if not properly cared for. In the wild, they often take the nests of *E. melpoda*, but also construct their own "maternity-rooms": round nests from dry grasses, leaves, moss, and some small feathers; sometimes sand, charcoal, and peat mold. They also construct—as *E. troglodytes* and *E. melpoda* do—small nests in the immediate vicinity of the breeding nest; these can be regarded as decoys. In order to gain breeding success, it is advisable to have 3 or more pairs in the same aviary. For more details see *E. troglodytes*. It is interesting to note that male and female feed their young every two hours. Egg foods are not appreciated, but insects are a must all year, especially during the breeding season.

38 ESTRILDA TROGLODYTES
Red-eared waxbill, gray waxbill or coralbeak

Classification Order Passeriformes, Family Estrildidae.
Characteristics Length: 10 cm (4 in). Mouse-brown with some gray on the head. Crimson eye line. Tail black, throat whitish with a vague pink sheen. Underside grayish white with a pink sheen. Eyes brown, beak scarlet, legs brown.
Habitat Semi-arid areas and swamps.
Distribution Senegal to Sudan and northern Ethiopia.
Captivity They are amusing little birds that quickly make themselves at home in indoor and even in large outdoor aviaries. They are always on the go, giving out a shrill little song that is not particularly pretty but has a certain charm. Out of the breeding season the sexes are difficult to tell apart, but this changes when the breeding time starts. The color of the male becomes a much more intense red, and his eyebrows become darker. He then goes through his display, holding a blade of grass or some such thing in his bill, dancing in circles around the female. Their bullet-shaped nests should be built in a hidden area of the aviary—a closed nesting box, for example. Three to five eggs are laid and then incubated alternately by the male and female, generally, for periods of 3 hours each. After 11-12 days the eggs hatch. The young leave the nest after 2 weeks, but, like many other birds, continue to take food from the parents for a while longer. They must be kept indoors during the winter. For food see firefinch.

39 ESTRILDA ASTRILD
Common, or St. Helene, waxbill

Classification Order Passeriformes, Family Estrildidae.
Characteristics Length: 11.5 cm (4½ in). Like *E. troglodytes*. Upperparts with dark little bars; underparts washed with pink; abdomen carmine, again, with little bars. Undertail coverts black. Crimson eye band. Eyes brown, beak red, legs brownish-red. The female is somewhat smaller, with lighter markings and with less pink on the abdomen. The bill is red; the eye band shorter. Undertail coverts brownish.
Habitat Grassland and cultivated areas.
Distribution Africa, south of the Sahara; Madagascar, Mauritius, St. Helena, and New Caledonia; this species now reported feral in Spain. There are 5 subspecies.
Captivity Sometimes these birds lay only one egg; at other times they may lay 5 or more, but then one must assume that more than one hen is using the same nest. In the aviary, the cock builds a bullet-shaped nest from grass and straw, primarily by himself. It is generally well-concealed in a thick bush. They will also use nest boxes, which should be hung high. After about 10 days the young are hatched, and another 2 weeks later they fly out of the nest. Nevertheless, the parents actively continue to feed them for quite some time. Insects and soaked seeds are essential; so is bathing (and this basically applies to all waxbills). During the breeding period, it is best to house just one pair in an aviary to avoid troubles.

40 ESTRILDA CAERULESCENS
Red-tailed lavender

Classification Order Passeriformes, Family Estrildidae.
Characteristics Length: 10 cm (4 in). Gray-blue; upperparts darker. Cheeks and throat lighter gray. Black belly with white on the sides. Rump, undertail coverts, and tail red. Little black periophthalmic ring. Eyes brown, beak red with black tip, legs light brown. Females are somewhat duller.
Habitat Bush and cultivated areas.
Distribution West Africa, from Senegal to northern Cameroon and southwestern Chad.
Captivity These birds are peaceful, and quite quickly become tame enough to eat from the hand of their keeper. They are acrobatic and amusing to watch. They breed well and regularly, particularly if there are no other birds of the same variety in the same aviary. In order to build their nests, they need a large amount of material (like the zebra finch). The young leave the nest after 2 weeks, but will be taken care of by both parents for quite some time. During the winter, these beautiful little birds must be kept in a warm area. Give them universal food, a good variety of egg mixture, ant eggs, egg yolk, finely cut mealworms, white worms, greens (lettuce, endive, chicory, chickweed, and such), and cuttlefish bone. The ant pupae can be given fresh as well as in the dry form. This food is indispensable, particularly during the breeding season.

41 URAEGINTHUS BENGALUS
Red-cheeked cordon bleu

Classification   Order Passeriformes, Family Estrildidae.
Characteristics   Length: 11.5 cm (4½ in). Upperparts mouse-brown; cheeks, throat, sides, breast and uppertail coverts sky blue. Tail duller blue. Crimson ear patches. Abdomen whitish-brown. The female lacks the red ear patches. Eyes brown, beak red with a black tip, legs yellowish-brown.
Habitat   Open country and cultivated areas.
Distribution   From Senegal to Ethiopia and south through eastern Africa to Katanga and Zambia.
Captivity   Excellent, lively aviary bird. Imported birds must be carefully acclimatized; a warm (25°C) indoor and roomy aviary or large cage is essential. They breed all year, but it is best to allow only 2 broods, during May to September. They build oven-shaped nests of fine grasses and feathers, but also accept half-open nest boxes. Both sexes incubate, for approximately 13 days. The young leave the nest after about 17 days. The young males attain the ear patch after about 5 months. Live food is necessary; especially aphids, ant eggs, and spiders.

---

42 URAEGINTHUS ANGOLENSIS
Angola cordon bleu or blue-breasted waxbill

Classification   Order Passeriformes, Family Estrildidae.
Characteristics   Length: 11.5 cm (4½ in). Almost identical to *U. bengalus*; these birds, however, lack the red ear patches. The blue is much brighter. Females have creamy underparts, but are difficult to distinguish from other female cordon bleu, although their beaks are usually a brighter pink. Eyes brown, beak red with a black tip, legs light brown.
Habitat   Scrub country and cultivated areas.
Distribution   From the Zaire to Tanzania (Africa); introduced into Zanzibar and São Thomé.
Captivity   The male has a nice strong song. They build their free grass nests in thick bushes, but will also use half-open nest boxes. The female lays 3-4 eggs. Live food is necessary. Sometimes antagonistic towards *U. bengalus*.

43 GRANATINA (URAEGINTHUS) GRANATINA
Violet-eared waxbill

Classification Order Passeriformes, Family Estrildidae.
Characteristics Length: 11.5 cm (4½ in). Chestnut. Violet ear patches. Wings brownish-gray with red margins. Forehead and tail coverts blue; chin, throat, vent, and tail black. The tail has bluish edges. Eyes reddish-brown, beak purple with a red tip, legs purple-gray. The female is duller, with grayish upperparts and yellowish underparts. Her throat is whitish. Lilac ear patches. No blue on the under-tail coverts.
Habitat Thorn scrub country and arid areas; in small flocks or pairs. Quite often together with *U. angolensis*. They build their nests in thorny bushes.
Distribution From Angola to Zambia (Africa).
Captivity These beautiful birds need a roomy aviary. They will not survive in temperatures below 21°C, and are therefore ideal for indoor aviaries and such. In addition to small seeds (grass seeds, spray millet), live food is essential all year. For more details see *Uraeginthus* species.

44 LAGONOSTICTA SENEGALA
Red-billed firefinch

Classification Order Passeriformes, Family Estrildidae.
Characteristics Length: 9 cm (3½ in). Crimson. Light brown wings and tail. Little white spots along the sides of the breast. Eyes brown, beak red, legs light brown. The female is brownish-gray with a crimson mask. Reddish uppertail coverts. Brown tail with crimson edges. Some white spots on the sides of the breast.
Habitat Cultivation and human habitation.
Distribution Western part of Africa.
Captivity This species is a rather shy bird which prefers to stay on the ground; somewhat withdrawn. They must be most carefully acclimatized, but, since this is quite difficult to do (many have a poor coat of feathers), my advice is that you buy only those birds that are aviary bred. Birds that are not yet acclimatized find it difficult to tolerate drafts and cold. They fare best at an even temperature of 19°C. In closed nest boxes they build a "cradle" from the same materials as the avadavats; rarely will they make a free nest in the bushes. When a nest box is hung in a little thicket, the birds will accept it sooner than a nest box hung up against one of the walls of the aviary. The female incubates the 3-4 eggs about 11 days. When the offspring are hatched, an extra amount of live food, greens, and egg foods are essential.

45 HYPARGOS NIVEOGUTTATUS
Peter's twin-spot

Classification Order Passeriformes, Family Estrildidae.
Characteristics Length: 11.5 cm (4½ in). Crown and nape brownish-gray; throat and chest crimson. Back brown with crimson sheen; darker wings. Rump, middle-tail feathers and uppertail coverts crimson. Inner webs black, outer webs crimson. Further underparts black with white spots, particularly on the flanks. Eyes brown, beak gray, legs reddish-brown. The female has a gray head; chest and throat are orange. Underparts gray with white spots, especially on the sides.
Habitat Bushy country, near rivers or forest edges. They feed primarily on the ground.
Distribution East Africa.
Captivity Nice birds in a community aviary; they are not aggressive and come to breed as long as they have live food, dry and soaked small seeds, maggots, ant eggs, egg food, and such. They like to build their nest in half-open boxes near the ground in thick bushes. The female lays 3-4 eggs; incubation time 14 days. The young leave the nest when they are 18-20 days old.

---

46 MANDINGOA NITIDULA
Green-backed twin-spot

Classification Order Passeriformes, Family Estrildidae.
Characteristics Length: 11.5 cm (4½ in). Red-orange face; deep olive-yellow uppertail coverts; some olive-yellow on throat, upper breast, and neck. Olive-green undertail coverts. Black underparts with white spots. Eyes brown, beak black with a red tip, legs brownish. The female is duller and a paler orange on the face.
Habitat Forest edges and thickets; in small groups. They feed mainly on the ground.
Distribution Mozambique (Africa). There are 2 subspecies, of which the Schlegel's twin-spot (*M. n. schlegeli*) of West Africa has a bright red face and a reddish chin and breast. The Chubb's twin-spot (*M. n. chubbi*) is from East Africa, with a red face and a golden-yellow chin and breast, often washed in orange.
Captivity Lively, hardy birds which feed mainly on the ground. A thickly planted aviary is necessary. They are friendly towards other birds, hence excellent for a community aviary. During the breeding season, live food is essential. For more details see *Hypargos niveoguttatus* and the *Uraeginthus* species.

47 ORTYGOSPIZA ATRICOLLIS
Common, or black-chinned, quail finch

Classification Order Passeriformes, Family Estrildidae.
Characteristics Length: 10 cm (4 in). Upperparts mottled brown. Forehead and cheeks black. White chin and areas around the eyes. Throat black. Underparts grayish with black and white bars. Abdomen yellowish-brown. Eyes brown, beak red, legs brownish. The female is duller and has small brown bars on the head.
Habitat Swamps, bogs, marshland, and other wet areas; in small flocks or family parties. During the breeding season in pairs.
Distribution Africa, south of the Sahara to Angola and Damaraland; in many species and subspecies.
Captivity Small, terrestrial birds, with short tails and strong, long legs. They have a whirring flight. The aviary floor can best be covered with high grasses, patches of granulated peat moss, and such. They are far from strong, and extra care must therefore be taken: feet must be kept clean, they must have small seeds that are offered on the ground, and, during the breeding season, live food (ant eggs, chopped mealworms, greenflies etc.) must be available on a daily basis. The female lays 4-6 eggs in a little nest near the ground in a grass tussock. Incubation about 11 days. The young leave the nest after approximately 2 weeks, but will still be fed by both parents for quite some time.

---

48 AMANDAVA (STICTOSPIZA) FORMOSA
Green avadavat

Classification Order Passeriformes, Family Estrildidae.
Characteristics Length: 10 cm (4 in). Upperparts olive-green with a golden sheen on the rump and uppertail coverts. Tail black. Underparts greenish-yellow, with dark green and white bars on the sides. Eyes brown, beak red, legs pinkish. The female is duller, with a grayish hue on the underparts and face.
Habitat High grass, sugar-cane fields, and other cultivated areas. They build their globular nests in cane fields or long grass tussocks.
Distribution Central India.
Captivity Attractive and hardy aviary bird. Recently imported birds must be first housed in a warm, roomy indoor aviary (22°C); after approximately 6 weeks they can be placed in a well-planted outdoor aviary. During the fall and winter, they must be housed indoors again. The female usually lays 4-5 eggs in a free, bullet-shaped nest. The species will certainly come to brood if their aviary offers the necessary privacy. The rest of its care parallels that of the strawberry finch.

49 AMANDAVA AMANDAVA
Strawberry finch or red avadavat

Classification   Order Passeriformes, Family Estrildidae.
Characteristics   Length: 10 cm (4 in). The male brown-red, with scarlet sides of head, throat, and underparts. Tail black; wings and tail coverts with numerous white spots. Rump scarlet. Eyes brown, beak red, legs pink. The female is reddish-brown with many white spots on the wings; uppertail coverts red. Breast yellowish-gray. This species has a seasonal change of plumage. During the breeding season, the male is brown-red; outside this period, he resembles the female.
Habitat   Scrub jungle and cultivated areas.
Distribution   India, Pakistan, south Nepal, southeastern Asia, Moluccas, and probably also Java (Indonesia). There is a variety in China which has even more vivid red coloring. There are 3 subspecies.
Captivity   Year long the male's song comes through with a clear tone. The female also can be heard to sing, particularly when she has no mate, but her song is less ebullient. During the breeding season the pair is enjoyable to watch. In their interesting courtship display, the male, bursting into full song, spreads his tail feathers and dances around the female. The gratifying results one can get with a good couple make these birds very suitable for breeding. The female lays 6-8 eggs in a little nest made of long fibers, hair, feathers, and grass. They will usually use nest boxes in the aviary, but they also like to build a nest in a dense bush. The cock builds the nest by himself, but the hen will incubate the eggs for 11-12 days; in the meantime, the fiery cock will defend the nest valiantly against all inquisitive eyes. After about 20 days, the young will fly out of the nest. Their beaks are still black at this time. The coloring changes start at around 3 weeks. After about 9 weeks, the new coloring is completed, but the birds will not really attain their true, adult coloring until 2 years old. During this period, the immature plumage often still shows many variations, so that different parts of the body may be red, yellow, brown, or white; only after two years will the color remain fast. This species can be quite troublesome towards other birds during the breeding period. It is advisable to house them separately at this time. Live food is essential all year.

Top: male
Bottom: pair of strawberry finches
(right, the male; left, the hen)

50 AMANDAVA SUBFLAVA
Golden-breasted, or zebra, waxbill

Classification Order Passeriformes, Family Estrildidae.
Characteristics Length: 9 cm (3½ in). Olive-brown above; bright yellow below. Red rump; orange breast. Red streak through the eyes. Eyes brown, beak coral red, legs brown. The female is duller in coloration.
Habitat Grassland and cultivated areas.
Distribution Africa, south of the Sahara, except the extreme south.
Captivity This easy-to-keep bird can stay in an outside aviary during the summer, but—like the avadavat and firefinch—it must spend the winter in a warmer area (around 18°C). This species does not adapt easily to captivity, and the breeding results are rare, which is a pity because the beautiful birds are so decorative in the aviary. In their bulky nest, a few eggs are sometimes laid, but unfortunately these are generally unfertilized. If, after about 12 days of incubation, the eggs develop, then feed the birds as you would the firefinch. During the breeding season, these birds may be quarrelsome with other birds; but, if the aviary is not too densely populated, and there is enough plant life to provide hiding places for those birds that want it, there should be no difficulty.

---

51 PADDA ORYZIVORA
Java sparrow or rice bird

Classification Order Passeriformes, Family Estrildidae.
Characteristics Length: 14 cm (5½ in). Pale blue-gray; head black with white cheek patches. Black tail. Eyes brown, beak pink, legs flesh-colored. The female is somewhat smaller; narrower crown and a more regularly tapered bill. The base of the male's bill is more swollen and a brighter red.
Habitat Rice and bamboo fields; in large flocks.
Distribution Java, Bali, and various neighboring islands (Indonesia); introduced into Sri Lanka, southern Burma, Zanzibar, St. Helena, among other places.
Captivity Currently a very popular bird! Several mutations have already been developed. The white, pied, and brown mutations have gained quite a following, and in 1973 I came across a blackheaded Java sparrow in Belgium. These birds are ideal aviary inhabitants. They prefer using half-open nest boxes (30 × 25 × 25 cm) or beechwood blocks (the entrance hole should have a diameter of 5 cm). If nothing is done to prevent it, the birds will breed throughout the year, which, of course, could lead to egg-binding problems. Limit the breeding period from May through July and no more than four clutches per season. The incubation period is 12-15 days. If the aviary is fairly peaceful, with only a few fellow inhabitants, success is guaranteed. To discourage fighting, do not hang the breeding boxes too close together.

52 LONCHURA (LEPIDOPYGIA) NANA
Madagascar mannikin, nana, bib finch or African parson finch

Classification Order Passeriformes, Family Estrildidae.
Characteristics Length: 9 cm (3³/₄ in). Olive brown; black lores, throat, and chin; gray underparts mixed with brown on the belly. Sexes are alike. Eyes brown, upper mandible black, lower mandible gray-blue, legs horn-colored.
Habitat Bush country, grassland and farmland, often near villages.
Distribution Madagascar, in groups of about 40 birds.
Captivity These birds—rare in the United States—are easy to breed in a well-planted aviary. The male dances before its hen and sings a soft, pretty song consisting of 4 phrases, repeated 3 or 4 times. They also like to chase each other as well as other birds, especially when the latter come too close to their nest. For this reason, I prefer to keep them in a small separate aviary, instead of in a community one, although they are not aggressive birds. Their nest is usually built in thick bushes. They also accept nest boxes. The female lays 3-4, sometimes up to 7 white eggs. Incubation time 12 days. After 21 days, the young leave the nest, but will be cared for by both parents for another 12-14 days, before they become independent. They do not attain full adult plumage for 2 years. During the breeding season, live insects and germinated seeds are essential.

53 LONCHURA (SPERMESTES) CUCULLATUS
Bronze-winged mannikin or hooded finch

Classification Order Passeriformes, Family Estrildidae.
Characteristics Length: 9 cm (3¹/₂ in). Head, neck, and throat black; upperparts dark brown. Uppertail coverts and sides with dark brown stripes; underside buff; scapulars metallic green. Eyes brown, beak gray (the upper mandible is darker), legs dark gray. The beak of the female is often more regularly tapered than the male's.
Habitat Open country, farmland, and near villages.
Distribution Africa, south of the Sahara, to Angola and Zimbabwe; also the islands of Pemba, Zanzibar, Mafia, Comoro Islands, and certain islands in the Gulf of Guinea.
Captivity These are very friendly, lively little birds, although they can be and usually are aggressive in the breeding season, even attacking larger birds. The male dances and sings a barely audible purring call during the spring and summer. They don't breed easily, however. To increase chances of breeding success, a well-planted, quietly situated outdoor aviary, housing this species only, should be provided. Commercial nest boxes and a wide variety of building materials (dry grass, hay, wool, hemp, moss, etc.) are necessary. The 4-6 eggs will hatch in 12-13 days; both sexes share the task of rearing their young. After 18 days the young leave the nest, but both parents continue to feed them for another 14 days. After this time, however, they must be separated from their parents, to prevent fighting.

54 LONCHURA (SPERMESTES) BICOLOR
Black and white, Fernando Po, or black-breasted mannikin

Classification Order Passeriformes, Family Estrildidae.
Characteristics Length: 10 cm (4 in). Black, glossed with bronze green; lower breast and the remaining underparts white; flanks with white scalloping. The sexes are alike. Eyes brown, beak dark gray, legs black.
Habitat Forests and secondary growth.
Distribution For the nominate race *bicolor*: West Africa (lacks the stripes on wings and rump). The subspecies *nigriceps*, sometimes called Rufous-backed mannikin, is from the east coast of Africa; the bird has a brown back. *L.b.poensis*, from Fernando Po, has many white spots on the wings; while *stigmatophora* has a black-brown back. The *L.b.woltersi*, which lives south of Zaire, has an extremely brown back. In the south, *rufodorsalis* occurs, with a fox-brown back and white underparts. The smallest subspecies is *minor*, from the north of Africa.

Captivity The cock has a soft song. They are reputed to be fairly good breeders and not quarrelsome, except toward their own kind, when housed in a well-planted aviary together with other small finches. The usual commercial nest boxes are necessary. The building materials that can be offered are grass, hay, wool, and coconut fiber. The hen will lay 3-4 white eggs, which are incubated by both parents for about 13 days. The young leave the nest when they are about 2 weeks old.

---

55 LONCHURA (SPERMESTES) ATRICAPILLA
Black-headed, chestnut, or chestnut-bellied, munia; or black-headed nun

Classification Order Passeriformes, Family Estrildidae.
Characteristics Length: 11.5 cm (4½ in). Head and upper breast, vent, and undertail coverts black; rest of the body chestnut; red-brown on the uppertail coverts. Eyes brown, beak blue-gray, legs dark blue-gray. Sexes are alike.
Habitat Swamps, sometimes in large groups.
Distribution India, especially in the southern parts.
Captivity This species will only breed very sporadically. Sometimes they will use the deserted nests of canaries and finches, but only when the aviary offers lush greenery, especially in the form of reeds, tall grass, and corn. Having a few flagstones on the aviary floor will assist the birds in keeping their nails in shape. The birds will not tolerate inspection during the breeding cycle. Supply them with perches located high in the aviary, and give them plenty of insects, cuttlefish bone, weed seeds, universal food, greens, canary-chick-rearing food, and stale bread soaked in milk or water. The hen lays 4-6 eggs; incubation time 12 days. After 21 days, the young leave the nest.

56 LONCHURA (ODONTOSPIZA) CANICEPS
Gray-headed, or pearl-headed, silverbill

Classification Order Passeriformes, Family Estrildidae.
Characteristics Length: 12 cm (5 in). Head gray; cheeks and throat are covered with small white spots. Mantle and underparts pinkish light brown; rump and uppertail coverts white; wing coverts gray; tail and wings black. Sexes are alike, although the cock is slightly richer in coloring and has larger white spots. Eyes brown, beak gray-blue, legs dark gray.
Habitat Dry country, with low and thorn bushes, high grass, and weeds.
Distribution Southern Ethiopia to Tanzania.
Captivity The courtship behavior and the singing of the male is, as with the majority of these finches, the most reliable indication of sex. They are very friendly towards other birds in an aviary, even towards birds of their own kind. Females are even tolerant of nest inspections. In a large, well-planted aviary, good breeding results are often achieved. They build large free nests in bushes or in wooden commercial nest boxes. If there is an abandoned nest available, however, they will prefer it to a nesting box. The hen lays 4-6 eggs; incubation time 12-13 days. After a month the young leave the nest. Fifteen days after flight, young males have been observed carrying out the nuptial display. Pairs are difficult to determine, therefore, it is wise to buy 6-8 birds at the same time and "let them do the searching."

---

57 LONCHURA (EODICE) CANTANS
African silverbill or warbling silverbill

Classification Order Passeriformes, Family Estrildidae.
Characteristics Length: 11 cm (4½ in). Light, sandy brown with indistinct little stripes. Darker on tail and wings; light on belly and undertail coverts. The sexes are alike. See *L. malabarica*.
Habitat Savannahs, farmland, and near villages; nests are often found under roofs and/or in the walls of the huts occupied by the natives; also in low shrubs.
Distribution West and central Africa; in 4 subspecies.
Captivity These birds are easy breeders and can be placed in community aviaries as well as in large cages. The best breeding results, however, are obtained in aviaries where they can be by themselves. The aviary (or cage) should be very quiet as they are susceptible to disturbance. Nest control therefore is taboo. The hen lays 3-4 eggs; both sexes incubate them for 12-13 days. After 21 days, the youngsters leave the nest. Fifteen to twenty-one young from one pair in one season is not only possible but relatively common. Three broods per year, however, produce the best young, and also lower the risk of egg binding. Silverbills are extremely suitable foster parents for finches that don't require insects. They prefer greens, millet, and especially spray millet as a treat. They can be crossed with *L. malabarica*, *L. punctulata*, and *L. striata* var. *domestica*, among others.

58 LONCHURA (EODICE) MALABARICA
Indian silverbill

Classification Order Passeriformes, Family Estrildidae.
Characteristics Length: 11 cm (4½ in). White rump and brown on top; African silverbills are light on top and have a pale buff-colored rump. The sexes are alike, but the hen has a somewhat smaller head. The male sings, although very softly. Eyes dark brown, upper mandible gray-blue (darker in *L. cantans*), lower mandible light gray-blue; legs pinkish or blue-gray.
Habitat Mainly in open country, in gardens, parks, and orchards.
Distribution India, Afghanistan, and Sri Lanka.
Captivity These birds are extremely suitable for cages and community aviaries. A true pair will build a free small nest in a bush or in a commercial wooden nest box. They are inoffensive towards their own kind as well as towards other birds. Two males or two females may behave like a true pair. This species is not too hardy, so it should be kept indoors during the winter months. In captivity the birds like to use old weavers' nests which they provide with a long and narrow entrance. The hen lays up to 10 and sometimes 12 eggs. Neunzig (1921) talks about 25 eggs, of two hens using the same nest; an occurence that happens quite often in a community aviary. Both parents incubate the eggs for 12-13 days. After 21 days, the young leave the nest. Three broods per year is ideal.

---

59 LONCHURA PUNCTULATA
Spice bird or spice finch

Classification Order Passeriformes, Family Estrildidae.
Characteristics Length: 11.5 cm (4½ in). Chocolate brown; darker brown on the head; underparts lighter brown and white on the abdomen. Breast and flank feathers with dark brown edges (scaly). Sexes are alike, but the male's beak is somewhat thicker and heavier; the head is larger and broader. Young birds don't have any scaly appearance.
Habitat Grassland, parks and gardens.
Distribution India, Sri Lanka, southeastern Asia, south China, Taiwan and Hainan, through Greater and Lesser Sundas (except Borneo) to Sulawesi (formerly Celebes) and the Philippines; introduced into Australia.
Captivity These birds are well known for their appealing nature and the modest demands they make upon the bird keeper. In aviaries as well as in glass enclosures, these birds thrive and breed. The male sings a song so softly we cannot hear it, but by the proud thrust of its head we can see that he is engrossed in it. They are almost always in motion. In the winter, they can be brought inside to a frost-free area, but this does not imply that they cannot tolerate temperate zones. Experience has shown that, if they are given an outside aviary with a sturdily built night enclosure (containing felt-lined nest boxes, which also serve as sleeping places), they can spend the winter outdoors.

60 LONCHURA FRINGILLOIDES
Magpie mannikin

Classification Order Passeriformes, Family Estrildidae.
Characteristics Length: 11.5 cm (4½ in). Head, flanks, rump, upper tail coverts and tail glossy black. Wings dusky, underparts off-white. The feathers of the mantle are brown. Typical lancet-shaped tail. Eyes brown, upper mandible of beak dark blue-gray, lower mandible light blue-gray, legs dark gray. The sexes are alike.
Habitat Jungle grassland and cultivated areas; in small groups.
Distribution Africa from Senegal to Somalia, and south to Natal.
Captivity These birds can be quite aggressive during the breeding season, especially toward small waxbills. Their care and breeding cycle parallels that of the Bengalese. They must be brought indoors into a lightly heated area for the winter months, and must have access to insects during the breeding season.

61 LONCHURA STRIATA VAR. DOMESTICA
Bengalese

This bird is not found in the wild but was bred from the sharp-tailed munia (*L. acuticauda*) and the striata munia (*L. striata*). The Bengalese comes in various colors, and there are even some varieties that have a little crest. These birds are suitable as both aviary and cage birds. They have an excellent reputation as foster parents. If a breeder has a preference for a particular color, he will need to continue breeding just that particular color from 3 to 5 times. The breeding itself does not usually pose many problems. In a well-planted aviary or in a box cage, one can achieve very satisfactory results. However, do not disturb the breeding birds, even if they are known as birds that allow regular nest inspections, because you may well be disappointed; peace is a necessary condition. Supply them with ample nest boxes (half-open: 25 × 25 × 25 cm) and nesting material (coconut fibers and grass), because some birds simply allow other more aggressive birds to take an unfair share of these materials. It is best not to allow more than 4 broods per season and avoid winter breeding. A large clutch of perhaps 10 or more eggs indicates that your "couple" is really two hens; two cocks may also behave like a "couple," but obviously the lack of eggs will give their little game away! A normal couple will have a clutch of 5-7 eggs, incubated in about 18 days by both parents. After another 20 days, the young fly out of the nest.

62 LONCHURA MAJA
White-headed munia, mannikin, or nun

Classification Order Passeriformes, Family Estrildidae.
Characteristics Length: 12 cm (5 in). White head; upperparts chestnut; underparts black. Sexes are alike, but sometimes the male's head is brighter. Eyes brown, beak dark blue-gray, legs gray.
Habitat Grassland, sometimes in enormous flocks.
Distribution Malay Peninsula, Sumatra, Simalur, Nias, Java, and Bali (Indonesia).
Captivity These birds are very much in demand around the world. Although the breeding results from these birds are only average, it is eventually possible that a couple will breed if the cage is in a very quiet and restful spot. There is a better chance of breeding if a male munia (or mannikin, as it is sometimes called) is mated with a Bengalese. Once they start breeding, you can expect the young in 12 days; after 25 days or so, they leave the nest but still take food from the parents for a while. Their nails grow quite long (as is the case with all *Lonchura* species) and should be carefully trimmed twice a year; a job that is far from easy but necessary. The bird must have fresh bathwater daily.

---

63 LONCHURA MALACCA
Black-headed munia or three-colored mannikin

Classification Order Passeriformes, Family Estrildidae.
Characteristics Length: 12 cm (5 in). Head, upper breast, center of belly, and undertail coverts black. Rest of upperparts chestnut brown; reddish on tail coverts and tail. White lower breast and flanks. The sexes are alike. Eyes brown, beak blue-gray, legs dark blue-gray.
Habitat Grassland and cultivated areas; in sometimes large flocks.
Distribution India and Sri Lanka, through southeastern Asia, Sumatra, Taiwan, the Philippines, Sulawesi (formerly Celebes), and Java (Indonesia).
Captivity This bird is controlled by export regulations. It is extremely strong, lively, and excellent for the beginner. Feed is identical to the red-billed firefinch's; care is the same manner as for the spice finch.

64 LONCHURA CASTANEOTHORAX
Chestnut-breasted finch

Classification Order Passeriformes, Family Estrildidae.
Characteristics Length: 10 cm (4 in). Head grayish-brown with light spots; dark brown mantle and wings. Yellowish rump and uppertail coverts. Yellowish tail. Black throat, chin, and face. Chestnut breast with lower black edges; the sides of the lower breast are black. White belly and undertail coverts. The sexes are alike. Females somewhat duller. Eyes brown, beak blue-gray, legs gray-brown.
Habitat Grassland, cane fields, reed beds, and along the coastal districts of north Australia. Destroys cereal crops.
Distribution Papua New Guinea, Vulcan Island, north and eastern Australia; introduced into New Caledonia, Society Islands, and elsewhere.
Captivity Amicable aviary bird. Before the breeding season starts, the male dances in front of his mate, drawing himself up to his full height, while hopping up and down on his branch or perch. They are very good birds for beginners, but it must be said that they practically never breed. There has been some success in crossing them with several mannikins, striata munia, Indian silverbill, masked grassfinch and zebra finch. They are pleasant, tolerant birds that never get into arguments and bear up quite well in most circumstances. They also need fresh bath water daily and nail care. According to Harman (see bibliography), some of the hybrids are fertile.

65 AIDEMOSYNE (POEPHILA) MODESTA
Cherry, or plum-headed, finch

Classification Order Passeriformes, Family Estrildidae.
Characteristics Length: 10 cm (4 in). Upperparts brown, with white spots on the wings. White face and neck. Purple-red crown; dark red chin. Brown uppertail coverts with white bars. Black tail with white spots on the outer feathers. Underparts white with small brown bars. Eyes dark brown, beak black, legs light brown. The female lacks the dark spot below the bill.
Habitat Gardens, shrubs, grassland, near water. Outside the breeding season in large groups, together with *P. bichenovii*.
Distribution Parts of Queensland and New South Wales; sometimes in Victoria (Australia).
Captivity Friendly and lively bird, suitable for a large, well-planted outdoor aviary. For some strange reason, these birds can suddenly drop dead, without a clear cause. They are sensitive to low temperatures. The female lays 4-6 eggs in a small, 15 cm long nest constructed from long grass, coconut fibers, and feathers; it is situated near the ground. Male and female remain very nervous. Avoid disturbances. In order to obtain good breeding pairs, give the birds the opportunity to choose their own partners. As soon as the nest is completed, remove all building materials (the same applies when they use a nest box). The incubation time lasts 12 days. The young leave the nest when they are 20-22 days old. Ripe and half-ripe seeds, berries, greens, and a variety of live food are necessary.

66 STIZOPTERA (POEPHILA) BICHENOVII
Bicheno's, or double-barred, finch

Classification Order Passeriformes, Family Estrildidae.
Characteristics Length: 8 cm (3 in); the smallest of all Australian grassfinches. Light brown, with fine bars. Black wings with white dots. Tail black; rump white. Forehead dark brown; two black bands across breast and neck. Throat, face, and underparts white, with a buff sheen. Eyes dark brown, beak gray, legs dark gray-brown. The female is duller.
Habitat Long grass and scrub (pandanus), near water; also in cane fields, parks, and gardens; in 2 subspecies.
Distribution Eastern New South Wales, Queensland (except the southwestern parts), northern areas of Northern Territory, and northwestern Western Australia.
Captivity An extremely friendly and peaceful aviary bird that must be housed indoors during fall and winter. They are often found on the ground, and it is advisable to have a leaf-mold compost heap in one of the corners. This heap should give the birds the opportunity to look for insects, satisfying their urge for scratching. This species builds its own little nests from grass and feathers, in thick shrubbery, or uses a nest box. The female lays 4-5 eggs, which are incubated for 14 days by both sexes. During the night, both partners sit on the nest. In addition to insects, standard seed mixture is needed. They drink by sucking, as do zebra finches.

---

67 TAENIOPYGIA (POEPHILA) GUTTATA
Zebra finch

Classification Order Passeriformes, Family Estrildidae.
Characteristics Length: 10 cm (4 in). Gray-blue head and neck; drab gray-brown back; dark gray-brown wings; blue-gray chest with black wavy markings; the lower parts of the chest are black; sides orange-red with round white spots; belly beige-white; tail black with white diagonal bands; white "moustache"; orange-red ear spots; under the eye a black band marking the front edge of the ear spot. Eyes red, beak deep red, legs yellow-brown. The female is gray above with a gray, sometimes almost white, ear spot. Throat, neck, chest, and sides gray.
Habitat Open woodland and grassland; arid interior in spinifex and mulga; near water; in big flocks all year.
Distribution Australia, except coastal areas of New South Wales and Victoria. A subspecies is found in Timor.
Captivity Social, lively, hardy and easily tamed (as are practically all *Poephila* species) are the qualities of the zebra finch. Excellent for all types of aviaries and large cages. Prolific breeders in outdoor aviaries, but only 3-4 broods per season are recommended. Remove all nesting materials (grass, plant fibers, feathers, wool), as soon as the nest is completed, to prevent further construction. The free nest is bottle-shaped, with an entrance tunnel. They like to use all types of nest boxes and such. The hen lays 4-5 eggs, which are incubated by both sexes for about 13-16 days. The young leave the nest after 20-22 days.

68 POEPHILA ACUTICAUDA
Long-tailed finch

Classification Order Passeriformes, Family Estrildidae.
Characteristics Length: 15-18 cm (6-7 in). Like *P. cincta*.
The black tail has two long central feathers like fine
needles. Eyes dark brown, beak yellow, legs red. The
female has slightly smaller markings; her call is lower in
pitch and softer.

Habitat High in eucalyptus trees and open forests; rarely
in open grassland and scrub country. Always near
watercourses.
Distribution Northern and northwestern Australia; in 2
subspecies.

Captivity Extremely sociable in the wild, but sometimes
troublesome in an aviary. Can best be kept with larger
birds in a well-planted aviary. They must be housed indoors
during fall and winter. The female lays 5-6 eggs; the sexes
alternate the incubating for 13 days. Give the birds as
many different nest boxes as possible; they must be
positioned high behind natural cover and far apart. They
will construct roosting nests as well, so be sure to provide
enough building materials. Sometimes different pairs will
sleep together in those nests. For more details see *P.
cincta*.

---

69 POEPHILA CINCTA
Black-throated, or parson, finch

Classification Order Passeriformes, Family Estrildidae.
Characteristics Length: 10 cm (4 in). Silverish-gray head.
Black throat and lores. Fawn back, brownish on the wings.
Black tail and bar over the rump. White uppertail coverts.
Breast and underparts cinnamon; white under the tail.
Black patch on the sides. Eyes dark brown, beak dark gray,
legs flesh-colored.

Habitat Forest, woodland, and scrubby country; near
watercourses; and open plains. Near the coast in small
flocks.
Distribution Cape York to South Queensland and the
New South Wales border (Australia); 3 subspecies.

Captivity Sociable, but sometimes aggressive in
captivity. They need space; hence a large, well-planted
aviary is necessary. More pairs together (that means at
least 3, never 2) stimulate social behavior and nest
building. They build a bottlelike nest of grass, feathers,

and plant fibers, with an entrance tunnel, but prefer using a
nest box or the old nests of other birds. They like to have a
choice, so supply plenty of housing facilities. The female
lays 5-9 eggs; both sexes incubate for approximately 13
days. The young leave the nest after 3 weeks and are fed by
both parents. In addition to small ripe and half-ripe seeds,
insects, greens, soaked white bread, soaked and
germinated seeds and cuttlefish bone are essential.

70 POEPHILA PERSONATA
Masked finch

Classification Order Passeriformes, Family Estrildidae.
Characteristics Length: 12.5 cm (5 in). Chestnut, darker on the wings; rosy-brown cheeks, neck, and underside white upper and undertail coverts. Black band across the lower back to the sides. Eyes dark brown, beak pale yellow legs light brownish-pink. The black mask of the female is smaller.
Habitat Timbered scrubland and grassy plains, near watercourses. Due to its constant search for water, also in gardens and parks; in sometimes large groups, composed of pairs (their pair bond lasts throughout the breeding season).
Distribution Northern Australia. The subspecies *leucotis* with some white under the eye, is confined to the east coast of the Gulf on Cape York. Two subspecies.
Captivity Excellent, sociable, but noisy birds, which need a large, well-planted aviary. They live mainly on the ground in search for food, but spend their mating season high between the branches of dead scrub and trees. Their nest is bulky, close to the ground, and constructed from grass feathers, fibers and wool. In the nest-sides pieces of charcoal are incorporated (for hygroscopic reasons). The female lays 4-6 eggs; both sexes incubate for 13 days. For more details see other *Poephila* species.

71 CHLOEBIA GOULDIAE
Gouldian finch

Classification Order Passeriformes, Family Estrildidae.
Characteristics Length: 14 cm (5½ in). Scarlet head, bordered with a narrow black band, followed by a broad turquoise-blue band. Throat and chin black. Breast deep purple, followed by golden-yellow. Neck, wings, and tail green. Undertail coverts white. Black tail. Middle tail feathers like needle points. Eyes brown, beak white with a red tip, legs pinkish. The female is duller and her bill becomes dark gray during the breeding season. In addition to the red-headed form, there is a black-headed form (most common in the wild) and a yellow-headed form (quite rare)
Habitat Grassy plains with trees, near watercourses; also in mangrove swamps and thickets.
Distribution Northern Australia.
Captivity These social birds, of which there are several mutations (e.g. blue, lilac, and white-breasted), must be housed in a dry and warm (30°C) aviary, at a humidity of approximately 70 percent. They use a hollow log or half-open nest box which they line with grass or coconut fiber Some pairs are prolific breeders, but for others Bengalese must be used as foster parents. During the molt, the birds must have protein rich foods, vitamins, minerals, soaked and just-sprouted small seeds, etc. Avoid white millet, as it causes illness and even death among the Goulds. The female lays 3-8 (5-6) eggs, which are incubated by both partners for about 14 days. The young leave the nest after about 21 days.

72 ERYTHRURA PSITTACEA
Red-throated, or red-faced, parrot finch

Classification Order Passeriformes, Family Estrildidae.
Characteristics Length: 12.5 cm (5 in). Red face, upper parts of breast, rump, and tail; rest parrot-green. Eyes dark brown, beak black, legs light gray-brown. The female is duller with less red on the face.
Habitat Grassland and scrubbery.
Distribution New Caledonia.
Captivity Friendly but nosy aviary birds, which become tame in a short while, as long as they are housed in a large, well-planted aviary. A rich variety of insects is essential all year, in addition to greens, ripe and half-ripe grass and other small seeds, and commercial egg and rearing foods. The birds like to use half-open nest boxes or old nests of other birds. The female lays 4-5 eggs, which are incubated by both partners during the day; at night only the hen incubates, while the male sleeps on a branch near the nest. Incubation time 13 days. They don't take nest inspections very well. The young leave the nest after about 3 weeks. When bred in small cages, it is of the utmost importance to take the young away from the father 2 weeks after they have left the nest; he can become hostile towards them.

73 ERYTHRURA TRICHORA
Blue-faced parrot finch

Classification Order Passeriformes, Family Estrildidae.
Characteristics Length: 13 cm (5¼ in). As *E. psittacea*, but with a cobalt-blue face. The female is duller in coloration.
Habitat Coastal plains, high mountain ranges, rain forests, and mangroves.
Distribution Sulawesi (formerly Celebes), Moluccas, Palau and Caroline Islands, Papua New Guinea and many neighboring islands, and the northern coastal areas of Australia. Also on Guadalcanal, Baules Island, New Hebrides, and Loyalty Islands.
Captivity Suitable only for a warm and well-planted aviary. They can become quite temperamental and aggressive, especially the males, when kept together with several pairs. Their pear-shaped nest has a side entrance. They like to use all kinds of half-open boxes; they are known to breed continuously if not stopped by taking the nest facilities away. Only three broods per season should be allowed. The female lays 3-6 eggs. For more details see *E. psittacea*.

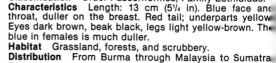

74 ERYTHRURA PRASINA
Pintailed parrot finch or nonpareil

Classification Order Passeriformes, Family Estrildidae.
Characteristics Length: 13 cm (5¼ in). Blue face and throat, duller on the breast. Red tail; underparts yellow. Eyes dark brown, beak black, legs light yellow-brown. The blue in females is much duller.

Habitat Grassland, forests, and scrubbery.
Distribution From Burma through Malaysia to Sumatra, Borneo, and Java (Indonesia).

Captivity Imported birds must have a rich variety of insects, greens, soaked ripe and half-ripe grass and other small seeds, etc. For more details see other *Erythrura* species. The nonpareil is an extremely delicate bird when first imported and needs careful management until established. Also, unlike other common parrot finches, it is not easy to breed.

---

75 NEOCHMIA (BATHILDA) RUFICAUDA
Star finch

Classification Order Passeriformes, Family Estrildidae.
Characteristics Length: 10-11 cm (4-4½ in). Vermilion face with small white spots. Light olive back and wings. Uppertail coverts red, again with white spots. Tail rufous. Olive-green breast and sides, heavily spotted; underparts pale lemon yellow. There is less red in the female; the underparts are grayish. Eyes dark brown, beak reddish, legs light brown.

Habitat Near water in tall grass, rice and sugar-cane fields, bushes and trees; often together with crimson finches.
Distribution Northern Australia; in 2 subspecies.

Captivity Peaceful, somewhat shy and quiet bird, but excellent in an aviary with other small finches. They spend a lot of time on the ground. During fall and winter, they must be housed indoors at room temperature. During the breeding season, a rich variety of insects, seeds, greens, and commercial egg and rearing foods must be available; they tend to throw their young from the nest when the food is not to their liking. The male becomes somewhat aggressive during the breeding season and will defend his nest with zest. Pairs like to build their own round grass nests rather than use a box. The female lays 3-4 eggs. Both parents incubate them for approximately 14 days. For more details see other Australian grassfinches.

76 STAGONOPLURA GUTTATA
Diamond sparrow

Classification Order Passeriformes, Family Estrildidae.
Characteristics Length: 12 cm (5 in). Grayish face; gray-brown upperparts and wings. Black lores and a broad black band crossing the chest; flanks black with white round spots. Uppertail coverts red; tail black. Underparts and undertail coverts white. Eyes dark brown, beak red, legs dark gray-brown.
Habitat Woodland, grassland, mallee, parks, and gardens; always near watercourses, in small groups. During the breeding season in pairs. They often nest in the lower part of nests of birds of prey. They also build bullet-shaped free nests.
Distribution Southern Queensland, eastern New South Wales to Victoria and eastern South Australia, and Kangaroo Island.
Captivity These hardy birds are not very active in captivity, so when they are placed in a roomy aviary, care should be taken that they do not become fat and pugnacious, and thus not come into breeding condition. Therefore, keep only one pair per well-planted aviary or large cage. They often bully smaller birds or interfere with their nests, breaking their eggs or killing their youngsters. The hen lays 5-6 eggs that are incubated by both sexes for 12-14 days. As the birds are quite sensitive, they won't always accept their partner; it is therefore advisable to let the birds do the "choosing."

---

77 PLOCEUS CUCULLATUS
Rufous-necked, black-headed, or village weaver

Classification Order Passeriformes, Family Ploceidae.
Characteristics Length: 18 cm (7 in). Head and shoulders black; nape and collar chestnut. Wings brown with yellow feather-edges; tail olive-brown. Other body parts orange-yellow. Eyes reddish-brown, beak brown-horn-colored, legs light brownish-pink. The female lacks the black head and is generally yellowish-brown with light grayish shoulders and brownish wings. Tail and wings have yellow edges. Outside the breeding season, both sexes are duller; the beak of male becomes pale horn-colored.
Habitat Bush, swamps, and around native settlements.
Distribution Senegal to central Africa. Other subspecies occur south of the Sahara, except the extreme south. The species has been introduced into Haiti and São Thomé.
Captivity Must be housed in a large, well-planted aviary. They are quite active, noisy, and aggressive and are best kept from small finches and such. One male with 6-10 females presents no problems, even when kept with budgerigars, small parrakeets, doves, starlings, etc. As they use plant materials to construct their nest, the majority of the plants in the aviary will be ruined very quickly. Therefore present a variety of building materials (raffia, fibers, grasses). For food see *P. vitellinus*.

78 PLOCEUS VITELLINUS (or velatus)
Half-masked weaver

Classification Order Passeriformes, Family Ploceidae.
Characteristics Length: 12-12.5 cm (5 in). Yellow; black face. Back olive with dark streaks. Wing and tail brownish-olive with yellow edges. Outside the breeding season the bird is brown above with dark streaks; the rump is olive-yellow, the head is olive. The female is olivaeceous-yellow above with dark streaks on the mantle. Chin and throat yellow. Underparts yellowish-buff, whitish on the belly. Outside the breeding season she is less green above and duller below. Eyes yellow, beak blackish, legs light brown.
Habitat Bush, scrubbery, and grassland. Nests in colonies in acacia groves.
Distribution Africa, south of the Sahara.
Captivity Hardy birds; more peaceful than village weaver species. Must be housed in a roomy, well-planted aviary, where they will weave their kidney-shaped nests with an extremely short, hardly noticeable tunnel. Live food is essential, in addition to millets; white grass, weed seeds; grains (oats and wheat), etc. During the breeding season, soaked and sprouted seeds are absolutely necessary, as well as small mealworms, maggots, and such.

---

79 PLOCEUS INTERMEDIUS
Masked weaver

Classification Order Passeriformes, Family Ploceidae.
Characteristics Length: 12.5 cm (5 in). Like *vitellinus*, but with a black forehead and forecrown. Outside the breeding season like *vitellinus* again, but with more yellow on the face. The females are like the eclipsed males, but with a more olivaceous-green tinge; outside the season duller with streaks on the upperparts. Eyes yellow, beak blackish, legs pinkish-brown.
Habitat Savannahs, often near watercourses; in small colonies (up to 10-12 pairs).
Distribution East and southern Africa.
Captivity Like the previous species, this bird is an excellent choice for the beginner. Repeatedly, you will be fascinated by the change in the cock's plumage after the breeding season; he will assume the plumage of his spouse, so that you will not be able to tell them apart. This is quite a change from the "wedding outfit" he wears during the breeding period. All these birds are only very moderate breeders in an aviary; in spite of their many woven, round nests with small tubular entrances (in the wild they often build low over water), which will continue to intrigue us, they rarely rear a good clutch.

80 PLOCEUS PHILIPPINUS
Baya weaver

Classification Order Passeriformes, Family Ploceidae.
Characteristics Length: 15 cm (6 in). Yellow forehead, crown, and nape. Black face and throat. Yellow breast. Upperparts gray-brown with dark streaks. Underparts soft gray. Eyes dark brown, beak blackish, legs light brown. The female is gray-brown with black-brown streaks; the rump is unstreaked. Outside the breeding season the male resembles the female.
Habitat Grassland; light forests; orchards; and other cultivated, arable land; in the last it can do considerable damage to seed crops.
Distribution India subcontinent; southeast Asia; Java, Nias (a small island west of Sumatra), and Sumatra (Indonesia); and Sri Lanka.
Captivity Aggressive bird that builds nest after nest in a large, well-planted aviary. The male constructs the long pendant entrance tunnel. For more details see the other *Ploceus* species.

---

81 EUPLECTES AFRA (or afer)
Napoleon weaver; yellow-crowned, or golden, bishop

Classification Order Passeriformes, Family Ploceidae.
Characteristics Length: 11.5-14 cm (4½-5½ in). Yellow; chin, cheeks, and breast black, the last with a yellow cross-band. Tail and wings brown. Eyes brown, beak blackish, legs pink-brown. The female is brownish, like a house-sparrow, with a buff eye streak. Outside the breeding season the male resembles the hen.
Habitat Swamps and grassland, near watercourses. They often build their oval nests, with a porchlike entrance, over water.
Distribution Africa, south of the Sahara; not in the extreme south.
Captivity If we keep more than one hen in a large, well-planted aviary together with one male, breeding results will certainly not be out of the question. These birds are fairly sensitive to drastic temperature changes. Plant corn, reeds, young acacias, and the like in their aviary. Insects are essential, as are small seeds (see *Ploceus* species), fruits, and greens. This hardy, amiable species is quite willing to come to brood. The female lays 2-4 green-bluish eggs. Incubation time 14 days. Only the female incubates and feeds the young, which leave the nest after approximately 3 weeks.

82 EUPLECTES HORDEACEA
Crimson-crowned bishop

Classification Order Passeriformes, Family Ploceidae.
Characteristics Length: 15-16.5 cm (6-6½ in). Like *E. orix*, but with an orange forecrown. Forehead, lores, cheeks, and chin black. Female almost identical to the female of the *E. ardens*.
Habitat Grassland, usually near watercourses.
Distribution Africa, from Senegal to Sudan, Angola and Zimbabwe; also in São Thomé, Zanzibar, and Pemba.
Captivity Likes to construct its nests against the mesh of the aviary (like many other weavers). Often aggressive towards other birds. For more details see other weaver species.

---

83 EUPLECTES ORIX
Grenadier weaver or red bishop

Classification Order Passeriformes, Family Ploceidae.
Characteristics Length: 12-15 cm (5-6 in). Forehead, crown, cheeks and chin, lower breast, and underparts black. Rest scarlet to red. Dark brown-grayish wings and tail with buff feather edges. Outside the breeding season, buff, dusky-streaked on breast and sides; a horn-colored bill. Eyes dark brown, beak blackish, legs light brown. Females resembles the eclipsed male, but the streaks are more pronounced.
Habitat Grassland, usually near watercourses.
Distribution Africa, south of the Sahara; in 4 subspecies.
Captivity A gregarious bird, which must be housed in a well-planted, large aviary. They build an oval nest, preferably between reeds or corn. The female lays 2-4 greenish-blue eggs. Incubation time 12 days; sometimes 14-15 days. The young leave the nest after 2 weeks. The female incubates, the male guards the nest. Insects are essential. For more details see other weaver species.

84 EUPLECTES PROGNE
Giant whydah

Classification Order Passeriformes, Family Ploceidae.
Characteristics Length: 60 cm (24 in) in the breeding season. Black with vermilion shoulders; buff-white wing bar. Wing feathers with buff edges. Out of season, at which time they lose their brooding feathers, 20 cm (8 in) in length; brown with streaked back; a white eyebrow, lores, and area around the eyes. Eyes dark brown, beak (out of season, horn-colored) and feet grayish. The female is similar to the male in winter plumage; she is smaller, however, and less streaked.
Habitat Swamps and grassy plains, near water.
Distribution South and eastern Africa.
Captivity Needs to be housed in a large aviary, so one can see the butterflylike flappings of the male before his mate during mating time. Although breeding successes are known, it remains difficult to raise young in captivity. Insects are a necessity. The female lays and incubates 3-4 eggs. Incubation time 14 days.

85 EUPLECTES ARDENS
Red-collared whydah

Classification Order Passeriformes, Family Ploceidae.
Characteristics Length: 39 cm (15 in) in the breeding season. Black with a red collar. The wing feathers have small light edges. Eyes dark brown, beak and feet black. The female is tawny on top with brownish-black streaks. Wings black with light feather edges. Yellowish head; whitish underparts. Bill horn-colored. The male outside the breeding season loses his long tail feathers and resembles the female, but he is more heavily streaked.
Habitat Grassland.
Distribution Africa, south of the Sahara.
Captivity Breeding in captivity is possible if kept in a large aviary without other birds. For details see giant whydah.

86 QUELEA QUELEA
Common quelea or red-billed weaver

Classification Order Passeriformes, Family Ploceidae.
Characteristics Length: 12 cm (5 in). Black forehead, cheeks, chin, and throat. Upperparts light gray with light streaks. Wings dark gray with light edges. Eyes brown, red periophthalmic ring, beak red, legs light brown-red. Out of the breeding season the male resembles the female, but he retains the red bill. The female is buff with a yellow beak, red outside the breeding period.
Habitat Savannah and cultivations; in usually large colonies.
Distribution Africa, south of the Sahara.
Captivity As *Euplectes ardens* and *Q. erythrops*.

87 QUELEA ERYTHROPS
Red-headed quelea

Classification Order Passeriformes, Family Ploceidae.
Characteristics Length: 11.5-12.5 cm (4½-5 in). Like *Q. quelea*, only with an entire crimson head. Chin black. The birds are darker outside the breeding season. Eyes dark brown, beak black, legs reddish-brown. The hen resembles the female common quelea.
Habitat Savannahs and open woodlands.
Distribution Senegal to Ethiopia, south to Angola, Natal, and Cape Province (South Africa); in sometimes large flocks, but not as common as *Q. quelea*.
Captivity Industrious builder, day after day. However, they seldom come to breed, although they have raised young in captivity on several occasions. They are best kept in a large aviary with open areas; in the corners plant reeds or corn. Insects are necessary all year, in addition to a tropical-seed mixture, greens, minerals, and vitamins.

88 STEGANURA (VIDUA) PARADISEA
Paradise whydah

Classification Order Passeriformes, Family Ploceidae.
Characteristics Length: 31-51 cm (12-20 in). Black with two long black central tail feathers. Chestnut band on the nape, extending across the chest. Underside white. Eyes brown, beak black, feet brown. Outside the breeding season the male almost resembles his hen, is 14 cm (5½ in) in length, somewhat brighter in coloration, and with brown streaks on the upperparts. The hen has shades of buff and dark brown, with some dark streaks.
Habitat Open grass country and scrubs.
Distribution Eastern and southern Africa.
Captivity The species, being parasitic, lays its eggs in the nest of the melba finch (*Pytilia melba citerior*). A pair of melba finches should be housed in a large aviary to improve the chances of achieving breeding results. Varieties of the paradise whydah are found in the eastern parts of Africa (see next species).

Top: female
Bottom: male

---

89 STEGANURA (VIDUA) ORIENTALIS
Broad-tailed paradise whydah

Classification Order Passeriformes, Family Ploceidae.
Characteristics There are different subspecies; they all differ from *S. paradisea* in neck and breast colors and in the shape of the tail. Restall (see bibliography) lists:
1. Broad-tailed paradise whydah (*S. o. orientalis*). Hind and sides of neck golden-buff, upper breast chestnut; tail, two central feathers short and oval; long pair only 13-15 cm (5-6 in). Host melba finch (*Pytilia melba citerior*).
2. Golden-naped paradise whydah (*S. o. kadugliensis*). Hind and sides of neck yellow, breast chestnut; tail fairly long and recurved. Host *P. m. citerior*.
3. West African paradise whydah (*S. o. aucupum*). Entire neck including upper breast tawny; tail similar to *S. paradisea* but not so long and not tapered. Host *P. m. citerior*.
4. Broad-tailed whydah (*S. o. obtusa*). Hind and sides of neck tawny, upper breast pale chestnut; four central tail feathers very broad and sail-like. Host *P. afra*.
5. Cameroons, or Uelle, paradise whydah (*S. o. interjecta*). Upper mantle, neck, and breast tawny; tail long and straight, broadening towards the last part. Host *P. phoenicoptera*.
6. Togo paradise whydah (*S. o. togoensis*). Neck and breast tawny; tail as long as *paradisea* but not graduated; it is no broader than that of the paradise whydah. Host *P. hypogrammica*.

90 VIDUA MACROURA
Pin-tailed whydah

Classification Order Passeriformes, Family Ploceidae.
Characteristics Length: 13 cm (5 in). Black face, upperparts, wings, and tail. Rest of body white. White band on the wing coverts. The female is black and brownish with six dark stripes on the head. The male resembles his hen outside the breeding season, although he is somewhat darker. Eyes dark brown, beak red, legs light brown.
Habitat Grassland and savannahs.
Distribution Africa, south of the Sahara.
Captivity Males can sometimes be quite aggressive. The species is parasitic; its hosts are *Estrilda astrild*, *Estrilda troglodytes*, and probably, *Estrilda rhodopyga* and *Estrilda melpoda*. It may be of interest to note that in the wild this male whydah has some 10-50 hens. All *Vidua* species require a good brand of tropical seed, many insects and insect substitutes, and fresh bathing water daily.

91 VIDUA REGIA
Queen whydah

Classification Order Passeriformes, Family Ploceidae.
Characteristics Length: 28-33 cm (11-13 in). Black forehead, crown, nape, and upperparts; neck and sides of head and underparts tawny. Eyes brown, beak and legs red. Outside the breeding season the males resemble their females, although some of them are darker. The female is brown with dark streaks on the upperparts; neck and head buff with a brownish streak on each side of the crown. Underparts grayish-white.
Habitat Dry thorny scrub or open grassy areas. They are often on the ground in search of insects and small seeds.
Distribution Southern Africa.
Captivity The host of this species, is the violet-eared waxbill (*Uraeginthus granatina*). For more details see *V. macroura*.

92 HYPOCHERA (VIDUA) CHALYBEATA
Senegal combassou

Classification Order Passeriformes, Family Ploceidae.
Characteristics Length: 10 cm (4 in). Black with a greenish glow. Brown sheen on wings and tail. Eyes dark brown, beak yellowish-white, legs reddish-brown. Black crown with buff streak, sides of head, and stripe over eyes. Blackish stripe near outersides of the eyes. The female has brownish upperparts with dark feather centers. Outside the breeding season the male resembles the female, although he is darker with more pronounced stripes.
Habitat Open country and grassland.
Distribution Africa.
Captivity Lively, friendly birds which must be kept together with *Lagonosticta senegala* (firefinch) if we want breeding possibilities, the combassou being parasitic. They sometimes make their own, usually poorly constructed, nests. For more details see firefinch.

93 PASSER LUTEUS
Golden sparrow

Classification Order Passeriformes, Family Ploceidae.
Characteristics Length: 14 cm (5½ in). Chestnut upperparts; yellow on the rump; underparts, head, and neck light yellow. Brownish-black wings; tail brown. Eyes dark brown, beak horn-colored, feet light brown. The female is pale brown with buff underparts.
Habitat Open country, in sometimes large flocks (up to 50 birds).
Distribution Northeastern Africa.
Captivity The hen lays 3-4 green-white eggs with gray and brown markings, which she deposits into a cup-shaped nest. The nest itself is made of grass and little twigs. These charming and lovely birds like cozy, community-style living, also evidenced by their community breeding in colonies. I have seen groups of 50 and more nests close together in just a few trees. In the aviary they prefer to build their nests in thick bushes, although they will also use nest boxes. The nesting boxes should not be hung higher than 2 meters. The breeding period takes place between May and November. The birds usually have 2 or 3 broods per season. The hen incubates the eggs for 10-13 days. After 2 weeks, sometimes sooner, the young leave the nest. Crossbreedings with the house sparrow (*Passer domesticus*) are known. Due to their pleasant song, their lively nature, and their tolerance even during the breeding season, these birds are very popular.

94 SPOROPIPES FRONTALIS
Speckle-fronted weaver

Classification Order Passeriformes, Family Ploceidae.
Characteristics Length: 11-12.5 cm (4½-5 in). Forehead and crown black with many little white spots. Nape, neck, back, and rump ashy-brown. The black wing and tail feathers have light ashy-brown to whitish edges. Lores, supercilium, ear covers, and sides of head light gray. Chin and breast grayish-white. Malar region (line bordering the ear coverts from beak to side neck) black with white spots. Underparts white. Eyes dark brown, beak yellowish-white, legs light brown. The sexes are alike.
Habitat Thorn scrub, but even in towns and villages. Very sociable. Usually in small flocks. Breeds in colonies.
Distribution Senegal to Sudan and south to Tanzania (Africa).
Captivity Although very sociable by nature, the species is rather quiet and timid in an aviary; extremely peaceful towards other birds. It is advisable to house a pair in a large, well-planted aviary and not in a cage (of any kind), as they will become inactive and sick. They need space. In the breeding season they may become somewhat aggressive towards birds that come too close to their nest. They use half-open nest boxes or old weaver nests; they also like to sleep in them during the night. The female lays 4-5 grayish-green or brownish-green eggs with dark brown markings. For more information see *S. squamifrons*. Insects are essential, especially in the breeding season.

---

95 SPOROPIPES SQUAMIFRONS
Scaly-crowned weaver

Classification Order Passeriformes, Family Ploceidae.
Characteristics Length: 10 cm (4 in). Black forehead and crown with numerous white little spots, especially on the forehead. Lores black. Around the eye a thin white ring. On either side of the chin a black stripe running towards the breast in a soft curve ("mustache"). Upperparts dove-gray, like *S. frontalis*. Wings and tail blackish-gray with white edges. Underparts whitish. Eyes dark brown, beak yellowish-pink, legs light brown. The sexes are alike, although the mustachial streak is sometimes larger in the males.
Habitat Thorn scrub, villages, and towns. See *S. frontalis*. These birds can survive for quite some time without any water intake.
Distribution Southern Africa.
Captivity Very attractive, noisy but peaceful, although they can become somewhat quarrelsome during the breeding season. In their behavior they remind one of sparrows. Their twittering song is nice to listen to. Although they are free breeders and build dome-shaped nests in thick bushes, they like to occupy half-open boxes, budgerigar logs, and old weaver nests. The female lays 5-6 olive-gray eggs with dark brown markings. Incubation time 12 days. After about 3 weeks, the young leave the nest, but will still be fed by both parents; they have a brown patch instead of a scaly crown, and the black lores are missing.

96 STREPTOPELIA RISORIA
Barbary dove, blond ringdove, ringdove, domestic ringdove, domestic collared dove, and fawn dove

Classification Order Columbiformes, Family Columbidae.
Characteristics Length: 23 cm (9 in). Light fawn with a pinkish suffusion on the breast. A typical black ring around the back of the neck. Eyes yellow, beak orange, legs pink. This bird is the domesticated form of the African collared dove (*S. roseogrisa*). There is a white variety called the "Java dove"; as the majority of the Barbary doves carry the white character in their genetic make-up, chances are that normal colored birds produce white offspring. There are also apricot-colored varieties and frilled forms, both recessive.
Distribution Domesticated; a "wild" colony can be found in the center of Los Angeles, California.
Captivity Friendly birds, even towards small finches and such. They present no problems as far as breeding is concerned; the hen may lay her 2 white eggs anywhere in the aviary if no breeding places are provided, such as flat baskets, cigar boxes, wire-mesh platforms, and similar nest pans. They use some small twigs and straw as building materials. Incubation time about 14 days. During the winter, these doves must be housed indoors at a temperature of about 10°C.

---

97 GEOPELIA STRIATA
Zebra dove

Classification Order Columbiformes, Family Columbidae.
Characteristics Length: 23 cm (9 in). Gray with a red shadow on the neck; upperside brown; sides with black and white stripes; a wine red spot on the chest. Eyes light gray or blue, beak gray, legs red-brown. The hen is similar, but smaller.
Habitat Open country with bushes and trees, near creeks and shrubland, in parks, gardens, and agricultural land.
Distribution From Malaya through Indonesia to Australia; introduced to Madagascar, St. Helena, the Hawaiian Islands, and many other places.
Captivity Friendly doves, which do not pose any danger for small birds. If we do not plant too many bushes in the aviary, we will see that these quick little birds spend a lot of time on the ground searching for seeds (grass and weed seeds), millet, and the like. They are not as likely to breed as the diamond dove, although we may well find their 2 little eggs placed in their flat nest creation in open nesting boxes and cigar boxes; if the aviary is located in very peaceful surroundings, there is a chance that a clutch will be successfully reared. Peace and quiet are absolute necessities. During the winter months, these birds should be housed indoors in a lightly heated location.

98 GEOPELIA CUNEATA
Diamond dove

Classification Order Columbiformes, Family Columbidae.
Characteristics Length: 19 cm (7½ in). Gray with tiny white dots on the wings. The female is slightly smaller than the cock, with a browner plumage, and more and larger white wing spots. The red-colored eyes are surrounded by a red periophthalmic ring. Beak horn-colored, legs red.
Habitat Mulga and woodland.
Distribution Australia.
Captivity This species requires a sunny cage or aviary, as they really enjoy sunbathing. They are lively, yet peaceful and easy to care for. However, when either a hen or cock is kept individually, they can be a nuisance, so it is important to keep them in pairs. The male can be distinguished from the hen as he spreads his tail during the courtship display. Limit the number of clutches to 4-5 per season. These doves prefer to use open nest boxes, since their own little creations are hardly safe—flat little nothings with many openings that can be peeked through. Their clutch consists of 2 eggs; usually producing a fledgling of each sex. The hen sits on the eggs before noon, while the cock has incubation duty after noon. Incubation time about 13 days. The young leave the nest after 10 days. After one month they have already achieved adult coloring, and at 2 months they possess their fully colored eye ring.

99 EXCALFACTORIA CHINENSIS
Painted, Chinese painted, or blue-breasted, quail

Classification Order Galliformes, Family Phasianidae.
Characteristics Length: 11.5 cm (4½ in). White cheeks with black border, throat black. White band across breast and sides of the neck. Chest and sides grayish-blue. Lower chest red-brown. The hen lacks all the white and black markings as well as the grayish-blue color on chest and flanks. Eyes hazel, beak black, legs yellow.
Habitat Swamps and grassland.
Distribution From India, Sri Lanka, China, Sulawesi (formerly Celebes), and the Moluccas to Australia.
Captivity These birds require heavy rations of live insects, especially in the breeding season. They build their nest on the ground, and it is often constructed with a small wall or roof to protect the nest from wind, etc. The hen lays 4-6 gray-olive or olive-brown eggs with black stripes and spots. Incubation time 16 days. When the young hatch, they look like small, active little balls of down. Only the hen incubates the eggs. If the cock does not pursue the hen (if he does he should be removed from the aviary), he will guard the nest, perhaps sitting nearby in a rather hunched-up position. After some 2 months the young have become adults and can no longer be distinguished from their parents, and should be removed.

100 NEOPHEMA BOURKII
Bourke's parrakeet

Classification Order Psittaciformes, Family Psittacidae.
Characteristics Length: 21 cm (8½ in). Pink; black-brown scalloping. Crown, neck, back, wings, and tail are auburn. Edge of wing blue, as is the underside of the tail feathers. Blue-white eye marking. Wing feathers with white band; outermost tail feathers blue-white. The female has a rounder head and usually lacks most of the blue coloring above the beak. After about 9 months the young achieve adult coloring. Eyes brown, beak shiny black, legs brown.
Habitat These birds are crepuscular and nocturnal to some extent. They occur in small groups, up to 10 birds.
Distribution New South Wales, Central Australia and Western Australia. Their range is difficult to define as they are migratory.
Captivity Once accustomed to climate and aviary, the hen will start to breed quickly; nest box 45 × 15 × 15 cm. The hen lays 3-4, sometimes 5-7, eggs, and incubates alone for about 18 days. The male will feed her during this time, and later the young as well. Each season a couple can rear 2-3 clutches. Young birds that fly out of the nest (after 4 weeks) are quite wild; keep a close watch on them as they may injure themselves flying against the wire or walls. This problem can be alleviated by placing plants against the walls and sticking some green twigs through the wire roof, etc. This species makes excellent foster parents for fellow species and members of the genus *Psephotus*.

---

101 NEOPHEMA SPLENDIDA
Splendid grass parrakeet or scarlet-chested parrot

Classification Order Psittaciformes, Family Psittacidae.
Characteristics Length: 21 cm (8½ in). Head and neck are sea-blue; upperparts green; underside yellow with red crop and chest areas (lacking on the female). Wings blue-green with bright blue and black colors. Tail green with yellow and black. Eyes brown, beak black, legs brown-black. The underside of the female is yellow; the breast has an olive-green shine; darker on back than the male; sides of head considerably less blue.
Habitat Inhabits dry scrubland. They are rare in the wild, but can sometimes be seen in large groups, usually feeding on the ground.
Distribution Western portion of New South Wales, northern parts of South Australia to the coastal areas of the Great Australian Bight, and inward in various colonies in Western Australia.
Captivity The female will start breeding quite quickly if a roomy nest box (see turquoisine) is hung in the outside flight; the bottom should be covered with a layer of moist turf and mulch, leaves, and other soft materials; leaves are often carried under the rump feathers. The female lays 2 or at the most 3-5 eggs. This species is friendly towards other birds; crossings with turquoisines and elegants are possible. Their soft song is virtually identical to that of the turquoisine, except that it is weaker.

102 NEOPHEMA PULCHELLA
Turquoise parrot or turquoisine

Classification Order Psittaciformes, Family Psittacidae.
Characteristics Length: 21 cm (8½ in). Sky-blue head, underside yellow-green, becoming lighter towards the tail. Neck, throat, and back green. Some red on the wings (lacking on the female). Blue band on wings and flight feathers. Tail coverts green. Outermost tail feathers yellow; underside of tail also yellow. Eyes black-brown, beak black, legs black-brown. The female has less blue on the head. Breast green-yellow; underside a faded yellow. Young males quickly develop the red on the wings; after 8-10 months they have achieved adult coloring.
Habitat This species lives in pairs or small groups in grassland and open woods; typical "dusk" birds.
Distribution Central Queensland south through New South Wales to the border of Victoria.
Captivity In early spring the female starts to inspect nest boxes (20 × 20 × 40 cm; entrance diameter 6 cm). Place moist turf, woodchips, and such inside the box. She usually lays 4-7, sometimes 8, eggs. After about 20 days the chicks hatch, and the male will then become active in bringing food for his offspring. Only specimens that have been locally bred may be kept outdoors during the winter. It is wise to remove the nesting boxes after the young of the second clutch have flown out. This species is not tolerant towards fellow parrakeets during the breeding season.

---

103 NEOPHEMA ELEGANS
Elegant grass parrakeet

Classification Order Psittaciformes, Family Psittacidae.
Characteristics Length: 23 cm (9 in). Golden yellow, less vivid in the female, which lacks the orange feathers on the belly. Yellow triangle between beak and eyes; small blue eyebrow; blue edges on the wing feathers; olive-green back; black flight feathers (brown in the female). Young males are a brighter yellow than the hens at the time they leave the nest, but do not yet have the band on the forehead. After six months the juvenile molting is completed.
Habitat This species lives in pairs or small groups, often not too far away from human habitation. They live near woods, on open grassland, and new plantations; they can often be found along the coast. They live mainly on grass seeds, although seeds of other plants are taken as well. They are migratory birds.
Distribution Southern New South Wales, western Victoria, South Australia, and southwestern Australia; also on Kangaroo Island.
Captivity The female lays 4-5 eggs. The care require by these birds parallels that of the other *Neophema* species. Various crossbreedings have been achieved, mainly with the turquoise, scarlet-chested, and blue-winged parrakeets. To ensure good breeding results, it is wise to provide deep nesting boxes (30 × 30 × 45 cm; entrance diameter 9 cm); cover the bottom with moist turf.

104 NEOPHEMA CHRYSOSTOMA
Blue-winged parrakeet

Classification Order Psittaciformes, Family Psittacidae.
Characteristics Length: 22 cm (9 in). Green, darker on back and shoulders. Bright green-yellow towards belly. Lores orange-yellow. Blue wings. Innermost tail feathers vivid orange-yellow. Blue band across the forehead continues to the eye. Many males have an orange-pink marking on the belly. The female is generally less vivid in coloring; she has a yellow-green glow woven through the blue. Smaller band on forehead. Flight feathers brown (black in the male). Eyes brown, beak blue-gray, legs brown-gray. It will take a full year for the young birds to achieve adult coloring.

Habitat They live in fairly large groups, and even during the breeding season a certain amount of community lifestyle remains. I have observed them in groups of 10-15 pairs during this period. These birds live in coastal areas, forested valleys, in sand dunes, swamps, grassland, tidal flats, etc.
Distribution Southeastern Australia, Tasmania, and the islands of Bass Strait.

Captivity These gentle birds can be tamed quickly and are very suitable for a community aviary; a couple will readily breed. The female lays 5-7 eggs; don't give her small nest boxes; they should measure at least 20 × 20 × 40 cm; entrance diameter 5-7 cm. For more information see *N. splendida*, above.

---

105 PLATYCERCUS ELEGANS
Pennant, or crimson, rosella

Classification Order Psittaciformes, Family Psittacidae.
Characteristics Length: 32-36 cm (12½-14 in). Red; throat, cheeks, and collar dark sky-blue. Wing coverts and tail blue. Flight feathers have a purplish-blue glow. Cloak feathers black, edged in red. The male has a slightly larger head and beak; young birds also tend to have this trait. Once the young are out of the nest, they generally look identical to the parents; sometimes they are a little greener. Eyes dark brown, beak grayish-yellow, often ending in a black point; legs grayish-brown. Females have a smaller upper mandible than the male.

Habitat These birds live in pairs or in groups concentrated in woody areas interspersed with fields and cultivated land. They spend a lot of time on the ground searching for food; they consume fruit and many destructive insects. Their not-altogether-unpleasant song is imitated by the famous lyre bird.
Distribution East and southeast Australia; introduced in New Zealand and Norfolk Island.

Captivity These hardy birds are not known to be the best breeders. The hen lays 4-8 eggs that take 21 days to hatch. The young leave the nest after 5 weeks. Once they have become independent, they will form—in the wild—their own group; they will never join a group that includes their parents. During the breeding season the parents like to feed their youngsters with earthworms.

106 PLATYCERCUS EXIMIUS
Red, eastern, or golden-mantled, rosella

Classification Order Psittaciformes, Family Psittacidae.
Characteristics Length: 32 cm (12½ in). Breast, shoulders, neck, and head bright red; less pronounced in the female. White cheek markings. Belly yellow with a green glow. Back green with feathers edged in green-black. Rump green-yellow. Large flight feathers and tail blue; the latter with a white band; central tail feathers green; feathers under the tail red. Eyes brown, beak gray-white, legs black-brown. The female's beak is smaller, the chest markings grayish white. Around the eyes grayish-brown feathers, which are always lacking in the male. Females are, however, often as brightly colored as males.
Habitat In large groups or in pairs on open terrain spotted with some trees and bushes; often near rivers. They spend much time on the ground; in cornfields or orchards they sometimes do considerable damage.
Distribution Southeastern Australia and Tasmania; introduced in New Zealand.
Captivity Excellent breeders and foster parents. The hen lays 4-8 white eggs. The male does not incubate, but he will feed the young. Incubation time about 22 days. After about 35 days, the fledglings leave the nest, and 10-15 months later they have achieved adult coloring. Once independent, they should be separated from their parents. Breeding results can be obtained when a pair is at least one year old.

---

107 PLATYCERCUS ICTEROTIS
Stanley's, yellow-cheeked, or western, rosella

Classification Order Psittaciformes, Family Psittacidae.
Characteristics Length: 26-28 cm (10-11 in). Crown, throat, breast, and belly bright red; flanks with a sprinkling of yellow feathers. Yellow cheeks. Back and rump green with black-scalloped coloring. Flight feathers blue-black; tail green and blue towards the tip; underside sky-blue. The female is smaller, and her coloring is less vivid; many have some green feathers on the belly and head and smaller cheek markings. After 60-65 days the young will begin to molt. Eyes brown, beak gray-white, legs black-brown.
Habitat Live in pairs or in small groups on the grassy plains, but can do damage when they visit fruit orchards and farmland. Roam in gardens and parks.
Distribution Southwestern Australia.
Captivity Once the female has laid eggs, remove the other nest boxes. She lays 4-6 eggs. Incubation time about 19 days; after a month the young leave the nest. Couples prefer to have an aviary to themselves (like all rosellas). Place moist sawdust and mulched wood inside the box. Outside the breeding period they are very tolerant of fellow species and exotic birds. Their song is quite pleasant. It is preferable to take them indoors for the winter to avoid frozen toes.

108 PLATYCERCUS VENUSTUS
Brown's, or northern, rosella

Classification Order Psittaciformes, Family Psittacidae.
Characteristics Length: 38 cm (15¹/₅ in). Crown and back of head brownish to black. Cheeks white with broad sky-blue markings on throat. Vague red glow on forehead. Back and wings black with broad yellow bands. Yellow rump. Primary wing coverts light blue with black. Flight feathers darker with brownish-green points. Tail blue-brown with dark edges, rimmed in white. Lower parts of belly red; underside tail blue with black point. Eyes black, beak light gray with a blue point, legs black-brown. Some Brown's rosellas either do not have the red on the forehead or have some yellow there instead. Others may have red on the yellow or black-scalloped belly.
Habitat These birds live in pairs or in small groups (up to about 10 pairs). In the breeding period each pair goes off alone. They prefer open woods, sometimes the edge of a mangrove swamp, or creeks and rivers.
Distribution Northwestern Australia; also on the islands of Melville and Bathurst.
Captivity Breeding and molting times often coincide; the breeding season starts in the winter. Remove the other nest boxes once the hen has made her choice; otherwise it may happen that she deserts hers (often with eggs in it) to start anew in another box. She lays 2 eggs; incubation time 21 days. A rare aviary bird in Britain, but quite common on the Continent and in the United States.

---

109 BARNARDIUS BARNARDI
Barnard's parrakeet or mallee ringneck parrot

Classification Order Psittaciformes, Family Psittacidae.
Characteristics Length: 32-34 cm (12-14 in). Blue-green; green dominates. Darker on breast, more yellowish on division of breast and belly. Dark green on back, green on rump; uppertail coverts are edged in blue. Heavy brownish-green tint on the head. Clearly visible red band on forehead; yellow neck ring. Wing curve blue; underneath the tail green-blue. Bluish-green on throat. Eyes brown, beak light gray, legs gray. The female has a smaller head and bill, and her markings are not as sharp. After 12 months the young achieve adult coloring.
Habitat These birds live in pairs or together in small groups of about 8-10 pairs. They prefer open woodland, near large rivers. They consider eucalyptus buds a treat and will give voice to some rambunctious screeching while eating them.
Distribution Eastern Australia.
Captivity Birds that are just 1 year of age can make a name for themselves by their good breeding abilities. The female lays 4-6 eggs and incubates alone. Incubation time about 20 days. Breeding period from mid-February to May. The young leave the nest after 5 weeks. These birds are not common in captivity.

110 PSEPHOTUS HAEMATONOTUS
Red-rumped parrakeet

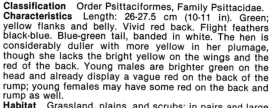

Classification Order Psittaciformes, Family Psittacidae.
Characteristics Length: 26-27.5 cm (10-11 in). Green; yellow flanks and belly. Vivid red back. Flight feathers black-blue. Blue-green tail, banded in white. The hen is considerably duller with more yellow in her plumage, though she lacks the bright yellow on the wings and the red of the back. Young males are brighter green on the head and already display a vague red on the back of the rump; young females may have some red on the back and rump as well.
Habitat Grassland, plains, and scrubs; in pairs and large flocks (up to about 150 birds). Sometimes they can be seen sitting in long rows on the barren rocks, singing to each other.
Distribution Southeastern Australia.
Captivity The female lays 4-7 eggs; incubation time 25 days. When the young are 1 month old they will leave the nest, but will still be fed for quite some time by both parents. Offer a roomy nest box: 25 × 15 × 35 cm; entrance diameter 6 cm. Once independent, young birds should be separated from the parents because the male will chase and possibly injure them. They will also not tolerate fellow species in the same aviary. This species makes excellent foster parents; also crossbreeding with other species of *Psephotus*, as well as with a few rosellas and possibly with the Barnard's parrakeet. The popular yellow-rumped mutation was first bred in 1935 (Britain).

111 PSEPHOTUS H. HAEMATOGASTER
Blue-bonnet parrakeet

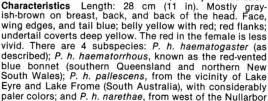

Classification Order Psittaciformes, Family Psittacidae.
Characteristics Length: 28 cm (11 in). Mostly grayish-brown on breast, back, and back of the head. Face, wing edges, and tail blue; belly yellow with red; red flanks; undertail coverts deep yellow. The red in the female is less vivid. There are 4 subspecies: *P. h. haematogaster* (as described); *P. h. haematorrhous*, known as the red-vented blue bonnet (southern Queensland and northern New South Wales); *P. h. pallescens*, from the vicinity of Lake Eyre and Lake Frome (South Australia), with considerably paler colors; and *P. h. narethae*, from west of the Nullarbor Desert, is smaller and colored deeper.
Habitat All subspecies are representatives of the dry savannahs. Research has shown that their numbers are slowly decreasing, as a lot of terrain is being converted to cultivated fields and grazing land. The birds live in pairs, though some live in small groups, except during the breeding season. They seek their food, which is mainly seeds and small insects, on the ground.
Distribution The dry interior of southeast Australia.
Captivity See previous species. The female lays 4-7 eggs. The species can only be housed and bred as a pair in a fairly roomy aviary by themselves; they are quite noisy, monkeylike, and active; will hybridize with red-rumped parrakeet, mulga parrot (*P. varius*), red rosella, and mealy rosella (*Platycercus palliceps*).

112 POLYTELIS SWAINSONII
Barraband's parrakeet or superb parrot

Classification Order Psittaciformes, Family Psittacidae.
Characteristics Length: 32-36 cm (12-14 in). Green, less bright in the female; bright yellow forehead, lacking in the hen; yellow throat and cheeks. Red blotch on throat. Flight feathers blue; tail green, margined in blue; underside black. Orange-yellow eyes, red bill, brown legs. The female's thighs show some red, and there is some pink underneath the tail; her eyes are brown. The young resemble the hen; the males have some red in the thighs, too, and may retain this, even after the first molt.
Habitat In open forest; they eat the blossoms and nectar of flowering eucalyptus, seeds, fruits, nuts, wheats, and berries; they are partly nomadic and occur in small flocks, even during the breeding season. They live mostly on the ground.
Distribution Mainly along the Murray and Murrumbidgee Rivers in New South Wales and bordering regions.
Captivity Peaceful; house them, however, in a roomy aviary by themselves. The female lays 4-6 eggs in a deeply hollowed tree trunk; cover the bottom of the hollow with mold, sawdust, and wood chips. Nest boxes of 2 m deep are also suitable. The male feeds the hen during the 20 day incubation time. After 33-35 days the young leave the nest and are independent after another 3 weeks. Crossbreedings with the king parrot, Princess of Wales, eastern rosella and red-winged parrot are possible.

113 POLYTELIS ALEXANDRAE
Princess of Wales parrakeet or princess parrot

Classification Order Psittaciformes, Family Psittacidae.
Characteristics Length: 35 cm (14 in). Crown and area around the eye a vague sea-blue. Yellow-gray-green on the back of the head and neck, shoulders, and back. Throat, breast, and part of the cheeks pinkish red. Bright sky-blue rump. Pinkish-red feathers around the legs. Underwing coverts green; wing coverts greenish-yellow. Yellow-green tail margined in blue-green; tips of tail feathers white. Eyes orange, encircled with red (not in the female); beak red, legs brown. The hen is grayish-blue; the entire tail is often shorter. Beak is not as red as in the male; there is less sky-blue on the rump. Not until they are 6 months old do the young start to show differences in color.
Habitat Arid scrub; nomadic. The species feeds on seeds of various grasses and breeds in hollow tree trunks, close to water.
Distribution Interior of western and central Australia.
Captivity The hen usually lays 4-6 eggs; incubation time about 3 weeks. Put mulched wood (from willow or poplar) in the nest box or hollow tree trunk, along with grass, wool, and hay. Place nest box or trunk at an angle of about 45°. Fasten some mesh on the inside so the bird can leave the nest without difficulties. After 35 days the young leave the nest, and after about 15 months they will be ready for breeding.

114 PSITTACULA KRAMERI MANILLENSIS
Ringneck parrakeet, Indian ringneck, or rose-ringed parrakeet

Classification Order Psittaciformes, Family Psittacidae.
Characteristics Length: 42 cm (16 in). Green with black collar and black band around the beak. Behind collar (lacking on the female) a red shine. Belly and undertail coverts yellowish-green. Uppermost tail feathers bluish-green with yellow tips. Eyes yellow-orange, beak red, legs black. After 2-3 years the young achieve adult coloring.
Habitat In gardens, parks, lightly timbered areas, farmland, etc.; also in the lowland arid zone of Sri Lanka. Sometimes in flocks of about 15,000 birds.
Distribution India, Pakistan, Nepal, and Sri Lanka; introduced to Singapore (1950/51).
Captivity The female lays 3-4 eggs; she starts nest inspection early in the year and will build the nest in about 3 days. She chews the wood shavings and wood chips, which have been placed in the nest box (25 × 25 × 40 cm; entrance diameter 8 cm), into the proper shape. The male feeds both female (who sits on the eggs) and offspring; after about a week the hen will help with the feeding of the young. Incubation time 22-24 days. Young independent birds should be placed in a roomy flight. Well-known mutations are lutino (sex-linked); blue (autosomaal recessive); albino; cinnamon (or isabelle); gray (dominant when paired to normal), among others.

---

115 PSITTACULA ALEXANDRI FASCIATA
Banded, pink-breasted, or mustache, parrakeet

Classification Order Psittaciformes, Family Psittacidae.
Characteristics Length: 37 cm (14⅘ in). Bright blue-gray head and black collar line. Cheeks outlined in black. Dark forehead, red collar, green back, green underside, and red breast. Tail blue with green seams; green wings. Bright yellow shoulder markings. Yellow iris; upper mandible blackish-red, lower mandible black. Grayish-yellow legs. The wine-red color on the female's breast continues higher towards the throat and neck, and the head is darker. The beak is black, but the upper mandible has an orange point. Young birds lack the red coloring and generally are grayer. Their beak is still black.
Habitat Sometimes in rice paddies and cornfields in large flocks (up to 10,000). Build their nest as high as possible in trees growing in the lowland plains and foothills.
Distribution From the northern parts of India and Nepal through Assam, Burma, the Andaman Islands, the southern portion of China and Indochina to Indonesia.
Captivity This noisy bird generally breeds from March to May or July, is very common, and inexpensive. Young birds are often kept in pairs in large cages, as they generally behave quietly. In the aviary, however, they sometimes can act quite wild and excited. Young birds can easily be taught to speak a few words. These birds are difficult to breed (see *P. krameri manillensis*).

116 PSITTACULA CYANOCEPHALA
Plum-headed parrakeet

Classification Order Psittaciformes, Family Psittacidae.
Characteristics Length: 35-37.5 cm (14-15 in). Pale green. Plum-colored head and wings; black seam around the head, followed by a bluish-green band. Dark green wings. Innermost tail feathers bluish-green; outer tail feathers green with pale yellow tips. Eyes brown, beak yellowish-white, legs grayish-brown. In the hen the red shoulder markings are missing; the neck band is lighter and grayish-purple. Young birds reach their adult colors after a full 2 years. Since young males resemble females before two years have elapsed, be very careful when purchasing these birds.
Habitat In jungles, but also cultivated areas.
Distribution India, West Pakistan, Nepal, Bhutan, West Bengal, and Sri Lanka; in 2 subspecies.
Captivity Before the birds commence breeding, cover the bottom of the nest box (20 × 20 × 30 cm; entrance diameter 8 cm) with wood chips and sawdust. The female lays 2-6 eggs, which only she will incubate. The male will feed the hen from his crop during the breeding cycle. After 21-23 days the young hatch; when 7 weeks old they leave the nest. Strangely enough, the hen will remain inside the box for another 8-20 days after the young have hatched, while the male feeds both wife and youngsters. Breeding results are obtained only when a couple have an aviary to themselves.

---

117 PSITTACULA EUPATRIA
Alexandrine parrakeet

Classification Order Psittaciformes, Family Psittacidae.
Characteristics Length: 45-50 cm (18-20 in). Green. Clearly visible black collar; back of the neck pink. Innermost tail feathers bluish-green with yellow-white tips. Eyes gray encircled with red, beak deep red, legs grayish-brown. The female is very similar; however, she lacks the black neck ring.
Habitat These intelligent birds live in small groups. Towards evening, however, all these groups flock together to spend the night in palm trees, separating again in the morning. A noteworthy fact is that once a group has been formed they generally remain together. The birds gnaw their own nests in trees.
Distribution Eastern Afghanistan south and east to Pakistan, north and central India, Nepal, Bhutan, Assam, Burma, Vietnam, Cambodia, Laos, Thailand, the Andaman Islands, and Sri Lanka.
Captivity The female lays 2-4 eggs. These birds can be quite easily led to breeding as long as they are housed in a roomy aviary by themselves. The nest box should be about 45 × 40 × 60 cm; entrance diameter 11-12 cm. Incubation time about 28 days; after 6-7 weeks the young leave the nest. Females often suffer egg binding. Providing they have a good shelter (to prevent the danger of freezing toes), these birds can remain outdoors during the winter. Only when kept in a cage can a young bird be taught to speak.

118 ELECTUS RORATUS
Electus parrot

Classification Order Psittaciformes, Family Psittacidae.
Characteristics Length: 35 cm (14 in). As both sexes are totally different in color, it was thought for a long time that they were two species. Dr. A.B. Meijer, of the National Museum of Natural History (Munich, Germany), discovered in 1874 that the male is predominantly green and the female red. The male's upper mandible is coral with a yellow tip, the lower mandible is dark to black; iris orange, legs gray. The beak of the female is black, the iris yellowish-white.
Habitat In woody and mountain regions and in rain forests up to 1,000 m; they are strong flyers and breed high in tree holes.
Distribution Moluccas, Ceram, Ambon, Sumba, Halmahera, Solomon Islands, New Guinea and adjacent islands, and northern Queensland (Australia); 10 subspecies.
Captivity Imported birds must be housed in warm (22°C) indoor aviaries (only one pair per aviary), and they must be given the opportunity to drink fresh water whenever they like. They need a daily diet of cooked rice, germinated and dry sunflower seeds, milk-soaked bread and/or rusk, sweet fruits, raisins, berries, flower buds, lettuce, dandelion, spinach, and chickweed. At first the birds commonly refuse all foods. Females are often quite delicate, more so than males. According to surveys there are fewer females than males in the wild.

119 ALISTERUS AMBOINENSIS
Amboina king parrakeet

Classification Order Psittaciformes, Family Psittacidae.
Characteristics Length: 36 cm (14 in). Head, neck, and underparts red; wings green, rump blue. Upper mandible red with a black tip; lower mandible black. The female has a smaller head and beak, and the edges of the smaller wing feathers are red. The young have green backs and white eye rings. Iris orange, legs brown-black.
Habitat In forests and lowland; often in midmountain areas up to 1,400 m, in pairs or singly.
Distribution Ambon, Ceram, Halmahera, Buru, Sula, Peleng (Indonesia), and northwestern Papua New Guinea; in 6 subspecies.
Captivity The female lays 3 eggs; brooding starts after the second egg. Incubation time 21 days; after 7 weeks the young leave the nest. Nest box 40 × 40 × 145 cm. In the winter and during the breeding season, these bird cannot thrive without fruit (oranges, apples, and berries), corn, millet, and greens. For more details see *A. scapularis*.

120 ALISTERUS SCAPULARIS
Australian king parrakeet

Classification   Order Psittaciformes, Family Psittacidae.
Characteristics   Length: 35-40 cm (14-16 in). The male has red on throat, head, and underside. The rump is blue, continuing to the uppermost tail feathers; balance of tail is dark brown, greenish-black on top. Wings and back are a dark grass-green; brown eyes with yellow irises; pinkish-red beak, edged in black; gray legs. The female is pale grass-green where the male has red colors, except for her belly, which is pinkish-red. The beak is gray-black. Young birds resemble the female, though the beak is yellow. After 6 months the sexes can be distinguished because the males will then have a shiny beak and a great deal less gray in the plumage than the females. After a year the males will start to show red on the breast and head, but it takes still another year before their adult coloring is complete and they are ready for breeding.
Habitat   The birds live either in pairs or small groups close to woods. Their song is not unpleasant. In the wild they thrive on seeds, berries, fruits, etc.; sometimes they can be rather destructive to cornfields.
Distribution   Eastern Australia from northern Queensland to southern Victoria.
Captivity   These birds need a large garden aviary (6 × 2 × 2 m), with a shelter of at least 4 × 4 m. This aviary may be constructed of wood, as they don't chew wood. Be scanty with scrubs. Ideal measurements for the nest box are 35 × 35 cm with a depth of 90–140 cm; place a thick layer, about 15-20 cm, of turf, wood chips, and mulched wood on the bottom of the nest box. The female lays 3-6 eggs; breeding season September-January. Incubation time 20 days; after 7 weeks the young will leave the box. This bird has been crossed with *A. choropterus*, *Aprosmictus erythropterus* and *Polytelis swainsonii*.

Top: male
Bottom: female

121 LORICULUS VERNALIS
Vernal hanging parrot

Classification Order Psittaciformes, Family Psittacidae.
Characteristics Length: 13-14 cm (5-5½ in). Both sexes are mostly green. The adult male has a sky-blue blotch on his throat. Rump red. Tail blue underneath. The beak is red with a yellowish tip, the iris is yellowish-white, the legs pale orange. The female's bill is pale orange, the iris is brown, and the legs are light brown.
Habitat In wooded regions and cultivated plantations in pairs or in large flocks during the blossoming of the trees, as nectar is part of their diet. They also like coconut palm toddy "which they take from the collecting pots, sometimes in such quantities that they become stupefied" (Forshaw, see bibliography).
Distribution Central and northern parts of India; Thailand.
Captivity These birds can best be kept in a large cage or indoor aviary. Breeding is difficult. A pair uses a small cardboard (budgerigar) nesting box; the female lays 3-4 eggs; incubation time 24 days. As nesting material they use strips of willow bark and such, which they carry to their nests tucked under their feathers. Due to their diet (nectar; boiled rice; soaked sultanas; ant's eggs; chopped-up, hard-boiled eggs mixed with biscuits; sweet apples; berries in milk soaked rusk; bananas; pears; opened figs, etc.) the excreta are liquidy. Clean cage, perches, and so on daily.

---

122 LORICULUS GALGULUS
Blue-crowned hanging parrot

Classification Order Psittaciformes, Family Psittacidae.
Characteristics Length: 13 cm (5 in). Both sexes are primarily green; the male has a blue blotch on his head and on the green back a yellowish glow. Throat, rump, and feathers just above the tail red. The beak is black, and the upper mandible extends over the bottom half. Eyes dark brown, legs buff-brown. The female lacks the blue on the head and the red throat, as do the young, which have brownish-red rumps and black bills.
Habitat Lightly wooded regions and evergreen forests, parks, gardens, orchards, and coconut plantations; in pairs or small flocks.
Distribution Peninsular Malaysia, Borneo, and Sumatra, with its outlying islands.
Captivity This birds sleeps in an inverted hanging position. When the males are at rest, they are sometimes heard to twitter a soft and distant song. Also, males, whether perching or resting, will usually hold their wings considerably lower than the females, showing off a noticable red stripe on the back. The female lays 3-4 eggs; incubation time 19-22 days. The male will feed the hen on the nest, but it is only the female that feeds the young. After 1 month they leave the nest which, by that time, has become extremely dirty. For more details see *L. vernalis*.

123 AGAPORNIS CANA
Madagascar lovebird or gray-headed lovebird

Classification Order Psittaciformes, Family Psittacidae.
Characteristics Length: 14 cm (5½ in). Upperpart green. Head, cheeks, throat, neck and parts of shoulder, and chest whitish-gray. Underparts light grass-green; wings dark green. Tail green with black feather tips. Chest has a hazy yellow glow which becomes darker towards wings and underside. The beak is whitish-gray, the eyes brown, the legs pale gray. The female is green; underwing coverts green. Young males are a more intense green on back and wings, and the gray can be seen quite early in life, sometimes while they are still in the nest.
Habitat These birds live in large flocks, mostly along the edge of forests. They do quite a bit of damage to farmland.
Distribution Madagascar; introduced to Rodriguez Island, Mauritius, Comoro Islands, Seychelles, Zanzibar, and Mafia Island; in 2 subspecies.
Captivity They are primarily seasonal breeders: November and December. The female lays 4-5 (in the wild up to 11) eggs. As the birds catch cold easily, they are best kept in indoor aviaries. The female will use a budgerigar nest box and will make a little "cushion" of various materials (dried leaves chewed into the desired shape and size) in the hollow of the nest. Grass, straw, strips of newspaper, bark of willow and fruit trees, larch needles, etc. are also accepted. Incubation time 22 days. The young leave the nest when about 5 weeks old.

---

124 AGAPORNIS PULLARIA
Red-faced lovebird

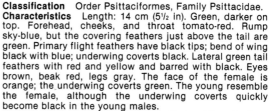

Classification Order Psittaciformes, Family Psittacidae.
Characteristics Length: 14 cm (5½ in). Green, darker on top. Forehead, cheeks, and throat tomato-red. Rump sky-blue, but the covering feathers just above the tail are green. Primary flight feathers have black tips; bend of wing black with blue; underwing coverts black. Lateral green tail feathers with red and yellow and barred with black. Eyes brown, beak red, legs gray. The face of the female is orange; the underwing coverts green. The young resemble the female, although the underwing coverts quickly become black in the young males.
Habitat Wooded regions in large flocks. They feed on grass seeds, leaf buds, figs, millets, or corn, generally leaving fields in a ravaged state. They carve their nests in the large, still inhabited tree nests of termites or in termite hills; a job primarily performed by the female. The "lodgings" should be imagined as a small tunnel with a widened, fairly round cavity, called a "kettle."
Distribution Sierra Leone, Cameroons, northern Angola, Uganda, and Rwanda (Africa).
Captivity Very hard to breed. The best method is using a big drum filled with moistened moss and then left to dry. Branches and twigs should be arranged on top and around it. The female lays 4-7 eggs. Incubation time 24 days; the young leave the nest when 6 to 7 weeks old.

125 AGAPORNIS ROSEICOLLIS
Peach-faced lovebird

Classification   Order Psittaciformes, Family Psittacidae.
Characteristics   Length: 16-18 cm (6¹/₂-7 in). Bright green; forehead, cheeks, chin, throat, and area just above the chest soft pinkish-red. Rump and uppertail coverts bright light blue; on the green tail some black and rust colored feathers. The beak is yellow to very pale green, the eyes are brown, the legs greenish-gray. The female is duller; the beak darker. Young birds are grayish-green in the beginning and lack the red coloring on the forehead. Full grown females are larger than males.
Habitat   In the wild in comparatively small groups, mostly in areas that are dry and grow leaf-shedding trees; usually near a body of water.
Distribution   Southwestern Africa; in 2 subspecies.
Captivity   This species transports nest-building materials between its back and rump feathers. The female lays 4-5 eggs; after the second egg the female commences to incubate for 22 days; after 4-5 weeks the young leave the nest box, but will continue to be fed (mostly by the male) for some time. They are excellent breeders and can breed and rear 3 clutches per season. Independent young should be housed in a separate, roomy aviary. Besides par blue mutations, which can also be found in the wild (and are recessive), there are many other mutations.

126 AGAPORNIS TARANTA
Abyssinian lovebird

Classification   Order Psittaciformes, Family Psittacidae.
Characteristics   Length: 15-16.5 cm (6-6¹/₂ in). Green with a red forehead and a red eye ring. Eyes brown, beak red, legs gray. The female lacks the red coloring on the head. Sometimes the small underwing coverts are greenish or brownish-black in color; in the male they are always black.
Habitat   In small flocks in mainly dry areas with evergreens; also in the immediate vicinity of cultivated land or in the sparse woods of the highlands, at a height of 2,000-3,000 m above sea level. They breed in all kinds of nooks, even in the nests of weaver birds, as peach-faced lovebirds do. Females carry nesting materials in their plumage to the nest, although some transport these in the beak.
Distribution   Southern Eritrea and southwestern Ethiopia; in 2 subspecies.
Captivity   The female lays 3-6 eggs; incubation time 24 days; the male takes care of feeding the hen on the nest. Once the young have hatched, the male feeds first the female, and she in turn feeds the youngsters. The fledglings are about 6-7 weeks old when they leave the nest box (25 × 20 × 18 cm; entrance diameter 5 cm, situated off-center about 3 cm from the top). Breeding results are obtained when each pair is housed separately, as other bird species and even fellow species are chased and attacked.

127 AGAPORNIS PERSONATA PERSONATA
Masked, white eye-ring, or yellow-collared, lovebird

Classification Order Psittaciformes, Family Psittacidae.
Characteristics Length 15.5 cm (6 in). Both sexes have a blackish-brown head with a yellow collar; throat and chest yellow with orange-red glow. The rest green with the exception of the blue rump, and the tail which shows a black and red band shortly before the ends on the outer feathers. Eyes brown, periophthalmic ring white, bill red, legs gray. The young look like their parents, although their coloring is somewhat duller, and the black in the plumage is not very bright.
Habitat Nomadic; it survives on the seeds of available trees and roosts in the crevices and crannies of baobabs. This bird will nest in Indian swifts' nests and breeds in the 7 cm space between the tiles of a roof and the boarding underneath. Often they will also nest under iron roofs, which retain much of the high heat radiated by the sun. Brood in colonies.
Distribution Northern Tanzania.
Captivity Males often scratch their heads with their feet prior to mating; females line the nests; they also weigh more than males (56 grams versus 50 grams). The hen lays 3-4 eggs; incubation time 21-23 days. The young leave the nest at 44-45 days of age. Provide more boxes than there are bird pairs; good boxes measure 50 × 25 cm. The hen enjoys a good supply of willow twigs. There are many color mutations, of which the recessive blue is very well-known.

128 AGAPORNIS PERSONATA NIGRIGENIS
Black-cheeked lovebird

Classification Order Psittaciformes, Family Psittacidae.
Characteristics Length: 11 cm (4½ in). Green; forehead and cheeks dark brown to black. Yellow-greenish throat sides and rear of the head; throat orange with a brown glow. A vague pink blotch on the chest. White eye ring; eyes brown, beak red, legs gray. The female is a little duller. The young look very much like the parents, although in their early life their colors are considerably duller. Some fledglings have black spots on the bills.
Habitat In the wild they live in all forests except evergreen; they are cheerful and fast and not particularly timid. I have observed these birds taking baths early in the morning and late in the afternoon in little streams and small waterfalls. Their distribution is relatively limited, being around 80 miles (130 kilometers) in diameter.
Distribution A small region in the northern portion of Zimbabwe, around the Zambezi River and the Victoria Waterfalls (Africa).
Captivity Have become rare in aviculture due to export restrictions in their country of origin. Excellent breeders. They are sweet and peaceful birds, even when housed with fellow species or other exotic birds. The hen lays 4-6, sometimes 2-8 eggs. Both sexes incubate the eggs; incubation time 16-21 days. After about 30 days the young fly out. The male does not feed the hen while she is sitting on the eggs. No color mutations are known.

129 AGAPORNIS PERSONATA FISCHERI
Fischer's lovebird

Classification Order Psittaciformes, Family Psittacidae.
Characteristics Length: 10 cm (4 in). Green; golden-yellow neck. Cheeks and throat orange. The top of the head is olive-green; forehead a lovely tomato-red. Rump blue, the tail green with sky-blue tips and an indistinct black band shortly before the end. The roots of the outermost feathers of the wings are brownish-red underneath. Eyes brown, beak red, legs slate-blue. The offspring look much like the parents except that their colors are somewhat duller, and the base of the upper mandible has brown markings.
Habitat This species lives at elevations of 1,000-1,700 m in small flocks. Their flight is straight and fast; in flight, the rustling sound of their wings can be heard, as can their high-pitched chirping. The species prefers to live in isolated clumps of trees with grass plains between them.
Distribution South and southeast of Lake Victoria (Africa).
Captivity This species is very sociable in an aviary. The hen lays 4-6 eggs; it takes 3-3½ weeks for the eggs to hatch. After 35-37 days the young will fly from the nest. After another 10 days, the youngsters are totally independent, and it is then best to separate them from the parents. There are many established mutations.

---

130 PSITTACUS ERITHACUS
African gray parrot

Classification Order Psittaciformes, Family Psittacidae.
Characteristics Length: 36 cm (14 in). Dove gray; white-grayish, naked face. Red tail and under coverts. Eyes yellow, beak black, legs dark gray. Head, beak, and body of female smaller; underside whitish-gray. Iris of male round; the female's elliptical. Iris of young black, changing to gray after a few months.
Habitat Forests, often in large flocks. During the night they sleep in tall trees particularly chosen for this purpose.
Distribution Central belt of Africa; in 3 subspecies of which the Timneh parrot (*P. e. timneh*) is occasionally imported; this bird is dark-gray with less red.
Captivity Talented imitator and usually very affectionate. Must be housed in a large cage (65 × 50 × 80 cm). Agitated birds oscillate their pupils and raise their nape feathers. They love to take showers in the rain. Breeding possibilities in large aviaries; the female lays 2-4 eggs, which she incubates for about 29 days. The male feeds her on the nest. After 10-11 weeks the young leave the nest, but will be foraged for by both parents for another 4 months. Nest box: 55 × 35 × 35 cm; entrance diameter 12 cm. Although birds engage in courtship behavior in their second or third year, females don't start breeding until they are in their sixth year. It is advisable to check newly imported birds for bacterial infections, especially salmonella (*Salmonella typhimurium*).

131 POICEPHALUS SENEGALUS
Senegal parrot

Classification Order Psittaciformes, Family Psittacidae.
Characteristics Length: 24 cm (9½ in). Green; gray head, yellow to orange underside. Pale green foreneck and upper breast. Eyes yellow, beak gray, legs brown.
Habitat Open forest, savannah woodland, and farmland; solitary, in pairs, or small groups; up to about 20 birds. Feeds on figs, bananas, nuts, seeds, corn, rice, and insects.
Distribution Western Africa; in 3 subspecies.
Captivity Friendly, somewhat timid bird. Young birds can learn to talk, although this can be a slow process. In a large aviary, breeding successes are possible. The hen lays 2-3 eggs, which she incubates for about 22 days. After 9-11 weeks the young leave the nest. Nest box: 25 × 25 × 25 cm; entrance diameter 6 cm. Excellent rearing foods are nuts, sprouting sunflower seeds, wheats and oats, apples, carrots, and corn on the cob. They have extremely strong beaks and are capable of quickly destroying wooden components in cages or aviaries. During the winter this species must be kept indoors at room temperature.

132 POICEPHALUS MEYERI
Meyer's parrot

Classification Order Psittaciformes, Family Psittacidae.
Characteristics Length: 22 cm (8¾ in). Grayish-brown with yellow on crown, bend of wing, underwing and thighs. Breast, belly, and undertail coverts greenish-blue; rump and uppertail coverts green. Eyes orange-red, beak and legs grayish-black.
Habitat Savannah, scrub, and all types of forests. Breed in woodpecker's nests, tree holes, etc. Live in pairs or small groups.
Distribution Central and eastern Africa; in 6 subspecies. The color differentiations are primarily on belly and rump.
Captivity Usually very shy, especially older birds. Young, imported birds are sometimes extremely nervous. Happily, there are recent breeding successes, as this species has only been known to aviculturists since the mid-1960s. The birds require a large aviary; the female lays 2-4 eggs; incubation time about 29 days. After 2 months the young leave the nest, but will be fed by both parents for quite some time.

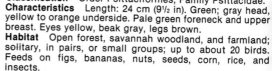

133 POICEPHALUS RUEPPELLII
Rüppell's parrot

Classification Order Psittaciformes, Family Psittacidae.
Characteristics Length: 22 cm (8¾ in). Male brownish-gray with sometimes a little white on crown and ear coverts. Yellow shoulders and bend of wing. Lower back, rump, and uppertail coverts beautifully blue in female; barely visible blue in male. Underwing coverts yellow. Eyes orange-red, beak dark gray, legs brown-gray.
Habitat Dry woodland and up to coastal plains; in small groups, high in tall trees.
Distribution Southwestern Africa.
Captivity Sporadically imported. Friendly little bird, especially in a large cage indoors. Some breeding successes have been accomplished (see *P. meyeri*), as well as hybrids between a male *meyeri* and a female *rueppellii*. Three eggs were laid and incubated by the hen. Only one young hatched and survived; fed by both male and female for about 2 months.

134 NYMPHICUS HOLLANDICUS
Cockatiel

Classification Order Psittaciformes, Family Psittacidae.
Characteristics Length: 30-35 cm (12-14 in). Grayish-blue; crest and head yellow; less bright on the female. Orange-yellow ear markings. White wing coverts; grayer on the female. Eyes brown, beak grayish-blue, legs dark gray. The female has dark ear markings and is duller in coloration.
Habitat Savannah and grassland; also urban areas.
Distribution Central Australia; rarer along the coastal regions. Introduced to Tasmania.
Captivity Graceful and peaceable birds that will readily breed in a roomy aviary when housed by themselves. The hen lays 4-7 eggs that take 20 days to hatch. The male incubates them during the day, and the hen at night. When the young are about 30 days old they leave the nest, but will continue to be fed by both parents for some time. Nest box: 35 × 20 × 45 cm; entrance diameter 6 cm. Do not make the entrance too high; the chicks like to stick their heads out of the nest box and make a peeping, "hissing" sound. Place a thick layer of sawdust on the nest bottom. The well-known budgerigar (*Melopsittacus undulatus*), also an "Aussie," can be kept in a cage (single or as pair) or in an aviary. Nest box: 20 × 20 × 25 cm; entrance diameter 4.5 cm. The 3-6 eggs are hatched in about 18 days. See bibliography for detailed books on these two important cage and aviary birds.

135 PROBOSCIGER ATERRIMUS
Great palm cockatoo

Classification Order Psittaciformes, Family Psittacidae.
Characteristics Length: 60 cm (24 in). Grayish-black with bare red facial patch. Strong, elongated upper mandible; smaller in female, as is her facial patch. Tongue red with a black tip. Eyes brown, beak blackish, legs gray.
Habitat Savannah woodland, tropical and monsoon rain forests; in small flocks. Even tiny seeds (in addition to nuts and seeds of pandonus palms) are taken, usually a few at a time, and put in a cavity of the lower mandible; one by one these seeds will be pushed—by the tongue— to the chisel edge of the lower mandible to be broken.
Distribution Cape York Peninsula (northern Australia), Aru Islands (Papua New Guinea), and nearby offshore islands; in 3 subspecies.
Captivity Gentle birds which occasionally come to breed in a large aviary (which should be built from very sturdy materials, as their beaks are extremely strong; fencing wire can be broken easily). The female lays one egg, which she incubates for about 33 days. The species uses hollow tree trunks or nest boxes 150 cm high and 40 cm in diameter, in which a 15-cm layer of nesting materials (chewed twigs) is placed by both sexes. A rare bird in Britain and Europe.

---

136 CALYPTORHYNCHUS MAGNIFICUS
Banksian, or red-tailed, black cockatoo

Classification Order Psittaciformes, Family Psittacidae.
Characteristics Length: 60 cm (24 in). Deep black with red tail patch. Female's tail barred with orange and yellow. Yellow on head and underparts. Eyes brown, beak dark gray, legs brownish-gray.
Habitat Dry scrubs, woodland, and dry mallee. They nest in holes of dead trees. Occur in groups, sometimes up to several hundred birds. Nomadic.
Distribution Eastern, northern, and western Australia; western Victoria and southeastern South Australia; in 4 subspecies.
Captivity Rare in aviculture, although quite popular in Australia. They are known to live for many years in captivity (40 years and more). The female lays 3-4 eggs, which she incubates for about 30 days. Both parents feed their young; usually twice a day. After 90 days the youngsters leave the nest; after 4 years they will have their adult plumage. Nest log: 2 m with an inside diameter of 40 cm. Place this at an angle of about 30 degrees and at a height of 2 m. A layer of twigs and rotten wood (30 cm thick) is advisable.

137 CALLOCEPHALON FIMBRIATUM
Gang gang cockatoo

Classification   Order Psittaciformes, Family Psittacidae.
Characteristics   Length: 34 cm (13½ in). Gray with whitish feather edges. Scarlet head and crest. Female gray with a gray head and (smaller) gray crest. Underparts with brick, white, and gray bars. Eyes brown, beak horn-colored, legs gray. After 1 year the males come into their adult plumage.
Habitat   Forest in the mountains; during the winter months in bush country, near farmland, parks, gardens, orchards, etc.; in pairs or small flocks. Sometimes in large groups, when there is a plentiful supply of food.
Distribution   Southeast Australia; introduced to Kangaroo Island.
Captivity   Requires a large aviary with lots of chewing materials; otherwise they start feather picking. They take the food with their left foot while standing on their right. Both sexes incubate the 2-3 eggs. Incubation time about 26 days. The young leave the nest after about 2 months. Nest box: 30 cm long and wide and 50 cm high. Breeding successes are still extremely rare. Not common in Britain and Europe.

---

138 CACATUA GALERITA
Great sulphur-crested cockatoo

Classification   Order Psittaciformes, Family Psittacidae.
Characteristics   Length: 50 cm (20 in). White; long sulphur crest, pale yellow on underwings and tail and around the ears. Eyes, beak, and legs blackish. Female's iris is red-brown.
Habitat   Savannah, scrub, mallee and woodland, close to water and farmland; in pairs during the breeding season, and in (sometimes large) flocks during the rest of the year.
Distribution   Northern and eastern Australia; Papua New Guinea, Aru Islands, and introduced to New Zealand, the Palau Islands and Ceramlaut and Goramlaut (Indonesia); in 4 subspecies.
Captivity   Hardy, intelligent birds. Partners that are kept together for some years will come to brood. The female lays 2-5 eggs, which are incubated by both parents; during the night by the female, during the day by the male. Young leave the nest after about 2½ months. Nest box 70 × 70 × 125 cm; entrance diameter 10 cm. For more details see *C. goffini*.

139 CACATUA SULPHUREA
Lesser sulphur-crested cockatoo

Classification Order Psittaciformes, Family Psittacidae.
Characteristics Length: 32-36 cm (12½-14 in). White; yellow to orange crest and ear coverts. Eyes black (reddish-brown in females), beak and legs black. The iris color of the young changes gradually after the second year from pale gray to black or red-brown.
Habitat Forest; often in farmland, around small villages, and near the coast; in sometimes large flocks.
Distribution Indonesia: Sulawesi (formerly Celebes), Lombok, Sumba, Sumbawa, Flores, and Timor; in 6 subspecies.
Captivity Friendly and intelligent birds which are willing to brood, usually during spring. Very social and always ready to learn some tricks. The female lays 2-3 eggs; incubation time 28 days. Both parents sit on the eggs; the female at night, the male during the day. The young leave the nest when about 3 months old, but will be fed by both parents for quite some time. As soon as the partners show new courtship behavior (the male circles the hen with bowing head movements), remove the young, as they are likely to be attacked by the pair!

---

140 CACATUA ALBA
Umbrella, or great white, or white-crested, cockatoo

Classification Order Psittaciformes, Family Psittacidae.
Characteristics Length: 40-45 cm (15¾-17¾ in). White; naked periophthalmic ring yellowish. Eyes black (red-brownish in female), beak and legs black.
Habitat Forest and around farmland; in pairs or small groups.
Distribution Northern and central Moluccas. Not much is known about this beatiful and gentle bird.
Captivity Friendly, quiet bird, which can be very long-lived. Breeding successes in an aviary are rare but possible. The female lays 2-3 eggs, which are incubated by both parents for about 1 month. After about 11 weeks the young leave the nest, but will still be fed for a relatively long time primarily by the male. Nest box (or barrel): 50 × 40 × 50 cm; entrance diameter 12 cm.

141 CACATUA MOLUCCENSIS
Moluccan cockatoo

Classification Order Psittaciformes, Family Psittacidae.
Characteristics Length: 50 cm (20 in). White with a soft pinkish tinge. Deep pink crest. Undertail coverts marked with yellow. Periophthalmic ring bluish-white. Eyes blackish, beak grayish-black, legs gray. Female has less pink, and her head is smaller; iris brown.
Habitat Coastal areas and on mountain slopes below 1,000 m; in small flocks. Can be extremely destructive in coconut plantations.
Distribution South Moluccas; introduced to Ambon Island. Feed on fruits, coconuts, berries, and insects.
Captivity Quite often available. Gentle but expensive bird; becomes very affectionate after a short while. As soon as matters arise that they don't appreciate, they start screaming and raising their crests. They are, in general, fairly good talkers and imitators. Breeding successes are possible only in large aviaries. Supply a few boxes of 120 cm height and 80 cm in diameter. The female lays 2-3 eggs. Both partners incubate the eggs for about 30 days. The young leave the nest after 3½ or more months. In 1968 two hybrids from *C. moluccensis* × *C. alba* were bred.

---

142 CACATUA LEADBEATERI
Leadbeater's, or Major Mitchell's, cockatoo

Classification Order Psittaciformes, Family Psittacidae.
Characteristics Length: 39 cm (15¼ in). White with a pinkish tinge on the underside. Red brow. Pinkish head. White, red, and yellow stripes on crest. Eyes dark brown (reddish-brown in female), beak white, legs gray. When the female young are approximately 3 years old, the iris becomes reddish-brown.
Habitat Thick mallee and arid country, sometimes close to water; in pairs or small flocks, usually families. Nest in hollow tree trunks (especially in red gum trees).
Distribution Interior of Australia, except the northeastern and southwestern portions; in 2 subspecies.
Captivity Require a large aviary. Birds bred in captivity become extremely tame; wild birds, however, remain cautious. They are far from excellent talkers. Fortunately, this species—which is becoming rare in Australia—often nests in a tree trunk or stout barrel. The female lays 3-6 eggs. Incubation time 25-30 days; both parents sit on the clutch; the hen during the night, the male during the day. Both parents feed their youngsters, which leave the nest after about 4 weeks.

143 CACATUA GOFFINI
Goffini's cockatoo

Classification Order Psittaciformes, Family Psittacidae.
Characteristics Length: 32 cm (12½ in). White with some pink on the forehead and yellow on the underside tail feathers; broad, naked and white periophthalmic ring. Eyes dark brown (reddish-brown in female), beak light grayish-white, legs gray.
Habitat Undescribed.
Distribution Tanimbar Island (Indonesia) and probably introduced to Tual, in the Kai Islands.
Captivity Plentiful and inexpensive during the 1970s they were therefore thought to be unsuitable as a pet. However, this species is one of the most intelligent and interesting of all the cockatoos. This gentle bird will come to brood in a large aviary, although not all pairs are willing to raise a family. The female lays 2-3 eggs. Incubation time about 30 days. The male usually sits on the eggs during the day; the hen at night. Nest box: 60 × 40 × 35 cm; entrance diameter 10 cm. Corn on the cob, millet spray, spinach, grated carrot, milk powder, sunflower kernels, and some grated cuttlefish bone are excellent, especially if one has chicks that require handraising.

144 CACATUA (EOLOPHUS) ROSEICAPPILUS
Galah, roseate, or rose-breasted, cockatoo

Classification Order Psittaciformes, Family Psittacidae.
Characteristics Length: 38 cm (15 in). Gray above, deep pink below. Small, whitish crest. Eyes dark brown (red in female), beak horn-colored, legs gray.
Habitat Savannah, open country, woodland, dry interior plain, farmland, parklands, and gardens. Never near the coastline; in pairs during the breeding season, otherwise in large groups. Feeds mainly on the ground and nests in hollows in eucalyptus tree trunks.
Distribution Australia, occasionally in Tasmania; in 3 subspecies.
Captivity One of the commonest cockatoos. Gentle, intelligent, and a good talker. The female lays 2-5 eggs. Incubation time 24 days; both partners incubate. After 7 weeks the young leave the nest, but will be fed (and preened) for another month. Two broods per season are common. The parents use small twigs and leaves to construct a nest lining. Nest box: 50 × 50 cm; 2.50 m deep. Use natural wood (with the bark still attached); entrance diameter 10 cm. During the breeding season germinated sunflower seeds, corn on the cob, oats, wheats, spray millet, and greens are essential, as is milk-soaked white bread.

145 ANODORHYNCHUS HYACINTHINUS
Hyacinth macaw

Classification Order Psittaciformes, Family Psittacidae.
Characteristics Length: 100 cm (39½ in); the largest living parrot. Deep blue; naked, periophthalmic ring golden-yellow; along the base of the lower mandible, a small, naked yellow area. The hen is usually smaller in size.
Habitat High in buriti palm trees, which can be found in swamps, near rivers, and lakes. They are not shy. Usually occur in pairs or small family groups.
Distribution Southern Brazil and western Bolivia.
Captivity Bred in captivity for the first time in Czechoslovakia (Bratislava), the pair used an old wooden nest box (150 × 150 × 180 cm). An exceptionally gentle, intelligent, and affectionate pet, although fierce towards strangers. Be aware that their beaks are exceptionally strong; they have approximately 300 pounds of biting pressure per square inch. Perches must be replaced on a regular basis. The bird is rare and therefore expensive. Protected species (Washington Convention).

---

146 ARA ARARAUNA
Blue-and-yellow, or blue-and-gold, macaw

Classification Order Psittaciformes, Family Psittacidae.
Characteristics Length: 90 cm (35½ in). Upperparts turquoise-blue; lower parts goldish-yellow. Forehead and crown greenish-blue. Bluish-yellow undertail coverts. Black collar beneath the face. Naked, white cheeks, bordered with some lines of small black feathers. Eyes yellow, beak and legs black. The female is smaller.
Habitat In some areas still quite common; in forests, savannahs, open country, in swamps and other spots close to water; in pairs of flocks. When operating in flocks, the couples stay together, even when they are on the wing. They nest in holes of dead palm trees.
Distribution Panama to northern Paraguay.
Captivity Very affectionate and highly intelligent birds that can learn to imitate and talk exceptionally well. Many young are reared in captivity, although it sometimes takes years before a pair begins to raise a family. The female lays 2-3 eggs; incubation time 25-28 days. The young leave the nest after they are about 3 months old. Nest box: 55 × 55 × 85 cm; entrance hole diameter 17 cm; use thick board (e.g., 4 cm). Provide all pairs with nest boxes year round; they like to use these for roosting. During the breeding season the birds may become extremely protective and therefore aggressive towards their owner.

147 ARA MILITARIS
Military, or great green, macaw

Classification Order Psittaciformes, Family Psittacidae.
Characteristics Length: 65 cm (25½ in). Olive-green; red forehead. Uppertail coverts and rump blue; bluish-red primary feathers. Cheek patches with small rows of small violet-brown feathers. Eyes yellow, beak dark gray, legs light gray. The female is slightly smaller. Young resemble the parents, but they are duller with a brownish tinge.
Habitat Dry forest and open woodland, in pairs or small flocks, up to about 20 birds. They leave their resting places—like all other macaw species—during the early morning to forage. They return to the same roosting spots in the evening. They live on nuts, berries, fruits, greens, seeds, etc.
Distribution Mexico to Argentina; in 3 subspecies.
Captivity An easily tamed, friendly bird with moderate talking ability. Only a few breeding successes are known. The female lays 2-3 eggs. Incubation time about 28 days. The young leave the nest after about 3 months. Pairs like to use barrels or drums as nesting places.

148 ARA MACAO
Scarlet macaw

Classification Order Psittaciformes, Family Psittacidae.
Characteristics Length: 85 cm (33½ in). Deep red with flesh-colored cheeks. Shoulders and wings yellow. Eyes yellow, upper mandible horn-colored with black at the base; lower mandible grayish-black; legs dark gray. The female is slightly smaller with a shorter, broader, and more curved beak.
Habitat Light woodland and savannah; in pairs, family parties, or flocks up to about 25 birds. They can often be observed flying in pairs, their wings nearly touching.
Distribution Southern Mexixo, Central America, and the northwestern section of South America.
Captivity Extremely sociable. There is a deep bond between the couples. Towards their keeper they are very affectionate, but they remain noisy (especially when frustrated or bored), and their earth-shattering screeches are a real drawback. As with all macaw species, the scarlet loves to bathe. It is interesting to watch a bird sitting in a rain shower slapping itself with its wings. Provide a large nest box (60 × 60 × 65 cm) all year, as they will use it as roosting place also. The female lays 2-3 eggs. Only the hen incubates, although the male sits beside her. After 3 months the young leave the nest. Oranges, bananas, sunflower seed, nuts, berries, carrots, calcium (cuttlefish bone), bread, tomatoes, and a daily supply of fresh twigs are essential.

149 ARA CHLOROPTERA
Green-winged, or marron, macaw

Classification Order Psittaciformes, Family Psittacidae.
Characteristics Length: 85 cm (33½ in). Dark red. Shoulder coverts and large upperwing green. Wings, rump, uppertail coverts and tail tip blue. Naked flesh-colored cheeks with red lines of small feathers. Upper mandible horn-colored with black-gray on lower sides of the base, lower mandible blackish. Eyes yellow, legs dark gray. The female is smaller and has a smaller head.
Habitat Hilly country and forest, in pairs or small groups. During the day they often stay in tree tops.
Distribution Eastern Panama to Paraguay.
Captivity Becoming rare in captivity and therefore expensive. In temperament they resemble the hyacinth macaw. Kind to children and pets, but easily frightened by sudden noises and movements. The female lays 2-3 eggs; incubation time 24-26 days. In the wild the young leave the nest after about 3 months, but in captivity it sometimes takes more than 100 days. This species hybridizes in the wild with the military macaw and the blue-and-gold macaw; in captivity, however, there is clearly more opportunity for successful hybridization.

150 ARA AURICOLLIS
Yellow-collared, yellow-naped, or Cassin's, macaw

Classification Order Psittaciformes, Family Psittacidae.
Characteristics Length: 38 cm (15 in). Dark green; black forehead; yellow collar on the back of the neck. Tail, primary and secondary wing feathers flashed with blue. White cheek patches. Eyes reddish, beak black, legs yellowish.
Habitat Swampland; in pairs or small flocks, but plentiful during dry weather spells.
Distribution Eastern Bolivia, Paraguay, northwestern Argentina, and Mato Grosso (Brazil).
Captivity Known for their sharp and high-pitched screech. Excellent pet with clownish behavior and a nice personality. The female lays 2-3 eggs; incubation time about 28 days. The young leave the nest after about 60 days. Breeding results are rare, however. Mixed fruits, vegetables, sunflower seeds, oats, and soaked corn are essential during the raising of the chicks. A hybrid yellow-collared x Illiger's macaw was raised successfully in 1978 (by Dan and Pat Mathews, USA). For further details see *A. severa*.

151 ARA SEVERA
Severa macaw

Classification Order Psittaciformes, Family Psittacidae.
Characteristics Length: 46 cm (18 in). Resembles the military macaw. Dark green with a blue crown and brown forehead. White cheeks with small feathers. Blue wings. Upperside of tail blue, mixed with green. Underwing coverts red. Underside tail brownish-red. Eyes yellow, beak gray-black, legs gray.
Habitat Tropical and swamp forests; often near rivers and lakes, in pairs or small flocks (up to about 25 birds).
Distribution Eastern Panama to the Guianas, south to the northern parts of Bolivia and to the southern parts of Brazil; in 2 subspecies.
Captivity Very affectionate pets which can even be kept in a large cage, although the birds should be allowed to "stretch their legs" daily for several hours. In an aviary breeding successes are possible. Present a few nest boxes of 45 × 45 × 45 cm and cover the bottom with a layer of damp soil, peat, and some moss. The female lays 2-3 eggs which she incubates for about 28 days. After 2 months the young leave the nest. During the whole year white seed, millet, hemp, nuts, berries, greens, and fresh branches are essential. All dwarf macaws are very sensitive to drafts and cold.

152 ARA MARACANA
Illiger's macaw

Classification Order Psittaciformes, Family Psittacidae.
Characteristics Length: 43 cm (17 in). Olive-green; orange-red forehead, followed by a green-bluish head. Red patch on belly and lower back. Wing blue and green. Tail blue. Naked cheeks yellow. Eyes reddish-brown, beak black, legs yellowish.
Habitat Forest, close to water, in pairs and small flocks. They have a distinctive flight pattern that is not straight (as with the other "miniature" macaws), but rather jerk up in a bucking motion.
Distribution Eastern Brazil and northeastern Argentina.
Captivity Excellent and affectionate bird, which tames easily, although many of them are (and remain) moody. They need a nest box year round (40 × 40 × 45-50 cm). It is used as roosting place, too. The female lays 2-3 eggs. Incubation time 27-29 days. The young leave the nest after about 3½ months. Provide the parents all year with bits of milk-soaked bread, seeds (millet, white seed, small sunflower seed, hemp, etc.), rice, universal food (with egg), and fresh twigs. The young should be fed a high-protein diet.

153 ARATINGA ERYTHROGENYS
Red-masked conure

Classification Order Psittaciformes, Family Psittacidae.
Characteristics Length: 33 cm (13 in). Green. Lores, ear coverts, area around the eyes, bend of wing, thighs, and outermost underwing coverts red. White periophthalmic ring. Eyes yellow, beak horn-colored, legs gray. Young birds lack the red head and thighs.
Habitat Valleys and arid areas.
Distribution Tropical zone of western Ecuador and northwestern Peru.
Captivity Beautiful birds but extremely noisy. Ideal in a large aviary. Sometimes—depending on the area—one can keep these birds free, like pigeons. Young birds tame easily and learn to speak a few words. Breeding box: 35 × 20 × 25 cm; entrance diameter 10 cm, which the birds will gnaw at during the breeding season, enlarging it substantially. The hen lays 2 eggs; incubation time 28 days; only the hen incubates. Nest control and other disturbances are taken badly. After 50 days the young leave the nest, but will be taken care of for another 3 months by both parents. Sweet fruits are essential the whole year.

154 ARATINGA LEUCOPTHALMUS
White-eyed conure

Classification Order Psittaciformes, Family Psittacidae.
Characteristics Length: 32 cm (13 in). Green with some red feathers on head, neck, and thighs. Bend of wing, carpal, and outermost lesser underwing coverts red; greater underwing coverts gold-yellow. White periophthalmic ring. Eyes orange, beak horn-colored, legs gray-brown. Young birds still have green wing coverts.
Habitat Light forests and mangroves, usually in small flocks or pairs.
Distribution Northern parts of South America, Guianas, Venezuela and eastern portion of Colombia south to northern Argentina and northern Uruguay; in 3 subspecies.
Captivity Very vigilant. Can only be housed in a large aviary with strong mesh, as their beaks are extremely powerful. Usually very noisy. They have the habit of commencing brooding early in the year. The hen lays 3-6 eggs; incubation time 4 weeks; after 9 weeks the young leave the nest. Nest box: 35 × 20 × 20 cm; entrance diameter 10 cm. It is a advisable to put moss in the box before the season starts. The birds don't take nest control readily; they react by screaming loudly and may even attack their owner.

155 ARATINGA JANDAYA
Jendaya, or yellow-headed, conure

Classification Order Psittaciformes, Family Psittacidae.
Characteristics Length: 30 cm (12 in). Golden-yellow head with small red feathers; throat area also yellow. Breast and belly deep red; the back and wings green; some of the wing feathers are blue. Rump red; tail green with yellow shine, margined with dark greenish-blue. Eyes brown, beak black, legs grayish-black. Birds that have not yet reached adulthood have less red on the face and breast; some have green spots on the breast.
Habitat Close to forests and young tree plantations, where they do a great deal of damage. They occur in pairs or small flocks (up to 16 birds).
Distribution Northeastern Brazil.
Captivity The female lays 3-4 eggs, which are incubated by both parents. Any bird that comes too close to the nest will be greeted with raised neck feathers and abrupt little nods of the head. A couple should be housed in a separate aviary. Breeding box: 25 × 25 × 35 cm; entrance hole should have a diameter of 8 cm; the bottom should be covered with a thick layer (up to 8 cm) of moist peat moss over which a layer of twigs should be placed. Incubation time 26 days; young leave the nest after about 8 weeks, but both parents will feed their young for another 5 weeks. Once the young have hatched, the parents should be given a plentiful amount of fruit and a rich variety of greens. These birds are rather nervous and noisy.

156 ARATINGA SOLSTITIALIS
Sun conure

Classification Order Psittaciformes, Family Psittacidae.
Characteristics Length: 30 cm (12 in). Deep orange on head and belly; breast and back yellow; small primaries with green edges; large primaries blue. Broad white periophthalmic ring, smaller on the hen. Eyes brown, beak dark-gray, legs gray. Young birds have more green and less orange; their iris is black. The hen has a little more green on the wings.
Habitat Open forests, savannahs, and palm groves; in flocks.
Distribution Northwestern Brazil, Guyana and southeast Venezuela.
Captivity Expensive bird, which is most likely conspecific with the Jendaya conure (*A. jandaya*) and the golden-capped conure (*A. auricapilla*). During the breeding season, males become extremely excited when one enters the aviary and checks the nest box. For the night these beautiful birds like to retire into a tree hole or nest box. Recently imported birds can't be kept at a temperature below 20°C. They have overpowering voices and like to gnaw wood. The female lays 3-6 eggs and incubates them for about 27 days. After 8 weeks the young leave the nest. Nest box 40 cm high, 25 cm wide, and 25 cm long; entrance diameter 8 cm. After they have left the nest, while they are still fed by both parents, young birds like to spend the night in the original nesting box.

157 ARATINGA GUAROUBA
Queen's, Bavaria's, or golden, conure

Classification Order Psittaciformes, Family Psittacidae.
Characteristics Length: 34 cm (13½ in). An overall brilliant golden-yellow, with green flight feathers. Eyes brown, beak pale horn-colored, legs pinkish-white. Young have green ear coverts and cheeks; through the yellow, green feathers are visible. The male has a larger upper mandible.
Habitat Tropical rain forests; usually in pairs or small groups, high in the tree tops.
Distribution Northeastern Brazil, south of the Amazon River.
Captivity This species is one of the rarest, most expensive, and most striking of all conures. The bird is uncommon in captivity. Only the hen incubates the 2-3 eggs, but usually the male roosts during the evening and at night with her in the nesting box. Towards their own species, they are tolerant, but not towards other birds. They love fruits, and in the wild their feathers are often stained with fruit juice. They prefer a long nest box or a hollow tree trunk (60-65/70 cm deep); the bottom should be covered with a layer of moist peat moss and dry leaves. Incubation time 28-30 days. The young leave the nest after about 45 days. The parents are very close, and the male often covers his partner with one of his wings, especially prior to mating.

158 ARATINGA ACUTICAUDATA
Blue-crowned conure

Classification Order Psittaciformes, Family Psittacidae.
Characteristics Length: 37 cm (14½ in). Green with yellow through the green on the underparts. Forecrown and forehead bluish. White eye ring. Eyes light brown, beak horn-colored, legs pink-brown.
Habitat Forest, close to farmland and orchards; sometimes in large flocks.
Distribution Northern Venezuela, eastern Colombia, and Brazil.
Captivity The hen lays 3 eggs in a long nest box or hollow tree trunk. Incubation time about 24 days. The young leave the nest in approximately 8 weeks and will be fed only by the male. They become very affectionate and even learn to speak a few words; I regard this species as one of the most intelligent of all the conures, although they have a rather overpowering voice. Sometimes young birds have red spots on the shoulders or on the edge of their wings; a color that is lacking completely in their parents. Hybrids between this species and *A. aurea* and *A. finschi* are possible. Fruits, berries, and such are essential.

159 ARATINGA CANICULARIS
Petz's, or orange-fronted, conure

Classification Order Psittaciformes, Family Psittacidae.
Characteristics Length: 24 cm (9½ in). Green; forehead orange; crown gray-blue. Sides of the head and throat olive-brown. Breast, belly, and underwing coverts yellowish-green. Periophthalmic ring orange-yellow. Eyes yellow, beak horn-colored, legs gray-brown. The iris of young birds is brownish, and the orange on the forehead less pronounced.
Habitat Forests. Nests in termite mounds abandoned woodpecker holes, and such. They occur in large flocks (up to and exceeding 200 birds). They live off fruits, figs, nuts, seeds, berries, blossoms, and insects.
Distribution Western Central America; in 3 subspecies.
Captivity The hen lays 3-5 eggs. Incubation about 30 days. After 6 weeks the young leave the nest. Only the hen incubates (after the first egg); during the night the male sleeps on the nest. Both parents feed the young. Nice birds, although their voice is loud and discordant. They become very affectionate towards their owner. Breeding successes are rare. Present a hollow tree trunk or a large nest box (40 × 35 × 40 cm; entrance diameter 10 cm). Hybrids with *Nandayus nenday* are possible.

160 ARATINGA AUREA
Golden-crowned, or peach-fronted, conure

Classification Order Psittaciformes, Family Psittacidae.
Characteristics Length: 28 cm (11¼ in). Crown yellow-orange, bordered with blue. Orange eye ring. Dark green neck and rump; the balance of the bird primarily pale with a yellowish-green belly. Blue shades can be seen shining through on wing feathers. Inside of the wings green to yellowish-green. Eyes orange to brown, beak and legs grayish-black. The young resemble the parents.
Habitat Savannah woodland and open country, in pairs or flocks (up to 30 birds). They are not shy.
Distribution South Surinam; Brazil, mainly south of the Amazon River; eastern Bolivia; north Paraguay; and the northwestern portion of Argentina; in 2 subspecies of which the *A. a. major* lives in the vicinity of the Paraguay River. This bird is somewhat larger than the nominate form.
Captivity The female lays 2-6 eggs. Both partners incubate the eggs; incubation time 26 days. After 50 days the young leave the nest box (35 × 22 × 25 cm; entrance diameter 8 cm). Two broods per season are possible. After the young have left the nest, remove all fellow species from the aviary, because the male will very actively defend his young. These birds become rapidly attached to their keeper and can even be taught to speak a few words. Hybrids with *A. canicularis*, *A. pertinax aeruginosa*, *A. solstitialis*, *A. jandaya* and *Myiopsitta monachus* are possible.

161 NANDAYUS NENDAY
Nandaya, black-headed, or black-masked, conure

Classification Order Psittaciformes, Family Psittacidae.
Characteristics Length: 30 cm (12 in). Green; blackish-blue cap. Light green color traversed with black below the eye. Some blue on throat and upper breast. Flight feathers bluish-black. Olive-green tail with bluish-black point; tail very dark green underneath. Thighs red. Eyes reddish-brown, beak blackish-gray, legs brownish-pink.
Habitat Savannahs, woodland, palm country, and rice fields; sometimes in very large flocks.
Distribution Paraguay, North Argentina, and southeast Bolivia. In the Mato Grosso often with *Myiopsitta monachus*. Nests in tree holes.
Captivity Providing their accommodation is roomy, these birds will breed quite readily. Do not hang the nest box (30 × 30 × 40 cm; entrance diameter 8 cm) too high, because they like sitting on top of them to watch the world go by, while making very loud commentary. When the female is incubating the eggs (25 days), the male sits for hours in silence on top of the box. The hen lays 2-5 eggs. During incubation the male likes to sleep on the nest at night. The young leave the nest after 7 weeks. This species can be kept together with finches and likes to take a bath or hop around in a rain shower. As a pet it can be tamed; it is regarded as a good talker.

162 PYRRHURA FRONTALIS
Red-bellied, or maroon-bellied, conure

Classification Order Psittaciformes, Family Psittacidae.
Characteristics Length: 26 cm (10 in). Green on top and back; sometimes clearly visible red feathers on forehead; the area around the eye brownish-yellow. Some blue on the wings, which are otherwise green; tail reddish-brown; abdomen brownish-red. Eyes dark brown, beak grayish-brown, legs gray. Eye ring white.
Habitat Forests, farmland, orchards, and corn fields; in sometimes very large flocks.
Distribution Southeastern Brazil, Uruguay, Paraguay, and northern Argentina; in 3 subspecies.
Captivity This bird can be kept in either a large aviary (often with other psittacines) or a roomy cage (by itself or as pair). When they first arrive, they are restless and sometimes quite wild, constantly flying against the wire or bars. It is therefore important that recently imported birds are housed in a roomy aviary with lots of shrubbery and left alone so that the other aviary inhabitants can make them feel at home. Once they become accustomed to captivity and the diet, they will grow very affectionate and will very likely soon come to take some delicious morsel from your hand. The hen lays 4-6 eggs—when housed in an aviary of at least 2 × 2 × 2 m, without any other birds. Incubation time 26-28 days. After 6-8 weeks the young leave the nest and will be taken care of by the male. In large aviaries a few pairs may be housed together.

163 PYRRHURA LEUCOTIS
White-eared conure

Classification Order Psittaciformes, Family Psittacidae.
Characteristics Length: 23 cm (9 in). Head, the area around the beak, and the sides of the face dark brown. Striking grayish-white line by the ears, and a reddish-brown crown. Neck and throat bright blue, shading to green. Black and white "semicircles" following the shape of the feathers run crosswise from the throat down almost to the abdomen. Belly reddish-brown; tail brownish; wings blue and green. Eyes brownish-red, beak grayish-black, and legs black. Yellowish-white cere.

Habitat High in trees of tropical and subtropical forests; in small groups, up to about 25 birds. They consume insects, larvae, and termites, as well as fruits and seeds.
Distribution North Venezuela and eastern Brazil. They have been introduced into the Rio de Janeiro Botanic Gardens.

Captivity Very pleasant birds and easily tameable. The female lays 5-9 eggs, which only she incubates. A closed nest box (possibly of beech) that measures 25 × 35 cm (entrance diameter 6 cm) would be ideal. Incubation time 22 days; after 5 weeks the young leave the nest. During the incubation time, the male stays on the nest at night and feeds his partner during the day. Once the young have hatched, I highly recommend you supplement the menu with soaked, stale white bread; cooked corn; sunflower seeds; boiled potatoes; a little hemp and oats, and, once a week, a sliced carrot.

---

164 DEROPTYUS ACCIPITRINUS
Hawk-headed parrot

Classification Order Psittaciformes, Family Psittacidae.
Characteristics Length: 35 cm (13¾ in). Green. Front of head white; back and nape maroon with blue edges. Breast and abdomen reddish with blue edges. At the base of the upper tail, a reddish patch. The female is smaller and has a smaller beak. Her eye ring is paler. Eyes yellow, beak grayish-black, legs gray.

Habitat Open tropical forests; not uncommon. Solitary, in pairs, or small flocks. They breed in hollow tree trunks, old woodpecker nests, and such.
Distribution Northern South America, east Venezuela, Guyana to the eastern parts of Ecuador, and the northern and parts of the southern banks of the Amazon River. Two subspecies. The *D. a. fuscifrons* has a brownish forehead.
Captivity The only parrot able to raise a fan of feathers on its head, which occurs when the bird is angry or extremely pleased. Tame birds like to raise their neck feathers as soon as they are scratched on the head with a finger. They are very gentle and lovable creatures, although expensive. They love a variety of foods: seeds, nuts, fruit—figs, grapes, oranges—fresh twigs of willow and fruit trees, etc. Breeding successes in captivity are rare. The hen lays 2-3 eggs, which only she incubates for 28 days. After 9 weeks the young leave the nest. A rather rare species in captivity.

165 RHYNCHOPSITTA PACHYRHYNCHA
Thick-billed parrot

Classification Order Psittaciformes, Family Psittacidae.
Characteristics Length: 38 cm (15 in). Probably related to the genus *Ara*. Green with yellow shine on cheeks and ear coverts. Forehead, bend of wing, carpal edge, and thighs red. Greater underwing coverts yellow. Eyes orange-yellow, beak black, legs gray.
Habitat Highland and pine forests. Feed on the cones of pines. Occur in pairs or small flocks. Nest in hollow tree trunks and woodpecker nests. Due to pine forest clearances, it is unlikely that this species will ever move back into southern Arizona and southwestern New Mexico.
Distribution Northern and Central Mexico; in 2 subspecies. The *R. p. terrisi* is somewhat taller and darker in color.
Captivity Very destructive in an aviary. Breeding successes are extremely rare. The hen lays 2-4 eggs; incubation time about 26 days. Only the hen incubates, although the male likes to go into the nest to stay with his partner. Young will leave the nest after about 85 days. In addition to sunflower seed, corn, white seed, hulled oats, and corn on the cob, *Pinus* seeds are essential, as well as fruits (apple, orange, papaya), a daily slice of whole-wheat bread, carrot, and some peanuts.

166 CYANOLISEUS PATAGONUS
Patagonian conure

Classification Order Psittaciformes, Family Psittacidae.
Characteristics Length: 45 cm (17¾ in). Mainly olive-brown; belly yellowish with a reddish patch. White eye ring. Eyes yellowish-white, beak gray, legs flesh-colored.
Habitat Rocky areas of the Andes. Nests in crevices and small hollows; the people of Argentina often call this bird the "bank-burrowing parrot," because it sometimes burrows up to 3 m deep into the limestone of a cliff or bank to nest. Sociable; lives in colonies, nesting close together.
Distribution Argentina, Chile, and Uruguay. During cold winters the species migrates as far as Uruguay. Three subspecies.
Captivity This species is usually very expensive; extremely noisy and destructive. Not suitable to keep with other birds. Needs a large aviary. The hen lays 2-3 eggs; incubation time 25 days. After 55-60 days the young leave the nest and are independant after another 3 weeks. Nest box: 75 cm long, 25 cm wide, and 25 cm high; entrance diameter 10 cm. After the young are hatched, the male commences to feed his offspring, but also spends quite some time on the nest. This species is very hardy and needs a daily supply of twigs (fruit trees and willow) and thick branches to satisfy its desire to chew. Strong netting and an aviary of metal is therefore essential.

167 MYIOPSITTA MONACHUS
Quaker, or monk, or gray-breasted, parrakeet

Classification Order Psittaciformes, Family Psittacidae.
Characteristics Length: 30 cm (12 in). Forehead, crown, and occiput grayish-blue; cheeks, and lores pale gray. Back of head, neck, back, rump, wings, and tail parrot-green. Eyes dark brown, beak brown, legs gray.
Habitat Lowland, open forests, along water courses, savannahs, woods, orchards, and farmland. Is released and/or introduced into many parts of the world.
Distribution Southern Brazil to central Argentina. A resident population introduced into southeastern New York, New Jersey, and Connecticut (USA); nests have been recorded in Massachusetts, Virginia, and Florida (USA).
Captivity Peaceful and pleasant bird which tames quite readily. Their reputation as screamers is somewhat exaggerated. The birds (the only species of parrot to build a proper nest) will be unlikely to breed unless their housing has very generous dimensions and shrubbery is plentiful. Their bullet-shaped nest is very large with an entrance protected with a small portico. The nest itself consists of two rooms. The 4-8 eggs are incubated by the hen in the "back room". The room that leads to the portico could be cosidered a "living room." Colony breeder. Incubation time 26 days. After 6 weeks the the young leave the nest. Uses nest boxes as well (15 × 30 × 45 cm; entrance diameter 8 cm). There are blue and yellow mutations available.

---

168 BOLBORHYNCHUS LINEOLA
Lineolated, or Catherine, or barred, parrakeet

Classification Order Psittaciformes, Family Psittacidae.
Characteristics Length: 17 cm (6¾ in). Green with black shell-shaped markings on the head, neck, back, rump, and along the wings. Feathers of the wings bordered with black. The smaller hen has the same black markings, although they are petite and less sharply defined. Eyes yellowish-brown, beak grayish-yellow, legs grayish-black.
Habitat Dense forests at an altitude of 2,000 m. They are excellent runners and will press themselves close to the ground in case of danger. They nest in hollow tree trunks and occur occasionally in large flocks.
Distribution Mexico, Panama, Colombia and Peru.
Captivity These gentle, pleasant-voiced, birds become tame very quickly and leave all signs of timidity behind. They have a strong constitution. The hen lays 4-5 eggs in a nest box (15 × 15 × 30 cm; entrance diameter 6 cm) incubation time 22-23 days. After 38 days the young leave the nest. Although the male doesn't brood, he is very involved and feeds his partner and later his young. The young are independent after about 6 weeks. The nest box will be used throughout the year as sleeping quarters. They do well in a community aviary and are basically very tolerant birds. When they become excited, they show their emotions by fanning their tail. They live on oats, panicum canary seeds, fresh twigs (apple, pear, and willow), fruit berries, and small insects.

169 BOLBORHYNCHUS AURIFRONS
Golden-fronted, or mountain, parrakeet

Classification Order Psittaciformes, Family Psittacidae.
Characteristics Length: 17 cm (6¾ in). Green; yellowish on the underside and around beak and eyes. Females and young lack the yellow. Eyes brown, beak horn-colored, legs brownish.
Habitat Coastal plains and Andean slopes, gardens, parks, orchards, and farmland; sometimes in large flocks. Nests in hollow tree trunks and sometimes in burrows excavated in banks (tunnels more than 2 m deep have been found with two-chambers one of which was used as a "maternity room").
Distribution Central and south Peru, central Bolivia, north and Central Chile, and northwestern Argentina. Four subspecies.
Captivity Friendly birds. Like to nest in budgerigar nest boxes or long, horizontally placed boxes (15 × 15 × 25 cm with a long entrance tunnel of 80 cm; entrance diameter 8 cm) with two separated chambers; only a small opening (diameter 8 cm) connects both chambers. Breeding successes however are rare. The female lays 3-4 eggs; incubation time 23 days. During the whole year, sunflower seeds, hemp, grass seeds, greens, and fruits (apple, banana, and orange) are essential.

---

170 BROTOGERIS VERSICOLURUS CHIRIRI
Canary-winged parrakeet

Classification Order Psittaciformes, Family Psittacidae.
Characteristics Length: 23-25 cm (9⅕-10 in). Primarily green, darker on breast and belly. Outermost wing-feather edges, epaulet, and primaries bright yellow. Underside of tail blue. Eyes dark brown, beak light horn-colored, legs pinkish-red. There may be some blue on the wings. Young birds are duller, particularly the blue and yellow hues.
Habitat In flocks, up to about 50 birds, close to forests and towns.
Distribution East and south Brazil, north and east Bolivia, Paraguay, and north Argentina.
Captivity One of the reasons these birds breed so well is their friendly and peaceful nature. The beechwood nest box (20 × 20 × 40 cm; entrance diameter 8 cm) should be equipped with a 4-cm-thick layer of moist peat moss. In order to assure the best possible breeding results, the nest boxes should be hung in the outside flight and not in the night shelter. The female lays 5-6 eggs; incubation time 23 days; after 7-8 weeks the young leave the nest. During the night the male stays on the nest. The young also like to sleep on the nest after they have fledged. Providing they receive good and proper care, the species can become tame in just a few weeks. It is a pity that they have a fairly loud, somewhat raucous call. The nominate form (*B. v. versicolorus* or white-winged parrakeet) is also found in captivity and requires the same care.

171 BROTOGERIS JUGULARIS
Tovi, bee-bee, or orange-chinned, parrakeet

Classification Order Psittaciformes, Family Psittacidae.
Characteristics Length: 18-20 cm (7^1/$_5$-8 in). Green; clear yellow patch on throat. Wing coverts greenish-brown; balance bluish-green. Primaries dark blue. Inside of wings bright yellow, except for a few large greenish-blue feathers. Eyes brown, beak grayish-black, legs dark flesh-colored. The young resemble the adult birds once they have lost their grayish nest down.
Habitat In pairs, small families or groups, up to about 30 birds in the woods. They will go up to about 1,400 m above sea level in the mountains—where they look for fruit, soft leaf buds, twigs, and berries. The young are also raised, for the most part, on soft fruits. They are fond of insects. Sometimes nest in termites' nests.
Distribution Southwestern Mexico to Colombia, Venezuela, east Ecuador, and northeastern Peru; in 2 subspecies.
Captivity Because of their pleasant nature, they make excellent aviary birds; they cannot tolerate draft and wind very well. During the winter months, they should be placed in a large cage indoors. The female lays 3-6 eggs; incubation time 21 days. After 35 days the young leave the nest box; budgerigar boxes are used as are 25-gallon drums (see *Agapornis pullaria*).

172 FORPUS COELESTIS
Celestial, or pacific, parrotlet

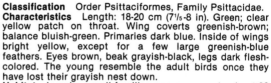

Classification Order Psittaciformes, Family Psittacidae.
Characteristics Length: 12 cm (4^3/$_4$ in). Green. Quite a lot of blue in the wings. Rump also blue; a narrow blue band runs along the back of the neck. Eyes brown, beak grayish-white, legs pinkish. The female lacks the blue in the wings, but has a blue rump and the blue neckband; much less clearly defined than in the male.
Habitat Woody areas, although thick rain forests are avoided. They operate in colonies, and breed in hollow trees or branches, holes in the ground, or in nests of the ovenbird (*Furnarius leucopus*).
Distribution West Ecuador and northwestern Peru; in 2 subspecies.
Captivity Can be kept with several pairs together as long as no breeding goals are pursued. Newly imported birds must be kept at room temperature. They like to attack each other's legs, especially during the breeding season. Ideal as cage bird; even breeding successes are possible. Present a pair with a normal budgerigar nest box and place some peat moss or wood shavings on the bottom. The hen lays 4-6 eggs which she incubates for 17-21 days. After about 30 days the young leave the nest. A good pair usually breeds twice or three times a year, starting in April. Many species (*F. cyanopygius*, *F. passerinus*, *F. xanthopterygius* among others) are very popular among aviculturists.

173 AMAZONA ALBIFRONS
White-fronted, or spectacled, Amazon parrot

Classification Order Psittaciformes, Family Psittacidae.
Characteristics Length: 27 cm (10¼ in). Green with dark-edged plumage. White forehead; blue crown. Lores and periophthalmic area scarlet. Red patch on primary coverts and alula. Eyes yellow, beak yellowish, legs pale gray. Wings are usually totally green in females.
Habitat Slopes, dry country, lowland, foothills, and lower mountains; sometimes close to water; in pairs or small groups, but also with thousands together in certain roosting spots. They live on figs, nuts, berries, blossoms, fruits, seeds, etc. It is reported that they are a pest to farmers. Little is known of their nesting habits.
Distribution Mexico to western Costa Rica; in 3 subspecies.
Captivity Very little is known about this bird. There are old breeding records available, but the only real successes have been extremely rare. Solitary, they can be excellent pets and good talkers, especialy when purchased young. Old birds remain noisy and will constantly raise their nape feathers when excited. The only way to accomplish breeding success is by placing several birds together in a large aviary where they can choose their own partners. Those pairs are then separated and placed in their own roomy aviary. Provide hollow tree trunks, barrels, or nest boxes of thick hardwood timber (35 × 35 × 45 cm; entrance diameter 10 cm).

174 AMAZONA VIRIDIGENALIS
Green-cheeked Amazon parrot or Mexican red-headed parrot

Classification Order Psittaciformes, Family Psittacidae.
Characteristics Length: 33 cm (13 in). Green. Feathers with black edges. Red forehead. Blue crown and blue around the ear coverts. Red wing coverts; primaries with blue tips. Green tail with yellow tip. Eyes yellow, beak pale yellow, legs green-gray. Young birds have a red forehead.
Habitat Woodland, along forests, and in low country. Generally near water. Like to forage in cypress or acacia trees, in pairs or large flocks.
Distribution Northern Mexico south to Veracruz.
Captivity Gentle birds; very popular with aviculturists. Usually fairly good talkers. Their courtship behavior—in the wild in March—is accompanied by much shrieking and pecking at each other. Hybridizing with *A. albifrons* succeeded in 1934; three of the four young survived. Provide a pair (housed in a good-sized aviary) with a roomy barrel or nest box (see *A. aestiva*). The female lays 2-3 eggs. Incubation time about 26 days. The young leave the nest after approximately 68 days. These parrots need large sunflower seeds, boiled maize (corn), some hemp, oats, wheat, white seed, millet, walnuts, hazel nuts, ground nuts, fruits, and greens year round. Various berries, such as black currants, rowan berries, bilberries, gooseberries, and strawberries, are essential.

175 AMAZONA FINSCHI
Finsch's, or lilac-crowned, Amazon parrot

Classification Order Psittaciformes, Family Psittacidae.
Characteristics Length: 32 cm (12½ in). Green; forehead and lores red; crown and neck blue. All feathers on the underside are dark edged. There is no red in the tail. Eyes orange, beak horn-colored, legs greenish-gray.
Habitat Wooded foothills and mountains; up to an altitude of 2,200 m. After the turn of the century, very common in flocks numbering several hundreds of birds.
Distribution Western Mexico; in 2 subspecies.
Captivity Bred in the US in the San Diego (Calif.) Zoo; the incubation time was 28 days; after 4 weeks the young were independent. One chick was handraised for 3 months (1951). Another breeding report stated that the young left the nest box after they were about 2 months old. Many birds are imported yearly. Recently imported young birds require boiled rice, corn on the cob, sprouting sunflower seeds, and a variety of fruits.

AQMSBUKQ
D PVKH

---

176 AMAZONA AUTUMNALIS
Yellow-cheeked Amazon parrot

Classification Order Psittaciformes, Family Psittacidae.
Characteristics Length: 35 cm (13¼ in). Green with black edges on the nape feathers. Red forehead and lores. Bluish crown, yellowish beneath the eyes. Red in small primaries. Eyes orange, beak yellowish, legs gray.
Habitat Lowlands; in flocks that may number from a few birds to over 100. The birds are extremely active during the day. They feed on fruits, berries, nuts, and seeds. They are especially numerous around the Amazon River basin.
Distribution Eastern and central Mexico and Brazil; in 4 subspecies.
Captivity Gentle bird, well-known to aviculturists; breeding successes are, however, very rare. The female lays 2-3 eggs; incubation time about 26-28 days. After approximately 10 days the young will open their eyes; at 7 weeks they already resemble their parents, and after 3 months they are independent. The birds like a closed barrel as "maternity room," with a nest opening 25 cm in diameter; or a nest log of 50 × 50 × 70 cm; opening diameter 15 cm.

AQMSBUKQ
D PVKH

177 AMAZONA AESTIVA
Blue-fronted Amazon parrot

Classification Order Psittaciformes, Family Psittacidae.
Characteristics Length: 36-38 cm (14-15 in). Green; bluish forehead, yellow throat, cheeks, and crown. Red or yellow bend of wing; wing coverts red. Eyes orange, beak blackish, legs gray. The heads of the young are a diluted green, blue, and yellow. The bend of wing (actually the upperwing edge) is much paler and the iris is black.
Habitat Wooded areas. Plentiful, although due to deforestation, their status has become dangerously affected.
Distribution Brazil, Bolivia, and Paraguay; in 2 subspecies.
Captivity Known as one of the most popular pets, with an excellent talking and mimic ability. Breeding successes are plentiful. The female lays 2-3 eggs, which she incubates for about 29 days. The male feeds her while she is incubating. Use a hollow log or nest box (40 × 40 × 150 cm) with a layer of peat mold. During the breeding season the pair is quite aggressive towards other birds, therefore they are best kept in roomy outdoor aviaries. After about 3 months the young leave the nest, but will continue to be fed for quite some time. Fruits, berries, greens, corn on the cob, and germinated sunflower seeds are essential, even outside the breeding season. At the time of writing (1984) there were pale blue, lutino, and pied-yellow hybrids.

---

178 AMAZONA OCHROCEPHALA
Yellow-fronted Amazon parrot

Classification Order Psittaciformes, Family Psittacidae.
Characteristics Length: 40 cm (15¾ in). Green; crown light golden-yellow. Red wing coverts, bend, and edge of wing. Eyes orange, beak grayish with orange on the side of the upper mandible, legs gray. There are many different color variations and possibly many subspecies.
Habitat Woodland, cultivated fields, forests, and savannahs; in pairs or flocks. Strong flyers. Feed on nuts, seeds (corn), fruits, berries, and blossoms. They nest in tree holes, termite nests, or in holes in the ground. During the breeding season copulation may occur several times per day.
Distribution Mexico, Central America, and tropical South America; in 9 subspecies.
Captivity Becomes very tame and is seldom malicious. Likes human company and is a very good talker and imitator, although not all specimens are intelligent. Breeding successes are still rare. Supply sturdy nest boxes of 45 × 45 × 75 cm; entrance diameter 14 cm. The female lays and incubates 2-3 eggs. Incubation time 28-30 days. The young leave the nest after about 75 days. There is an almost pure lutino in captivity, as well as a beautiful blue mutation (with a white forehead) of *A. o. panamensis*. This subspecies has a yellow forehead and a bluish sheen in the green neck feathers; it is well-known in aviculture primarily because the bird is highly intelligent.

179 AMAZONA VINACEA
Vinaceous Amazon parrot

Classification Order Psittaçiformes, Family Psittacidae.
Characteristics Length: 36 cm (14 in). Green; all feathers are black-edged. Forehead, chin, and lores red. Upper throat, breast and, sometimes, the abdomen, purple-red. Nape feathers bluish. Eyes orange-red, beak red with a horn-colored tip on the upper mandible, legs gray. The female is darker tinged, and the beak is less red. The young have pale red lores, and the beak is red only at the base; the iris is yellow.
Habitat Forest.
Distribution Southeastern Brazil and Paraguay.
Captivity Gentle, affectionate bird, but, as a rule, not a good talker. Only young birds are easily tamed. Due to deforestation their natural biotope is dangerously affected, and therefore the export of this species is forbidden. The bird is now on List B (Vulnerable) of the Washington Convention. There are still many pet birds in Europe and the US available, it is therefore time that aviculturists combine their efforts to save this species from extinction. The birds breed in captivity without too many problems. The female lays 2-3 eggs; both parents feed the young, which hatch after about 28 days. High-protein baby cereal and bread soaked in honey-water are essential during the breeding season; also necessary are sunflower seeds, monkey chow, fruits (banana, apple, tomato) and greens. Willow twigs are necessary throughout the year.

180 PIONUS MENSTRUUS
Blue-headed parrot

Classification Order Psittaciformes, Family Psittacidae.
Characteristics Length: 27 cm (10½ in). Green; head and neck blue; ear-coverts black. Undertail coverts red; large green tail tips. Eyes brown, beak blackish with red on the sides, legs greenish-gray. The young frequently have a red neck band; the beak is horn-colored. The young are much duller in coloration and don't as yet have the blue head feathers.
Habitat Lightly timbered country, farmland, foothills, forests. Sometimes in large flocks in search of ripe fruits or corn. During the breeding period in pairs.
Distribution Southern Costa Rica, Panama, North Bolivia and central Brazil; also found in Trinidad; in 3 subspecies.
Captivity Well-known and loved in aviculture for many years. Imported birds must be carefully acclimatized. Young birds especially become very tame and affectionate. Excellent as a cage bird because their voice is soft. In a community aviary friendly towards other species. The female lays 2-4 eggs; incubation time 26 days. Greens (dandelion, lettuce, chickweed, spinach), fruits, fresh branches, oats, millets, sunflower seeds, and ground nuts are essential. They use a normal wooden nest box (35 × 35 × 40 cm; entrance diameter 10 cm).

181 PIONUS MAXIMILIANI
Maximilian's, or scaly-headed, parrot

Classification Order Psittaciformes, Family Psittacidae.
Characteristics Length: 29 cm (11½ in). Like *P. menstruus*; with green head-feathers edged with blue. Blue throat band. Forehead and lores almost black. Naked periophthalmic ring with two white areas above and below the eye and two dark areas on either side of the eye. Red undertail coverts. Eyes brown, beak horn-colored with lighter colors on the edges, feet and legs gray.
Habitat Light forest and open woodland; in pairs or small or large flocks; groups of up to 50 birds have been seen.
Distribution Southeastern Brazil and northern Argentina; in 4 subspecies.
Captivity Relatively uncommon in aviculture. In an aviary a true pair comes to brood easily and is not aggressive towards keeper and other birds. For further details see *P. menstruus*.

---

182 PIONUS CHALCOPTERUS
Bronze-winged parrot

Classification Order Psittaciformes, Family Psittacidae.
Characteristics Length: 28 cm (11 in). Navy blue; white patch on the throat. Forehead feathers with pink edges. Red undertail coverts. Periophthalmic ring pink, and deep pink during the breeding season. Eyes brown, beak yellowish, legs brownish-pink.
Habitat Mountain forests, in pairs or small flocks.
Distribution Northwestern Venezuela, western Colombia, Ecuador, and northwestern Peru; in 2 subspecies.
Captivity Occasionally available. Gentle but nervous birds which sometimes come to brood in a small garden aviary, although large flights are recommended. Success, however, is not always guaranteed. Due to stress, they often preen each other's head to such an extent that after the birds have been separated it may take months before the lost feathers are properly replaced. The female lays 2-4 eggs; incubation time about 26 days. Although the hen incubates, the male spends time on the nest, sitting next to his mate. For more details see *P. menstruus*.

183 PIONITES MELANOCEPHALA
Black-headed caique

Classification Order Psittaciformes, Family Psittacidae
Characteristics Length: 23 cm (9 in). Green; black forehead and crown; lores and streak under the eyes grass-green; cheeks, chin, throat, ear coverts, nape, and hindneck yellow; breast and belly white; abdomen, thighs, and undertail coverts orange-yellow. Blue-gray periophthalmic ring. Eyes orange, beak grayish-black, legs gray. The female's eye ring is paler.
Habitat Savannahs and forests, near rivers, in flocks or family parties. Quite noisy.
Distribution Eastern Venezuela, northeastern Peru, southwestern Colombia, the Guianas, and north Pará (Brazil); in 2 subspecies.
Captivity Beautiful birds which sometimes have very powerful voices. Only young specimens can be tamed. Recently imported birds are extremely delicate, but once acclimatized they appear to be hardy. They must have a nest box to roost in (35 × 25 × 30 cm; entrance diameter 6 cm) which they will use as "maternity quarters" as well. The female lays 2-4 eggs; incubation time 23 days. After about 60 days the young leave the nest. During the breeding season males can be quite aggressive. Hybridization between the *melanocephala* and *leucogaster* has occurred. Germinated seeds (sunflower, millet, pine cones, etc.), fruits, berries, nuts, buds, and fresh branches are essential, especially during the rearing of the young.

184 PIONITES LEUCOGASTER
White-bellied, or white-breasted, caique

Classification Order Psittaciformes, Family Psittacidae.
Characteristics Length: 23 cm (9 in). Green. Yellowish-orange head, darker on crown and neck. White breast and belly; primaries bluish. Green abdomen and thighs. Yellow undertail coverts; periophthalmic ring pale pink. Eyes red, beak light horn-colored, legs pink.
Habitat Forests, near water; in pairs, family parties or small flocks.
Distribution Eastern Venezuela, eastern Peru, eastern Colombia, and parts of Guyana; in 3 subspecies.
Captivity Not as common as *P. melanocephala*. Both species, however, love to take a shower in the rain or a bath in an earthen dish. It is advisable to keep these birds indoors during the winter at a temperature of about 22°C. For further details see *P. melanocephala*.

185 CHALCOPSITTA ATRA
Black lory

Classification Order Psittaciformes, Family Psittacidae.
Characteristics Length: 32 cm (12½ in). Black with purple sheen. Eyes orange-red, beak black, legs gray.
Habitat Forest edges, savannahs, and grassland; in pairs or small flocks. They like to bicker in a high-pitched voice.
Distribution Papua New Guinea (Western Vogelkop), West Irian, and the islands of Batanta and Salawati; in 4 subspecies.
Captivity Quite aggressive towards other birds, but gentle when kept as pair in an aviary, although some mated couples remain dangerously aggressive. After acclimatization usually quiet and pleasant. During the winter they must be housed indoors (22°C), as they are very susceptible to cold and humidity. During the summer they must have the opportunity to roost in a large nest box (40 × 40 × 50 cm; entrance diameter 10 cm). The female lays 2 eggs; incubation time about 23 days. The young leave the nest when they are approximately 2 months old. Nectar, mixed with wheat-germ cereal, and milk are necessary on a daily basis during the breeding season. For food details see *C. duivenbodei*.

186 CHALCOPSITTA DUIVENBODEI
Duivenbode's lory

Classification Order Psittaciformes, Family Psittacidae.
Characteristics Length: 29 cm (11 in). Extremely colorful; dark brown with a golden sheen. Orange and yellow on forehead, throat, bend of wing, underwing coverts, and thighs. Blue-violet rump. The yellow markings on the outer tail feathers are often missing in females. Eyes reddish, beak black, legs dark gray.
Habitat Lowland, up to about 200 meters.
Distribution Northern parts of Papua New Guinea; in 2 subspecies.
Captivity Newly imported birds must be acclimatized with care and housed indoors at a temperature of about 24°C. The aviary must be long, e.g., 5-6 m minimum. Fruit pulp is essential all year: in a 2-liter plastic container combine 1 part pulp (apple, pear, strawberries, pineapple, carrots, cucumber) with 1 part each rice flour, commercial bird egg food and universal food, and baby cereal. Mix with blender and add 1 teaspoon glucose, 10 teaspoons honey, a tablespoon of a reliable multivitamin product, 1½ ounces of seaweed and 3 ounces of rose-hip extract. Add water until the mixture is the consistency of yogurt. Store in freezer, but serve it completely defrosted. In addition to this mixture, which must be presented twice a day (remove all old food), supply sunflower seed, millet spray, grass seeds, fresh branches, lettuce, chickweed, endive, raisions, grapes, corn on the cob, and cuttlefish bone.

187 CHALCOPSITTA SINTILLATA
Yellow-streaked lory

Classification   Order Psittaciformes, Family Psittacidae.
Characteristics   Length: 29 cm (11½ in). Dark green. Red forehead, crown, and lores, thighs, underwing coverts, and underside of tail feathers. Black ear coverts. Abdomen and neck with pale-green stripes; mantle and breast with golden-yellow stripes. On the sides of the breast red spots. Yellow band on flight feathers. Eyes orange-yellow, beak black, legs dark gray. The red is less extensive in females.
Habitat   Lowland, savannahs, and forests, usually near water; in pairs or small flocks (up to about 30 birds).
Distribution   Aru Islands and the southern parts of Papua New Guinea; in 3 subspecies.
Captivity   Breeding successes are rare. Care and feeding similar to other *Chalcopsitta* species.

188 EOS BORNEA
Red, or Moluccan, lory

Classification   Order Psittaciformes, Family Psittacidae.
Characteristics   Length: 25-30 cm (10-12 in). Red with blue vent and undertail coverts. Partly black and red primary and secondary wing feathers. Blue greater wing coverts. Eyes red, beak orange, legs dark gray.
Habitat   Flowering trees; in sometimes large flocks.
Distribution   Ambon, Saparua, Goram, Ceramlaut, Watubela and Kai Islands (Indonesia); in 4 subspecies.
Captivity   Gentle birds with a harsh voice. Once acclimatized they can be kept in an outdoor aviary. During the winter the birds must be housed inside, at about 24°C. They birds are very playful. They roost in a nest box (25-33 × 35 × 45 cm; entrance diameter 8 cm) and must be kept in pairs only, as they are aggressive towards other parrots. The female lays 2 eggs, which she incubates for approximately 24 days; the male sleeps in the nest, next to his mate, at night. Grass and weed seeds are essential. The young leave the nest after about 3 months, but will be fed by both parents for another 2-3 weeks. For diet details see Duivenbode's lory.

189 EOS SQUAMATA
Violet-necked, or violet-naped, lory

Classification Order Psittaciformes, Family Psittacidae.
Characteristics Length: 22-25 cm (9-10 in). Reddish to dull purple; bluish nape and throat band. Violet spot on the belly. Black markings on primary and secondary feathers. Red-purple uppertail coverts; underside red with brownish sheen. Eyes yellow to orange, beak orange-red, legs gray.
Habitat Coconut plantations and places with flowering *Erythrina* trees.

Distribution Schildpad Island, Gebe, Waigeu, Batanta and Mysol (Western Papuan Islands), and Halmahera (Indonesia).

Captivity These small lories are well-known, as they are playful, friendly, and not difficult to breed. In an indoor aviary with a long, outdoor flight, they often come to proper breeding results. The female lays 2 eggs; both parents incubate. Incubation time 24–26 days. The young leave the nest after 8–10 weeks, but receive much care after they have fledged. They molt after 8-10 months. Nest box: 25 × 25 × 45 cm; entrance diameter 8 cm. The bird must be fed baby cereal, honey, glucose, boiled rice, condensed milk, berries, soaked white bread, small pieces of carrot, and multivitamins; for more details see Duivenbode's lory.

---

190 LORIUS GARRULUS
Chattering lory

Classification Order Psittaciformes, Family Psittacidae.
Characteristics Length: 30 cm (12 in). Deep red. Wings and thighs brown-green. Bend of wing yellow, as are the underwing coverts. Pinkish band across the primary feathers. Uppertail feathers brown-green with blue tips. Eyes yellowish-brown to orange-red, beak orange, legs dark gray.

Habitat Around flowering coconut and palm trees; in pairs or flocks. Quite common.
Distribution Moluccas (Indonesia); in 3 subspecies.

Captivity Well-known in aviculture. Friendly and willing to breed. The female lays 2 eggs. Incubation time 26 days; the hen incubates during the day; at night both parents are in the nest; frequently the male only rests next to his mate, but doesn't incubate the eggs. After 2½ months the young leave the nest. The male can be hostile towards his young as soon as they have fledged. In addition to the food mentioned for the Duivenbode's lory, these birds must have access to fresh willow and fruit branches (preferably with blossoms), weed seed, chickweed, endive, and earthworms.

191 LORIUS LORY
Black-capped lory

Classification   Order Psittaciformes, Family Psittacidae.
Characteristics   Length: 30 cm (12 in). Red; blue hindneck band. Forehead, crown, and nape glossy black-purple. Wings bronze-green. Underparts of mantle dark blue. Yellow band across the flight feathers. Blue abdomen and undertail coverts. Eyes yellow to orange-red, beak orange-yellow, legs dark gray.
Habitat   Forests in lowland, sometimes up to 1,600 m; usually in large flocks. They live on nectar, insects, fruits, pollen, and seeds.
Distribution   Papua New Guinea, the Western Papuan Islands, and some islands in the Geelvink Bay; in 7 subspecies.
Captivity   Extremely popular birds; they are friendly (although they possess a harsh voice) and are willing to come to brood. They are fairly good talkers and can be kept alone in a cage. A pair will usually come to brood in an aviary with a lightly heated night shelter. The nest box must be made of thick wood (40 × 40 × 45 cm; entrance diameter 10 cm); they also use it as night quarters. For more details see Chattering lory.

192 LORIUS DOMICELLUS
Purple-capped, or purple-naped, lory

Classification   Order Psittaciformes, Family Psittacidae.
Characteristics   Length: 28 cm (11 in). Red with a black forehead and crown. Dark blue nape and hindneck. Wings brown-green; bend of wing with blue. Underwing coverts blue. Yellow band across underside of flight feathers, and one across the upper breast. Thighs violet-blue. Eyes brown to orange, beak orange, legs dark gray. Immature birds have black eyes and a black bill.
Habitat   Forests; usually in pairs.
Distribution   Ceram and Ambon Island (Indonesia); introduced into Buru.
Captivity   A well-known and loved lory. In a large flight with a roomy night shelter, they usually come to brood. The female lays 2 eggs; incubation time 24-26 days. After 11 weeks the young leave the nest. For more details see other lory species.

193 PSEUDEOS FUSCATA
Dusky lory

Classification Order Psittaciformes, Family Psittacidae.
Characteristics Length: 25 cm (10 in). Dusky olive-brown.
Yellow crown. Upper breast and hindneck feathers with
dull yellow edges. Yellow-orange throat band, and some
have a yellow band across the breast. Orange to yellow
abdomen and lower breast. Orange-red thighs. White rump
and back. Underwing coverts green, dark brown, and
yellowish. Undertail coverts bluish-purple. Two orange-
yellow bands across the flight feathers. Tail olive-yellow
with orange markings. Eyes red, beak dark orange, legs
dark gray.
Habitat Forest, savannah, and mountain ranges up to
2,000 m; in large flocks, which feed on flowering and/or
fruit-bearing trees.
Distribution Papua New Guinea, except the central area;
Salawati, on the western Papuan Islands; and on Japen
Island (Geelvink Bay).
Captivity Records show that even in a relatively small
cage (1 × 1 × 2 m) breeding is possible. The birds,
however, prefer a large aviary. They need a nest box of
25 × 25 × 45 cm; entrance diameter 9 cm. The female lays
2 eggs; incubation time 24 days. The young leave the nest
when about 10-12 weeks old, but will still receive food from
their parents for some time. After approximately 7 months
they have their adult plumage. For food details see Duivenbode's lory.

---

194 TRICHOGLOSSUS ORNATUS
Ornate lorikeet

Classification Order Psittaciformes, Family Psittacidae.
Characteristics Length: 25 cm (10 in). Dark green with
yellow-edged feathers on lower breast and belly. Dark blue
forehead. Red lores, chin, and breast; the last, with blue
edges. Yellow band on the neck behind the ear coverts.
Red occiput. Yellow underwing coverts. Eyes dark orange,
beak orange-red, legs greenish-gray.
Habitat Wooded mountain country, teak forest, and near
villages; in pairs or small flocks. Their food consists of
nectar, blossoms, pollen, fruits, greens, and some soft
seeds.
Distribution Sulawesi (formerly Celebes) and some
off-shore islands.
Captivity This small lory has become somewhat rare in
aviculture, although it was extremely popular in the 1960s
and early 1970s, and has a harsh voice; it must be carefully
acclimatized. The female lays 2 eggs; it is questionable
whether both parents incubate, although the male remains
in the nest during the night, sitting next to the hen.
Incubation time 26-27 days; after about 80 days the young
leave the nest.

195 TRICHOGLOSSUS HAEMATODUS MOLUCCANUS
Swainson's, rainbow, or blue mountain, lorikeet

Classification Order Psittaciformes, Family Psittacidae.
Characteristics Length: 30 cm (12 in). Dark blue to violet head with lighter-colored shafts. Nuchal collar yellowish-green. Breast scarlet with red and yellow markings. Abdomen dark blue. Flank red and yellow, edged with dark green. Thighs yellowish with green edges. Undertail coverts and underside of the tail yellow and green. Underwing coverts orange. Eyes orange-red, beak orange to dark red, legs greenish-gray to dark gray.
Habitat Lowlands, savannahs, woodlands, secondary forests, along water courses, and mountainous regions; also in gardens and parks in pairs or small (noisy) flocks.
Distribution This species is one of the 27 subspecies. *Moluccanus* inhabits northeastern Australia, eastern and southeastern Australia up to the Eyre Peninsula in the west, and Tasmania. At the Currumbin Sanctuary (near Brisbane), the birds are a real tourist attraction; so tame they sit on people's shoulders to take honey-soaked bread.
Captivity The majority of the breeding pairs are very prolific, as long as they are housed in a long aviary with a roomy night shelter; the temperature must be maintained at 24°C. The birds not only use nest boxes (25 × 25 × 40 cm; entrance diameter 8 cm), but also dig holes in the ground. The 2 eggs are incubated for about 24 days. For more information see the other lory species.

---

196 PROSOPEIA TABUENSIS TABUENSIS
Red-shining parrot

Classification Order Psittaciformes, Family Psittacidae.
Characteristics Length: 45 cm (18 in). Head and underparts crimson. Nape band blue, as are the primary wing feathers. Back, wings, rump, uppertail coverts, and tail green. Forehead, chin, and lores red. Eyes orange-red, beak black, legs dark gray. The young have a brownish iris and a yellow and black beak.
Habitat Rain forest, near villages; in pairs or flocks.
Distribution Kandavu (Fiji Islands) and introduced to Viti Levu.
Captivity Quite popular among experienced aviculturists, although the birds are protected under the Washington Convention, and therefore rare and expensive. Thanks to breeding successes, however, they are offered on the bird market quite regularly. They need wheat, white seed, milo, millet, sunflower seed, pine nuts, apple, blueberries, oranges, papaya, figs, lettuce, hydroponic barley, and bread. The female lays 2 eggs; incubation time about 26 days. They like a large natural log (50 × 50 × 65 cm; entrance diameter 10 cm) situated high in the (large) aviary flight.

197 TURDUS MERULA
Blackbird

Classification Order Passeriformes, Family Turdidae.
Characteristics Length: 25 cm (10 in). Male black with a yellow or orange beak. The female is dark brown, lighter on the underside; chin white; upper breast vaguely checkered. Brown beak. Eyes dark brown (the male has a yellow periophthalmic ring), feet gray-black. The young are more reddish and blackish speckled.
Habitat Gardens, orchards, parks, farmland, and woods.
Distribution Britain and Europe, northwestern Africa, and central Asia.
Captivity The male has a melodious song. A pair is easily kept in a well-planted aviary. The female lays 3-5, in rare instances 6 or more, green-blue eggs with red-brown and yellow-brown spots. Incubation time 2 weeks. After 14 days the young leave the cup-shaped nest (built with plant matter and lined with mud). Both parents feed the young fledglings another 2-3 weeks. During the breeding season live insects are essential. The Shama (*Copsychus malabaricus*) from the Indian subcontinent, southeast Asia, Hainan, and Western Indonesia, and the Pagoda Starling (*Sturnus pagodarum*), from Afghanistan, India, and Sri Lanka, require the same kind of care as the blackbird and the song thrush. Both need nesting boxes of at least $35 \times 25 \times 30$ cm. Both birds have a lovely song, and they can also imitate rather well. Can be kept in Britain only if aviary bred and close-rung.

198 TURDUS PHILOMELOS
Song thrush

Classification Order Passeriformes, Family Turdidae.
Characteristics Length: 23 cm (9 in). Upper parts brown sides and breast tawny with many small black spots. Reddish-brown tail; dark brown to black primary and secondary feathers; wing coverts with two wing bars. Young birds have a striped back.
Habitat Parks, gardens, and woods.
Distribution Britain and Europe, Asia, and northern parts of Africa. Introduced into New Zealand and New Hebrides
Captivity Prefers a large, well-planted outdoor aviary in which the female constructs a cup-shaped nest of dry grasses, fine twigs, and moss; she lines it with mud. The female lays 4-9 eggs, which are blue-green in color with small spots. Incubation time 11-15 days; both parents rear the young. A plentiful supply of garden insects is essential, as are mealworms, maggots, worms, moilusks, and spiders. It is necessary therefore to place a stone in the aviary upon which the birds can break the snail shells Fruits and insect mixtures are also a must throughout the whole year. Can be kept in Britain only if aviary bred and close-rung.

199 PYCNONOTUS CAFER
Red-vented bulbul

Classification Order Passeriformes, Family Pycnonotidae.
Characteristics Length: 21 cm (8½ in). Black head; the black throat gradually shades to brown; and the neck, shoulders, breast, and wings are brown with white feather seams. This results in a wavy effect on the breast and shoulders. The flanks and underside are gray-white; the back is gray, slowly shading to white. The undertail coverts are a rich purplish-red, and the tail is brown with white feather tips. Cheeks chocolate-brown. Eyes brown, beak black, and legs dark gray-black. The female is smaller and duller in coloring. The beak is somewhat narrower and larger. The head feathers can be raised into a crest; these crest feathers are raised particularly when the bird is angry or enthusiastic about something. It may sing very nicely at the same time.
Habitat Farmland, near villages, and up to 1,700 m elevation; in the winter they usually live in small groups.
Distribution From India to Indochina and Java.
Captivity These bulbuls are very sweet and tolerant towards fellow species and small birds, providing they are kept singly (no couples). During the winter months, they need to be housed in a lightly heated area indoors. If kept in a cage, this should measure at least 80 × 50 × 50 cm. The hen lays and incubates 3-4 eggs in a cup-shaped nest for 12-13 days. The birds prefer to use canary nests and fill these with a little moss, hay, grass, and coconut fibers.

200 PYCNONOTUS JOCOSUS
Red-whiskered, or red-eared, bulbul

Classification Order Passeriformes, Family Pycnonotidae.
Characteristics Length: 20 cm (8 in). Black crest with a metallic sheen, white ear markings with some red; a white throat and a brown neck. Breast and underside are white, brownish towards the flanks. Back and wings are brown, the tail is brown with white feather tips (outermost feathers only), and the undertail feathers are red. Eyes brown, beak black, and legs dark brown-black. The hen is browner and has less red on the cheeks. She is also smaller.
Habitat Wooded areas, but also in and around cities.
Distribution India to Indochina, southern China to Malaysia.
Captivity The 2-3, sometimes 4, eggs are hatched in a cup-shaped nest which is beautifully constructed with grass, moss, dry leaves, hay, coconut fibers, spider webs, and hair. The nest is built very close to the ground (75 cm), especially in thick shrubbery, but seldom in trees. Incubation time 12 days. The cock does not incubate nor does he feed the hen while she is incubating the eggs, but he will later feed the young. The male sings in a rather remarkable manner. Like all bulbuls, it is somewhat timid and withdrawn initially. Later these traits disappear, and it will even take food from the keeper's hand. The young leave the nest after about 16 days.

201 CHLOROPSIS AURIFRONS
Golden-fronted leafbird

Classification Order Passeriformes, Family Irenidae.
Characteristics Length: 20 cm (8 in). Blue throat and black eye stripe, cheeks, neck and breast, all with purple iridescence; crown yellow. The breast is bordered by a broad yellow band. The curve of the wing is blue. Back dark green, underside lighter grass-green; flight feathers brownish; tail green. Eyes brown, beak black, legs gray-blue. The black in the hen is less deep, and in general she is much duller in coloring and markings.
Habitat Forest and scrub.
Distribution Himalayan region in India; Burma and Sumatra.
Captivity This species sings beautifully and is also kept as a decorative bird in a cage in its native lands. Sometimes they tend to make a mess at the feeding dishes, since many have the habit of carefully inspecting the contents, piece by piece. They are somewhat quick-tempered. They enjoy bathing and drink a lot. The hen lays 2-3 eggs in a cup-shaped nest which is made of moss, hair, stalks, leaves, and such; usually placed in the fork of a branch; the nest is lined with small roots and moss. Incubation time about 14 days. The molt takes place in the fall, so they find fluctuating temperatures difficult to tolerate. Needless to say, they should be brought indoors during the winter months (about 18°C). This bird can be aggressive if housed with other species.

202 LEIOTHRIX LUTEA
Red-billed leiothrix or Pekin robin

Classification Order Passeriformes, Family Timaliidae.
Characteristics 15 cm (6 in). Head, neck, flanks, upper body, and uppertail coverts (with a white band at the tip) green-gray; top of tail blue-black. Beige stripe by the eye; throat bright yellow, shading to orange on the chest. Shoulder feathers, lesser wing coverts, and small flight feathers green-gray; the large flight feathers red with black and yellow bands; the underside a vague yellow. The head of the hen is not as deep in coloring. Eyes brown, beak coral-red (black at the base), legs brown-yellow.
Habitat The birds are very timid in open fields, preferring heavily wooded areas. They generally live together in small groups, and mostly in pairs during the breeding period.
Distribution From the southern Himalayas across northern Indochina (north to the Yangtze Valley), but particularly in the southern parts starting at 6,000 m above sea level.
Captivity They use canary "baskets," which must be placed in a half-open nest box. They will also build their own cup-shaped nest of straw, bark, moss, thin roots, and twigs. The nest box should be hung in a secluded location. The hen lays 3-4 eggs; incubation time 14 days. After approximately 13 days the young leave the nest but will continue to be fed by their parents for some time. When kept in a cage, this must measure at least 75 × 45 × 65 cm. The male sings beautifully.

203 ZOSTEROPS PALPEBROSA
Oriental, or Indian white-eyed, zosterops

Classification Order Passeriformes, Family Zosteropidae.
Characteristics Length: 10-14 cm (4-6 in). Pale olive-green above, becoming still paler at the sides. Head and neck also pale olive-green. Underside bright yellow; stomach grayish, and flanks brown-gray. Eyes brown, beak black, legs gray-brown. Young birds are greener and duller in coloration. White ring around the eyes.
Habitat These birds live in lowland woods, but can also be found at altitudes up to 1,660 m. In April they leave for their breeding grounds.
Distribution India, Sri Lanka, Indochina, and the Greater Sunda Islands.
Captivity Providing their care is good, they will breed in captivity quite regularly. They build a shallow, cup-shaped nest that is located in trees and thick bushes. It is constructed of moss, hair, spiderwebs, plant fibers, and such. The hen lays 2-4 eggs; incubation time 10-12 days. Both birds incubate the eggs. The young leave the nest after about 12 days. Birds find dramatic temperature changes and low temperatures difficult to tolerate. Bathing is an absolute must. They are best kept in a large cage (70 × 50 × 50 cm) or roomy aviary; are very tolerant towards other species, and become extremely tame with their keeper. Their song is not unpleasant. Place their food on a small table of some sort, about 40-60 cm from the ground. During the breeding season live insects are essential.

204 GRACULA RELIGIOSA
Hill mynah

Classification Order Passeriformes, Family Sturnidae.
Characteristics Length: 25 cm (10 in). Black. Fleshy yellow lobes. Eyes brown, beak and legs orange.
Habitat Woods and forests, always near water; in large groups.
Distribution Southeast Asia and Indonesia; introduced elsewhere.
Captivity This species is one of the most popular of all pet birds. Its ability to talk is unexcelled, and its rate of learning is amazingly rapid. The hen lays 2-3 eggs; both parents incubate the eggs for about 15 days, and the young will leave the nest after approximately 1 month. They are independent at 2 months. Breeding in captivity is rare, however. Supply starling nesting boxes throughout the year, but especially during the breeding season, and quite a lot of live food and fruit. Alone in a cage, a mynah bird gives lots of pleasure. Suggested minimum measurements for a cage are 90 cm (35½ in) long and 55 cm (22 in) wide and high.

205 TANGARA CHILENSIS
Paradise tanager

Classification   Order Passeriformes, Family Thraupidae.
Characteristics   Length: 13 cm (5 in). Head yellowish-green. Neck, shoulders, back, and tail black. Wings black, edged in purple. Rump red (in the eastern parts of their range, red and yellow). Wing coverts, sides of breast, and belly splendidly blue; the center of the belly black. Eyes brown, beak black, legs black-brown.
Habitat   Primarily lowland, up to about 1,500 m elevation, but also in forests and woodland.
Distribution   South America east of the Andes and south to Bolivia and southern Brazil.
Captivity   Because of their basically sweet and juicy food, their droppings are watery. Consequently the bottom of the cage (at least 150 × 80 × 60 cm) should be covered with absorbent paper towels or a few layers of newspaper or construction paper. Daily cleaning is essential in order to avoid diseases. Washing facilities in cage or aviary must always be present. Breeding results in captivity occur only sporadically in large, well-planted aviaries. They prefer to breed as high as possible in a variety of nest boxes already containing nesting material (coconut fibers, dead and live grass, leaves, moss, pieces of bark, wool, and the like). Quite often these very shy birds, which like to hide in corners on the ground, also choose to build their nest free in a thick shrub. The female lays 2-3 eggs; incubation time 13-14 days.

---

206 TANGARA FASTUOSA
Superb, or orange-rumped, tanager

Classification   Order Passeriformes, Family Thraupidae.
Characteristics   Length: 14 cm (5½ in). Black around the beak; head blue-green; neck band and back black. Shoulders and tail purple-blue with a light sheen. Rump and underside orange; undertail coverts black; the lesser wing coverts blue-green. Rest of body black. Eyes brown, beak black, legs brown-black. The hen has a greenish-blue head, but the rest of her coloring is less vivid, with the back being more green and bright yellow (male is yellow with orange).
Habitat   Forests. These species spend their time high in the crowns of trees, leaving only when they seek food. They breed together in small groups.
Distribution   East Brazil.
Captivity   A very tolerant bird, regularly offered for sale. It becomes tame rapidly. Nevertheless, I would advise you to allow them to breed only when kept in an aviary where there are no small exotic birds; it occasionally happens that they steal young birds from the nests. The hen lays 2-3 eggs; incubation time 14 days. They build their nest as high as possible; both sexes cooperate in the construction. The young leave the nest after about 3 weeks. Live insects are essential. After about one year the young gain adult plumage. Recently imported birds should be kept at a constant temperature of 25°C; this temperature can be gradually decreased to 20°C after acclimatization.

GLOSSARY

♂ Indicates a cock or male; the symbol represents the shield and spear of Mars, the Roman god of war.

♀ Indicates a female or hen; the symbol represents the mirror of the Roman goddess of love and beauty, Venus.

Addled fertile egg in which the embryo has died at an early stage.

Albino a mutation in which all pigments are absent, leaving only white; the mutant has reddish eyes and pinkish legs and toes.

Allele any of a group of possible mutational forms of a gene; short for allelomorph.

Autosome paired, ordinary (hence asexual) chromosomes, similar in both sexes.

Bacteria unicellular microorganisms with no nucleus which multiply mainly by division; live singly or in colonies.

Backcross to mate the offspring of a certain pair back to their parents.

Barred heads term used for budgerigars in baby plumage, whereby the barrings or stripes are extended close to the cere.

Biotope a limited ecological region; environment.

Breed see *Type*.

Broken cap the clear head area of a canary that is broken with dark feathers.

Buff and yellow types of feathers in canaries. Buff (also called *mealy*) feathers are bordered with white, creating a frosted appearance; this is not visible on yellow feathers.

Cap the whole top area of a canary's head.

Cell the smallest specialized unit of an organism consisting of nucleus and protoplasm.

Cere the fleshy swelling at the base of the upper mandible of parrots, parrakeets, and some birds of prey.

Character a distinguishing characteristic.

Chromosomes microscopic thread-shaped bodies, which are present in the cell, to which the genes are attached.

Class a group of related orders. A group of classes forms a phylum.

Clear without dark feathers. Also indicates infertile eggs.

Clutch the number of eggs produced or incubated by a hen at a single sitting.

Cobby bird with a short and thick body.

Colony a group of birds (of the same species) living together.

Colony breeding uncontrolled breeding in an aviary or bird room.

Color break a sudden genetic color change.

Color food a soft bird food, containing a red coloring agent.

Consort the plain-headed Gloster canary.

Contour a bird's outline.

Coppy another name for crest.

Corona see *Crested.*

Counterpart a similar mutation with a different ground color.

Coverts certain feathers (e.g., lesser wing coverts, undertail coverts).

Crestbred noncrested canary bred from one crested parent.

Crested a bird with a crest (corona); may be natural to the species (cockatiel) or the result of a mutation (corona).

Crop a pouchlike enlargement of the beginning of the digestive tract, in which food is stored or partially digested.

Crossing-over the exchange of genetic material (genes) between homologous (or related) chromosomes.

Dilute a plumage color paler than the normal shade.

Dimorphism the condition of having two different forms, e.g., differences in plumage coloration between males and females (e.g., weavers, whydahs).

Domesticated a bird species that has been consistently raised in captivity for many generations.

Dominant a visible trait or character that is produced by an allele, despite the presence of other genes (which are recessive).

Double buffing the mating of two buff-feathered birds.

Double character the same color character in a double quantity in the genetic makeup of a bird.

Double yellowing the mating of two yellow-feathered birds.

Down the soft, fluffy body covering of growing young birds; its chief function is heat conservation.

Egg binding inability of the hen to pass the egg.

Even-marked a bird with the same color markings or areas on both sides of its body.

F symbol for filial generation.

F_1 represents the first filial generation, produced from any specific mating.

F_2 denotes the second filial generation, produced from a mating of a male and a female from the F_1 breeding.

Factor a simple Mendelian trait; may be considered synonymous with gene (see *Gene*).

Family a group of genera with common characteristics. A group of families forms an order.

Fancy certain type breeds, particularly of budgerigars, canaries, and cockatiels; hobby.

Flight feathers the comparatively large and stiff wing feathers.

Flue the downy feathers next to the body.

Frosted see *Buff and yellow.*

Gamete, germ, or reproductive cell the spermatozoon produced by the male, and the ovum produced by the female.

Gene microscopic functional hereditary unit situated on a fixed location on the chromosome; controls the inheritable characteristics.

Genotype the hereditary composition of an organism, especially as distinguished from its physical appearance (see *Phenotype*).

Germ see *Gamete.*

Get chick or offspring.

Gizzard the organ—essentially an enlargement of the alimentary canal—in which a bird's food is ground up with the aid of small, sharp stones (grit) swallowed by the bird.

Grit finely broken shells, mixed with sand and stone.

Ground colors the basic colors of white or yellow on which all other colors are superimposed.

Habitat the physical environment of a bird.

Heredity that factor in evolution which caused the persistence of characteristics in successive generations.

Heterozygote non-purebred. Such birds occur when we cross two birds of different colors, thus endowing the offspring with a variety of colors, both visible and invisible, from their parents.

Hikers or runners budgerigars suffering from French molt. These birds are unable to fly.

Homozygote a purebred. The opposite of heterozygous is homozygous. Homozygous animals are purebred for a particular character. If we have a homozygous zebra finch, then this bird will possess no other qualities or characters other than those we observe from its outward appearance. Non-pure birds and purebred birds may sometimes be outwardly indistinguishable from one another.

Hybrid the offspring of a mating of two different species (see also *Mule*).

Hypostasis a condition in which the action of one gene suppresses or conceals the action of another gene, that is not its allele but that affects the same organ, part, or state of the body; e.g., the masking of the dominant pied head in opaline-factor budgerigars.

Inbreeding birds that are bred from closely related individuals.

Inheritance the process of genetic transmission of characters or characteristics.

Lacing a fine and dark color on a light ground in budgerigars.

Lethal gene a gene that causes the chick to die before it is hatched.

Line breeding the mating of blood-related birds in order to establish a line or strain.

Mantle the area between neck and back.

Mealy see *Buff and yellow*.

Melanistic possessing extra black pigment in the plumage.

Mule in Britain, the hybrid result of crossing canaries with certain British (wild) birds, e.g., canary × bullfinch, canary × goldfinch. In America, the term can refer to any cross involving a canary and other bird species.

Mutation the sudden chromosomal change of character or color.

Nest feathers the first feathers of a young bird (chick).

Order a group of related families. A group of orders forms a class.

Outcrossing the pairing of unrelated birds from different strains (see *Inbreeding*).

Ovary a female reproductive gland producing ova.

Pallid see *Dilute*

Parasite an organism that lives at the expense of a different organism, while contributing nothing to the survival of its host.

Phenotype the external appearance of an organism (see *Genotype*).

Phylum a group of related classes. A group of phyla forms a kingdom.

Pied describes a bird whose color is broken with light zones.

Pigment   a substance that gives feathers their colors.

Pin feathers   feathers still encased in their follicles.

Plainhead   a bird without a crest.

Progeny   offspring from a breeding couple.

P-symbol   symbol for parental generation.

Quill   the main shaft of a feather.

Recessive   a trait or character that is carried by an allele that has no visual effect. Paired recessive, however, is visible.

Red factor   the genetic factor introduced to canaries by crossing a canary with the red siskin.

Reproduction   the sexual or asexual process by which organisms generate others of the same species.

Reproductive cell   see *Gamete*.

Saddle   the upper back area.

Segregation   in genetics, the separation of paired alleles in meiosis (the method of division of cells characteristic of germ cells).

Self   all one color.

Sex chromosomes   either of a pair of chromosomes in the germ cells that combine to determine the sex of an individual. The male bird has two X chromosomes, the female one X and one Y chromosome.

Sex linked   recessive characters that are carried by a sex chromosome. Such characters are passed from mother to son.

Sexual coloration   characteristic color difference between male and female.

Sexual dimorphism   when markings and/or coloration differ in both sexes, e.g., Senegal combassou or pin-tailed whydah.

Single character   bird possessing only one single quantity of a certain character in its genetic makeup.

Sperm   the male germ cell, usually a nucleated cell with a long, thin, motile tail (spermatozoon).

Splayed legs   deformed legs that spread outwards, especially in budgerigars.

Split   if a heterozygous (not-purebred) bird is bred for a particular quality, then for the sake of convenience it is listed by the visible color as well as its recessive or individual color. A heterozygous bird that is outwardly white but carries gray would be classified as a white/gray bird or a "white-blooded" bird, which means "white out of gray" (e.g., in zebra finches). No matter what we call it, the meaning is clear. The different names can well lead to confusion, so in this book we use the terminology generally used in bird breeding literature—the term "split." In our example then, we have white split gray (white/gray).

Stance   the posture of a bird.

Sterile   incapable of reproducing sexually; infertile.

Strain   a group of organisms of the same species, having distinctive characters but not usually considered a separate breed or variety.

Suffusion   the overlaying of one color by another color.

Testis   a male reproductive gland responsible for the production of male germ cells or sperms.

Tours   special song notes by roller canaries.

Vent   anus.

Wild type   the species as found in the wild.

Zygote   the cell formed by the union of a male and a female gamete. The beginning of a new individual.

BIBLIOGRAPHY

Bates, H. and Busenbark, R. *Finches and Soft-billed Birds*. Neptune, N.J.: T. F. H. Publications, Inc., 1978.
—*Parrots and Related Birds*. 3rd ed., Revised and expanded by Dr. Matthew M. Vriends. Neptune, N.J.: T.F.H. Publications, Inc. 1978.
Brockmann, J. and Lantermann, W. *Agaporniden*. Stuttgart: Verlag E. Ulmer, 1981.
Forshaw, Joseph M. *Australian Parrots*. 2nd ed. Melbourne, Australia: Lansdowne Press, 1981.
—*Parrots of the World*. 2nd ed. Melbourne, Australia: Lansdowne Press, 1981.
Harman, I. and Vriends, Dr. Matthew M. *All About Finches*. Neptune, N.J.: T.F.H. Publications, Inc., 1978.
Hoppe, D. *Amazonen*. Stuttgart: Verlag E. Ulmer, 1981.
Kronberger, H. *Haltung von Vögeln—Krankheiten der Vögel*. 4th ed. Jena, D.D.R.: V.E.B. Gustav Fisher Verlag, 1979.
Lint, Kenton C. and Alice Marie. *Diets for Birds in Captivity*. Dorset, England: Blandford Press, 1981.
Low, Rosemary. *Parrots, Their Care and Breeding*. Dorset, England: Blandford Press, 1980.
Petrak, M.L., et al. *Diseases of Cage and Aviary Birds*. 2nd ed. London: Bailliere Tindall; and Philadelphia: Lea & Febiger, 1982.
Restall, Robin L. *Finches and Other Seed-eating Birds*. London: Faber and Faber, 1975.
Rutgers, A. and Norris, K.A. *Encyclopedia of Aviculture*. Vols. 1, 2, & 3. Dorset, England: Blandford Press, 1972.
Vriends, Matthew M. *Australische Papegaaien en Parkieten*. 2nd ed. Utrecht, The Netherlands: Het Spectrum, 1984.
—*Breeding Popular Cage and Aviary Birds*. New York: Howell, 1984.
—*The Complete Budgerigar*. New York: Howell, 1984.
—*The Complete Cockatiel*. New York: Howell, 1983.
—*Encyclopedia of Loverbirds*. Neptune, N.J.: T.F.H. Publications, Inc., 1978.
—*Handbook of Zebra Finches*. Neptune, N.J.: T.F.H. Publications, Inc., 1978.
—*Papegaaien en Parkieten*. Best, The Netherlands: Zuid Boekproducties, 1983.
—*Papegaaien en Parkieten uit Afrika, Azië en Zuid-Amerika*. Baarn, The Netherlands: Kim/Hollandia, 1981.
—*Popular Parrots*. New York: Howell, 1983.

INDEX OF ENTRIES

(The numbers refer to the entry number)